BLACK
CAMPUS
LIFE

SUNY series, Critical Race Studies in Education

Derrick R. Brooms, editor

BLACK CAMPUS LIFE

THE WORLDS BLACK STUDENTS MAKE
AT A HISTORICALLY WHITE INSTITUTION

ANTAR A. TICHAVAKUNDA

Published by State University of New York Press, Albany

This book is freely available in an open access edition thanks to TOME (Toward
an Open Monograph Ecosystem)—a collaboration of the Association of American
Universities, the Association of University Presses, and the Association of Research
Libraries—and the generous support of the University of Cincinnati.

Printed in the United States of America

For information, contact State University of New York Press, Albany, NY
www.sunypress.edu

Library of Congress Cataloging-in-Publication Data

Name: Tichavakunda, Antar A., author.
Title: Black campus life : the worlds black students make at a historically white
    institution / Antar A. Tichavakunda.
Description: Albany : State University of New York Press, [2021] | Series:
    SUNY series, Critical Race Studies in Education | Includes bibliographical
    references and index.
Identifiers: ISBN 9781438485911 (hardcover : alk. paper) | ISBN 9781438485928
    (ebook)
Further information is available at the Library of Congress.

10 9 8 7 6 5 4 3 2 1

For Gran and Pop-Pop. I did my best work.

Contents

THE ENGINEERING SCHOOL COMMUNITY

THE MAINSTREAM WSU COMMUNITY

Illustrations

Tables

Figures

Acknowledgments

Writing, in many ways, is an act of faith. First and foremost, I thank God for using me as a vessel for any good that comes out of this work. This book was a community effort. I have to acknowledge, however, my mother. Thank you for talking to me every day, listening to me rant about things only a mother would listen to, and supporting me in every way possible. Thanks for the smiles in your voice. Thanks dad for helping me keep things in perspective and your support. Thanks for giving me a powerful name and teaching me to be proud of who I am and where we are from. Thanks Aziza for being you. Thanks Lynnie for your constant positivity and support. To all of my family, thank you for always welcoming me with open arms even when research, schooling, and work makes it tougher to get back home. I am because we are.

In writing this book, I was deeply reflective of and grateful for my schooling. I am a proud product of DC Public Schools. My experience navigating DC Public Schools and being taught and coached by people who nurtured and loved me shapes my work. To my teachers from Shepherd Elementary School, Alice Deal Junior High, and Benjamin Banneker Academic High School—thank you. Thank you to my professors at Brown— Carla Shalaby, Diana D'Amico Pawlewicz, Kenneth Wong, Thomas Lewis, and Corey Walker—who believed in me, pushed me, and planted the seed of doing research. Further, it was also at Brown where I got my first taste of Black student life at a predominantly White institution. I would not have been interested in this topic were it not for the amazing friends I made at Brown and the Monster Alpha Gamma Chapter of Alpha Phi Alpha Fraternity Incorporated.

My friends are my adopted family. Every day I am reminded of how lucky I am to have so many good friends. Shouts to Shepherd Park. I am also fortunate to have made such great friends in graduate school and as a professor. You all are my world. Thank you all for putting up with me and my needy to obnoxious ways. Thank you for reading drafts, being my biggest fans, and forcing me to celebrate every little win. Thank you all for believing me when I did not believe in myself and for being my therapists before I had one (and helping me see that therapy was okay). I have leaned on you all more than you know.

I am eternally grateful to my advisor/mentor/coach/friend, William G. Tierney. More than just getting by, I have wanted to make you proud. Thank you for pushing me to write this book, for your mentorship, and for working with me. Thank you to my mentors who read the earliest drafts of this work, especially Zoë Corwin, John Slaughter, and Pierrette Hondagneu-Sotelo. You all continue to inspire me and have laid the foundation for this book.

I, of course, have to acknowledge my editor Rebecca Colesworthy. Thank you for shepherding this work and helping me understand what writing a book is about. I also am appreciative of the Critical Race Studies in Education series editor, Derrick Brooms. Thank you for your incisive feedback as well as your friendship and mentorship. And to the readers who engaged with the first iterations of a junior scholar's first book—thank you. Your feedback and reflections took this work to the next level.

Thanks to my favorite NSBE chapter, my focal participants. You all inspire me. When I was writing by myself for hours on end, I thought of you all. I wrote my hardest because of you—because I could not let you all down and because I witnessed your resolve to succeed no matter how hard you had to work. Outside of making this research possible, you all treated me like family—especially after I paid my NSBE dues. The title of NSBE dad is one I will forever wear with honor.

1

Learning About Campus Life from Black Engineering Majors

Negroes love and hate and fight and play and strive and travel and have a thousand and one interests in life like other humans. When his baby cuts a new tooth, he brags as shamelessly as anyone else without once weeping over the prospect of some Klansman knocking it out if and when the child ever gets grown.

—Zora Neale Hurston, *Art and Such,* 1938

I joined other first year students in the tradition of walking through Brown University's Van Wickle Gates in Fall 2007. Brown's 7 percent Black population was different from the majority Black public high school I graduated from in Washington, D.C. As a Black student on a predominantly White campus, race shaped much of my collegiate life. The parties I went to, the fraternity I joined, the classes I took, the leadership positions I held, and the friends I made were informed by my societal positioning as a cisgender Black man. My experience as a Black student on a predominantly White campus was complex, difficult in many ways, but full of life.

The difference between my undergraduate experience and what I often read about Black collegians led me to this work. Research and popular media centering on Black collegians' experiences on predominantly White campuses often highlight the racist experiences Black students shoulder. From White nationalists marching through campuses, to campus police profiling Black students, to seemingly monthly videos of students and

1

faculty wearing Blackface or saying the n-word, to the more insidious, everyday racial slights Black students hear on campus in the form of microaggressions—racism shapes the campus experience for many Black students. If you ask me if racism influenced my time at Brown, my answer would be, "Of course." I can recall the sting of White peers averting eye contact with me outside of class. I can recall the sick feeling of wishing I had said something in response to the question White students often levied at me, "Hey, you're on the basketball/football team, right?" I can recall replaying these moments over and over in my head long after they happened. Research examining racism's hold on campus remains vital.

Yet, if you ask about my experience at Brown in general, my answer would be more complex. I would tell you about the impromptu freestyle rap battles in Harambee, the Black affinity residence hall. I would tell you about how my friends and I, under the name Pain Revisited, won Brown's Intramural Basketball Championship. I would tell you about the professors who advised me when I was unsure of my economics major and encouraged me to follow my passion for education. I would tell you about the life my friends and I made in spite of, and sometimes because of, the state of race relations on campus. Much of the work about Black students' campus experiences overlooks the complexities, contradictions, and richness within Black student life I once experienced. My time at Brown shaped my approach to *Black Campus Life*—I walk the tightrope of acknowledging both the permanence of racism and the agency of students. I wrestled with theory and research on Black people in higher education to make sense of a group of Black engineering majors' lives at one historically White institution (HWI)[1]—West Side University (WSU).[2]

Studying Black Campus Life through Social Worlds

Black Campus Life explores how students experience four overlapping, yet distinct, social worlds. Students' involvement in these worlds, I argue, shapes how students perceive campus race relations and how students foster a sense of engagement on campus. Engagement is understood as the time and effort students expend on their higher education experience, both in and out of the classroom (Quaye et al. 2019). Early in my research, participants led me to the idea of studying social worlds. In conversation with the president of WSU's Black Student Union (BSU), for example, I expressed my interest in learning more about the school's Black community.

"Which one?" she asked, before delving into idiosyncrasies of different groups such as the student athletes, engineers, and members of sororities and fraternities—all within the WSU Black community. Similarly, Catherine, the director of the Black Cultural Center at WSU, said, "The [racial] climate also depends on what communities the students are attached to." By better understanding the social worlds students traverse, we can better understand campus life and how to support students.

Campus life is expansive—including the experiences of living in residence halls, meeting with advisors, skipping or attending class, hitting up parties on the weekend, going to sporting events, and everything in between. Campus life encompasses students' campus cultures, traditions, and experiences from the everyday to the extraordinary (Stevens et al. 2008; Jack 2014). All students experience campus life in some fashion. Research on campus life, however, has historically revolved around White students (e.g., Armstrong and Hamilton 2013; Boyer 1987; Horowitz 1987; Moffatt 1989). Black students are typically addressed in an assigned race relations or diversity chapter. To be sure, a corpus of work examines Black students' experiences in HWIs (e.g., Griffin et al. 2016; Griffith et al. 2019; Harris and Patton 2017). While a growing body of literature exists (e.g., Brooms 2017; Charles et al. 2009; McCabe 2016), less often do researchers explore Black campus life *beyond* students' experiences with racism.

This book begins with and centers Black student life. Black students have varied and full experiences on campus, outside of instances with racism, that are often underexplored. During my research, students continuously reminded me that campus life—even for a seemingly homogeneous group of Black engineering majors—was far from a uniform experience. How students understand race relations on campus and experience campus life at WSU was shaped by the social worlds they traversed. Social worlds are the dynamic campus communities and cultures that are made of shifting relationships between students, staff, faculty, and other campus stakeholders. To better understand the complexity and nuances of social worlds, I provide a preliminary glimpse here of two of the social worlds examined in greater depth in later chapters—the Black community and the Black engineering community.

◆ ◆ ◆

Monday evenings are busy for the Black WSU community. The Black Student Union (BSU) meets at 6p.m. and National Society of Black Engineers

(NSBE) meets at 7p.m. Both meetings last an hour. NSBE members who attend the BSU meetings usually leave early, around 6:45p.m., giving them time to walk to their NSBE meeting, chat with other members, sign in, and, hopefully, get a plate of free food. Sometimes the food is provided by NSBE with funds from the school of engineering. Other times the food is provided by Intel, Facebook, or whichever company is giving a talk at the meeting. For students eager to save a "swipe," or meal credit, food is a welcomed incentive to attend meetings.

Nearing the end of the spring semester, organizations often hold executive board elections for duties the following academic year. The last Monday in March, BSU held elections. Four women ran for BSU president. Near the beginning of the semester, upwards of seventy students would come to BSU meetings, with students forced to sit on the steps or share seats. The turnout for the election, however, was low. Only twenty-eight students were in the room, six of which were men.

Standing behind a podium at the front of the room, a first-year with curly, dark hair just reaching her shoulders, began, "My name is Imani. I'm a transfer student from Oakland." "Aaaayyee!" a couple of students, perhaps from the Bay Area as well, exclaimed upon hearing where she was from. The speeches shared similar arcs—they described their experience as Black students at WSU and then provided some ideas of what they wanted to do with BSU during their tenure in office. Imani spoke of the role of BSU in her short time at WSU so far, confessing, "This is the first time I felt like an individual as opposed to a walking minority." She also critiqued a diversity outreach video created by WSU that seemed to only highlight students' experiences with microaggressions, arguing, "Our experience is heightened by microaggressions, but we are not defined by them."

"We are also very invested in the community. We don't want to see it flop," Nia, a junior, sporting a combed out, almost perfectly spherical afro, told the audience in her speech for president. "The community" she was referring to was the WSU Black community. A uniting theme of the meeting was heterogeneity in Blackness. The audience and candidates seemed to wrestle with the underlying question, "How can BSU bring more Black students together?"

During the question and answer segment, an Ethiopian student in health sciences asked, "There's a sizable portion of students that don't feel like BSU represents them. What do you all think about that?" Nia responded, "I mean, everyone has their own personal journey in identity. BSU is here to support Black students but it's not just that identity." Taylor, who was running for co-president along with Nia, added, "We want to make sure we aren't creating an environment just for one narrative." Nodding, Nia finished her thought, "Yeah, you know, member orgs are important. That's where everyone finds their niche. Like that's why we have NSBE." Conspicuously absent in the audience, however, were the Black engineers.

Less than a half-hour later, the NSBE meeting began. Twenty-seven Black undergraduate WSU engineers, nearly half of the entire Black undergraduate engineering school population, were in attendance. None of the engineers in the room were aware of the BSU election that had transpired.[3] Their attention was preoccupied with their pre-election meeting where each executive board member would provide a description of their role and responsibilities within NSBE. When executive board members walked to the front of the room to explain their positions, the NSBE president changed the PowerPoint slide to a professional headshot of the corresponding member.

Erving's picture flashed on the screen and he walked to the front to describe his role. Before he could speak, Charlie interjected, "Everyone else is wearing suits. Where's yours, man?" Erving was only wearing a button-up shirt in his headshot. Reflexively, Erving replied, "You should've seen my shoes," inciting laughter. Thomas's picture also caused a ruckus. In his picture, Thomas, donning a serious look, wore a black suit, white shirt, and purple tie. The high-definition photo accentuated his high cheek bones. "Boy you look like a chocolate vampire!" Robert chided. Thomas laughed, rolling his eyes, and waited for the members to stop laughing so he could describe his position.

At the close of the meeting, I joined a conversation with Thomas, Robert, and Johnson about a new Kendrick Lamar song. I changed the topic during a lull in the conversation, asking why they never go to BSU meetings. The three gave almost a collective shrug. Robert said he had class at the same time and, "It's low-key, a women's group." They generally agreed on the idea that their identity of Black engineers was so specific that NSBE resonated more than any other organization concerning their Black engineering identity. "We're not just Black," Johnson added. He continued, "BSU kind of promotes a certain narrative about Black students." More than their words, their actions manifested tensions of intragroup diversity. Without knowledge of the speeches given by BSU members earlier that night, the NSBE members I talked with spoke to the very issues BSU candidates addressed.

◆ ◆ ◆

Black Campus Life is as much a story of Black engineering majors at WSU as it is a story of the nuances and complexities of campus life in general. How students invest their time—and what they deem important—shapes their campus experience. Black engineers attending both BSU and NSBE meetings, for example, would have weekly back-to-back, hour-long meetings on Monday nights. Social worlds, as I show throughout this work, inform the spectrum of students' campus experiences, including organizational involvement, coursework, or even partying. In other words, the social worlds students are attached to shape how they spend their time.

WSU, like other college campuses, is comprised of overlapping and shifting social worlds. Social worlds have their own modes of engagement (see Table 2.2). As I explain later, Black students, for example, are not necessarily members of the Black community; membership entails certain practices. Students can find belonging and engagement in various worlds within the same campus. Black engineering participants were attached to WSU through smaller, often Black, social worlds. The various social worlds students traverse shape their complex, even contradictory, perceptions of campus. Depending on the social worlds a student traverses, a student might feel both "at home" yet out of place, or validated yet neglected on the same campus. Similarly, a Black student attending an HWI can understand campus as both racist and inclusive. I grappled with such tensions in studying Black engineers' campus lives, examining how they foster a sense of engagement and experience the campus racial climate at an HWI.

Racial Realities on Campus

Race matters in higher education. From the impact of structures such as affirmative action (Patton 2016), to the everyday cross- and intraracial interactions (e.g., Bonilla-Silva 2019; Gilkes-Borr 2019; Harper and Quaye 2007), to organizational involvement (e.g., Brooms 2018; Park 2014), race shapes student life. Scholars interested in such racial realities on campus often employ the concept of *campus racial climate* (Hurtado 1992). A campus racial climate is "part of the institutional context that includes community members' attitudes, perceptions, behaviors, and expectations around issues of race, ethnicity, and diversity" (Hurtado et al. 2008, 205). The campus racial climate framework provides language and tools to pin down the abstract nature of campus race relations. For example, beyond describing a campus climate as "chilly" or "friendly," scholars and students can also identify people, practices, or relationships that shape the climate.

Students often experience the same campus differently depending on their race. For example, Black students attending HWIs tend to perceive the racial climate in a more negative manner than their White peers (Harper and Hurtado 2007). From campus spaces (Inwood and Martin 2008) to campus security (Dache and White 2016; Jenkins et al. 2020), Black students and other racially marginalized groups tend to experience sites and systems on the same campus in a more negative manner than their White peers. Depending on their race, students can view the very same campus in contradictory ways. It is more than possible for a White student to view a campus in a wholly positive manner—friendly, welcoming, diverse, and without any racial friction—and a Black student, on the same campus, to view the university in a negative manner—hostile, alienating, overwhelmingly White, and racist.

Racism is not just a nonblack student calling a Black student the n-word or a professor wearing Blackface on Halloween. Racism manifests in different, interconnected forms. At the same time, racism is both macro and micro, institutional and individual, material and symbolic, outright and subtle, as well as structural and intrapersonal (e.g., Bonilla-Silva 2019; Essed 1991; Feagin and Sikes 1994; Pillawski 1984). Scholars interested in studying the everyday forms of racism use *microaggressions* as a core concept. Microaggressions are subtle visual, verbal, and nonverbal insults about race that can contribute to some students' feelings of marginalization (e.g., Pierce et al. 1978; Solórzano et al. 2000). While microaggressions are varied, an example might be a White student telling a Black student, "You're not like other Black folk. You're different." Another example might be the note of my experience I mentioned at the beginning of the chapter—specifically, how nonblack students assumed I played on a sports team for no other reason than my race. Given the often subtle nature of racism, I refer to microaggressions throughout the book.

The unique historical moment during which I collected data for *Black Campus Life* is also worth noting. I began collecting data soon after the presidential inauguration of Donald Trump—a period of racial dissonance. The logics of race in American society, for some, seemed to be flipped on its head. An increase in hate crimes, emboldened White supremacists wearing Trump's "Make America Great Again" hats, and racist and sexist language invoked by the president seemed to stoke the flames of racial animus (see Feinberg et al. 2019). Less than a decade earlier, Barack Obama, the first Black president, had ushered in talks in mainstream media of the possibility of a postracial society where race no longer serves as a mark of oppression. Racism's hold on society, however, remained firm. If any assumed that Obama's presidency marked the end of racism, high-profile extrajudicial murders of Black people as well as the continued protests concerning race on campuses served as a rude awakening. Black college students mobilized at universities across the nation using social media and protests to highlight racist, inequitable conditions on their campuses (Racial Tension 2015). Similar protests continued throughout my process of data collection.

Examining Two Crises

This study examines the intersection of two crises, up close, from an ethnographic lens. The first is the United States' "quiet crisis," stemming from the nominal gap[4] between the United States' presumed need for workers with science, technology, engineering, and math (STEM) backgrounds and the limited production of graduates in STEM fields (Slaughter et al. 2015). Perhaps less quiet in nature, scholars also characterize race relations and diversity in higher education as a crisis (see Smith et al. 2002). From the integration of previously White colleges and universities in the mid-twentieth century to present-day campus protests concerning hostile racial climates at HWIs—campuses continue to reckon with the problem of the color line. As scholars of race and equity continue to demonstrate, the educational experiences of Black people attending HWIs can be, in a word, "agonizing" (Feagin et al. 1996). Issues with the racial climate spill over into STEM classrooms at HWIs. From limited numbers (Hurtado et al. 2010), to experiencing racialized insults and stereotypes in the classroom (e.g., Burt et al. 2018; McGee and Martin 2011), to feeling like "aliens" in STEM classes (Winkle-Wagner and McCoy 2016), Black people are further marginalized in STEM.

The immediacy of both issues draws the attention of scholars, policymakers, and activists alike. Because of this urgency, perhaps, researchers focus on outcomes, asking, "How can we get more Black students graduating with engineering degrees?" Little is known, however, of a critical piece in solving this puzzle—the daily life of Black engineering majors at HWIs. For example, research indicates that student engagement and belonging influences the persistence of Black engineering majors at HWIs (Harper 2010; Strayhorn 2012), but how is engagement manifested in daily life?

Project Description

I conducted a year-long ethnography of Black engineers at a selective HWI, West Side University (WSU). Black students comprise 5 percent of the undergraduate population at WSU. Even more minute was the percentage of Black students in Caldwell, the school of engineering—only 2 percent or fifty-eight students (see Table 1.1). WSU and its school of engineering are particularly useful for study in the temporal moment because the undergraduate population is technically a majority-minority school in terms of race. Studying race relations in a majority-minority school is especially important given the increasingly diverse American higher education and societal context. While gaps persist in racial representation, the demographics of student populations are changing, likewise shaping campus racial dynamics.[5] As such, *Black Campus Life* examines how Black students majoring in engineering or computer science at the same institution experience the campus racial climate in a majority-minority context.[6]

An ethnographic study of how Black engineers foster a sense of engagement because of, and/or in spite of the campus racial climate and

Table 1.1. WSU Engineering Undergraduate Full-Time Student Composition

Racial/Ethnic Identification	Percentage
Unknown	1%
Pacific Islander	>1%
Black	2%
White	34%
Asian-American	26%
Latinx*	14%
Native American	>1%
International*	18%
2 or more races*	5%

*Race not listed

Source: Data compiled from the American Society for Engineering Education.

Note: Percentages are rounded to nearest percent.

institutional structures, presents an opportunity to learn more about student engagement, heterogeneity within Black engineering majors, as well as the lived experiences of Black people at HWIs. Thus, the larger purpose of this work is to gain qualitative understanding of how Black students in engineering and computer science at an HWI experience and shape the campus racial climate and seek out or create mechanisms of engagement.

I used National Society of Black Engineers (NSBE) meetings at WSU as an initial site to meet Black engineers. My identity as a younger Black person in my mid-twenties likely aided in my ability to build rapport with students. With extended contact with students, I conducted 113 interviews and more than 180 hours of observation. I also interviewed nearly 77 percent of the entire Black undergraduate engineering population at WSU. More information concerning my data-collection, analysis, and positionality can be found in the appendix.

Studying Black Student Life

University chapters of NSBE and Black Student Unions are examples of Black social worlds that scholars often refer to but rarely research. While guided by the stories of the students I talked to, my decision to include and begin with Black students' social worlds was also informed by the sociology of E. Franklin Frazier. To better understand the context of race relations in America, E. Franklin Frazier (1968) argued that scholars needed to study "the social world of the Negro" (50). Living and publishing during the early to mid-twentieth century, Frazier noted the capacity in which Black people came in contact with Whites. While interracial contact was more frequent in the North, Frazier (1968) noted that, in the South, "the life of the Negro outside his economic relationships with Whites revolves chiefly about the organized social life of the Negro community" (52). I began my research with a similar assumption—that, with the exception of courses or campus-wide events, the social lives of some Black students attending HWIs might be anchored in Black social worlds on campus.

Sylvia Hurtado's (1992) foundational work, "The Campus Racial Climate: The Contexts of Conflict," provides a framework for the study of campus race relations. Given the urgency of campus racial climate studies, most research analyzing campus climate similarly begins with conflict, or how students challenge or experience racism (see Harper and Hurtado

2007). Too often, however, scholars neglect the Black campus social worlds in climate studies. Rarely do scholars endeavor to examine what makes a campus climate positive for students, students' racial lives outside of conflict, or how students themselves shape the campus racial climate.

Studying Black collegians through an ethnographic lens is particularly important because scholars often rely on one-time interviews to study Black students' experiences (see Harper 2014). Similarly, campus racial climate research, while sometimes qualitative, is rarely ethnographic (see Hurtado et al. 2008). Through an ethnography, I was able to interview students who might not otherwise be interviewed. Yet, even in ethnographies of campus life, Black life is underexplored.[7] By virtue of my identity, however, I was uniquely positioned to begin this study in the Black campus community, a social world previously unexplored by, or perhaps even off-limits to other scholars. I was often mistaken for a Black engineering major myself. Partly because of my identity, I achieved a level of closeness that other scholars could not. As a result, I can tell a story that other scholars cannot.

Thinking with Theories

Ralph Ellison, after moving to New York City, recounted enjoying the freedom of sitting wherever he pleased on buses. While still haunted by memories of sitting in the back of segregated buses in the Jim Crow South, Ellison began to see that, in the back of buses, he enjoyed more space and a view of the happenings on the bus. He wondered "to what extent had I failed to grasp a certain degree of freedom that had always existed in my group's state of unfreedom?" (2003, 626). Ellison's reflection informed how I studied agency and Black students' lives. Even within Jim Crow segregation, Black people, to some degree, had agency. Ellison meditates upon the freedoms he enjoyed without discounting oppressive conditions. Taking cues from Ellison, I argue that despite racist conditions at HWIs, Black students are agentic, capable of surviving, enjoying, and even shaping the campus experience for their unique needs. I use Pierre Bourdieu's Theory of Practice and Critical Race Theory as tools to understand both the objective structures that create a state of unfreedom for Black students, as well as their behaviors within, and sometimes against, such structures.

USING PIERRE BOURDIEU'S THEORY OF PRACTICE

I use Pierre Bourdieu's sociological work to understand students' networks, cultures, and the relationship between students' agency and structures (Bourdieu and Passeron 1990; Gonzales 2014). Bourdieu was a French sociologist who was very concerned about societal reproduction, especially the taken-for-granted structures, relationships, and customs that perpetuate inequality. His theory is useful in understanding how objective societal structures inform the subjective behaviors exhibited by individuals. Bourdieu's work is also helpful in explaining why some groups engage in specific behaviors while others do not. In thinking with Bourdieu, I engage with complex questions of behavior and culture such as, "Why do some students feel more comfortable in the NSBE community than the Black community?"

Black students, as I mentioned, are often seen as generally experiencing the campus climate more negatively than their White counterparts (see Harper and Hurtado 2007). Informed by Bourdieu, however, I analyze how personal histories of Black engineers and the unique setting of a selective HWI contributed to their practices and unique understandings of campus. Bourdieu provides the tools to analyze how some Black students' backgrounds of attending elite, predominantly White and private high schools, for example, informed their campus experience and which social worlds they were drawn to. Drawing from Bourdieu's Theory of Practice, I similarly show how the social worlds students are attached to shape students' mechanisms of engagement and perceptions of the campus racial climate.

CRITICAL RACE THEORY

I use Critical Race Theory (CRT) to understand the context of racism in American society and on WSU's campus. CRT came about as a response to Critical Legal Studies—a legal framework created to challenge the law's role in reifying class hierarchies. A group of scholars argued that Critical Legal Studies scholars unduly focused on class and diminished the role of racism (Delgado and Stefancic 2012). Kimberlé Crenshaw, one of the leaders of the CRT movement, critiqued Critical Legal Studies for "its failure to come to terms with the particularity of race" (Crenshaw et al. 1995, xxvi). Drawing from CRT and the legal field, Gloria Ladson-Billings and William Tate IV first introduced CRT to education in 1995.

As a framework, CRT is at its best when its lens is directed toward identifying racism and the racialized nature of different aspects of education. As Zeus Leonardo (2013) suggests, the Critical Race scholar holds that "race is always in play, never irrelevant" (21). The CRT lens sees racism as ordinary and deeply engrained within society. CRT informed how I viewed Black students' experiences with race and how they encounter racism in a world where racism is permanent. I am indebted to the many scholars, who for so long, have asserted and analyzed how race and Blackness in particular matter in education (e.g., Allen 1992; Davis 1994; Feagin et al. 1996; Fleming 1984; Harper 2012; Hurtado et al. 2008; Ladson-Billings and Tate 1995; Patton 2016; Tierney 1999). Because of their work, I am able to do something different. I accept racism as a given, adopting racial realism—a core proposition of CRT—as an analytic lens.

Racial realism is premised upon the recognition of the permanence of racism in society and education. Derrick Bell (1992), who coined the term *racial realism,* argued that a racial realist perspective "enables us to avoid despair, and frees us to imagine and implement racial strategies that can bring fulfillment and even triumph" (373–74). Bell (1992) offers four points to understand racial realism. First, the path to racial progress and civil rights is not linear. As time continues to pass, for example, the racial realist does not assume that society will naturally become less racist or that the societal standing, wealth, and life outcomes of Black people in America is bound to positively change. Second, racial realism focuses on the material conditions of Black people rather than the ethics or attitudes of nonblack others. Analyzing racist ideologies is important, but racial realism refocuses on the material, everyday lives of Black folks in order to strategize creative ways to support them. Third, while racism is permanent, one can find fulfillment in the struggle against racism itself. In focusing on the process—the struggle and resistance against racism—rather than outcomes, one can avoid despair and continue challenging oppressive structures. Lastly, Bell argues that anyone fighting against racism and for social justice must be realistic about racism's hold on society to avoid idealism. While Bell offers points that can be applied to social justice and advocacy work, racial realism can also be applied to how one goes about research. A racial realist perspective frees scholars to imagine new questions. From a racial realist perspective, questions concerning the existence of racism such as, "Does racism play a role in higher education?" are already answered in the affirmative. What other questions, then, might we ask? I use racial realism to show the multitude of ways—from the positive to the negative to the mundane—that race matters in students' everyday lives. I therefore use racial realism as an analytic tool throughout *Black Campus Life*.

Race and racism lie at the center of a CRT analysis. However, CRT also supports an antiessentialist view of race, examining how race intersects with other identities such as sexual orientation, class, language, and gender (Crenshaw 1991; Delgado and Stefancic 2012). As such, while a CRT analysis engages with intersecting identities, they are understood through a lens of race and racism. Similarly, in this project, while I attend to various identities, examining how class and gender intersect with race, I prioritized race in data collection and analysis. This, of course, is not to say gender or other identities do not matter and do not shape the campus experience. I engage with students' various intersecting identities throughout the text. Yet, in attempting to paint a broader portrait of Black engineering students' campus lives, I could not provide the rich, intersectional analyses that comes from narrowing on a more specific population such as Black men or Black women (e.g., Brooms 2017; Winkle-Wagner 2009). My point, however, is that my analysis is limited as my protocol was mainly preoccupied with race.

MAKING BLACK LIVES MATTER IN RESEARCH

I began this chapter with a passage from the novelist, ethnographer, and critic Zora Neale Hurston. She points out that "Negroes love and hate and fight and play and strive and travel and have a thousand and one interests in life like other humans" (as cited in Hunter et al. 2016). Despite the preponderance of racist violence and terrorism, Hurston asserts that Black people's lives do not singularly revolve around racism. In a similar manner, I assert that Black students are more than the manner in which they cope with hostile racial climates. As Hunter and colleagues (2016) noted, "[S]ocial science scholarship on Black urban communities . . . so rarely captures the life that happens within them, and thus the matter of Black people's humanity" (2). The same can be said of research on Black students attending HWIs. Black students are people leading normal lives—they go to the gym, party, have lunch, watch TV, etc. By only focusing on the difficult experiences of a group, we inadvertently make them one-dimensional.

A product of Fisk and later Harvard University, Du Bois himself experienced life uniquely as a Black man at an HWI. While not explicitly focusing on his time at Harvard, a young Du Bois began his *Souls of Black Folk* highlighting his experience being one of the few Black people in majority White settings. Describing his interactions with seemingly well-meaning White people, behind their conversation starters—"I know an excellent colored man in my town; or . . . Do not these Southern outrages make your blood boil?" (1903)—was a more fundamental, unasked question, "How does it feel to be a problem?"

Whether implicitly or explicitly, scholars studying Black students' experiences at HWIs continue to reckon with the question posed to Du Bois—how does it feel to be a problem? Such work is a necessity given the permanence of racism in American society and the unwillingness of some to seriously consider that race matters. Yet, research stemming from the problem status of Black people will be limited in the questions asked, stories told, theories used, and conclusions made. How, for example, might a group of Black engineering majors at a selective HWI cast themselves? Consider the second NSBE general body meeting I attended at WSU, which I briefly highlight next.

◆ ◆ ◆

Nina, the vice president of WSU's NSBE Chapter, introduced two representatives from Twitter. Students had a double incentive to come to the NSBE meeting that evening—free food as well as the chance to hear from employees from a big company. Thirty-six students, all Black, were in the audience. At least three split their attention between computer programming assignments on their laptops and the guest speakers. Others paid little attention to the talk because they were in fields of engineering that Twitter was not interested in recruiting.

One of the representatives, a Black man wearing faded blue jeans, black sneakers, and a navy blue T-shirt with the Twitter logo on it, explained the specifics of his computer programming job as well as how he landed at Twitter. We listened in awe as he explained how he came to America as a refugee and how his grandfather was a chief in a town in Sierra Leone. "I started at Best Buy, just loading stuff," he explained, and by a stroke of luck, his manager overheard him explain a tech product to a customer and recommended he move to the Geek Squad department. "From there, I started doing coding meet-ups and eventually started working for Amazon. Left there, and here I am," he explained. Seeking to fill in some gaps in his story, Charlie, a senior, asked, "So what did you major in, in college?" "I was self-taught," he replied. He scanned the students for another hand to answer more questions. Charlie raised his eyebrows in surprise. I heard some muffled "Wow's." I looked at Johnson and caught him doing a quick dab,[8] signifying how the representative just shocked everyone. Anthony said, "Okay, Black excellence!" Johnson texted me shortly after, "Where did they find this super negro? He's a prince and a genius. lol."

Ayana, the NSBE president, thanked the Twitter reps for coming, saying, "And to close this meeting, in true NSBE fashion . . ." On cue, all of the students stood from their seats. In unison they recited the NSBE mission, "To increase the number of culturally responsible Black engineers who excel academically, succeed professionally, and positively impact the community." While chatting with other NSBE members, Johnson said, "I felt like the Black guy was kind of stuntin' on us. Like I get he was trying to show that we can do anything, but yeah. Not at all relatable. But Black excellence for sure." Anthony added, "Right! Self-taught . . ." he laughed, "it's like we were trying to get him to tell us how we could get there too, but it's like he didn't understand."

◆ ◆ ◆

We miss stories like this, I believe, if we begin with the question levied at Du Bois, "How does it feel to be a problem?" We might miss the heterogeneity not only in Blackness, but also in engineering. We might miss the leadership of Black women, how Black students manage intense workloads, make use of resources available to them, and understand success in their fields. While Du Bois's question remains relevant, I argue that there is something more about Black students' experiences that we might learn from when we recognize their agency, accept racism as a given, and appreciate that the whole of their campus lives are not reducible to responses to racism.

The Organization of *Black Campus Life*

Black Campus Life can be understood as a tour of WSU student life through the lens of a group of Black engineers. Chapter 2 sets the stage for the remainder of the text, providing temporal context, describing relevant WSU history as well as the school's current state of race relations and engineering. Chapters 3–11 are divided into four parts. Each part represents a different campus social world—the Black community, the Black engineering community, the engineering school, and the mainstream campus community. I explain how students experience the racial climate and foster a sense of engagement in each social world. I also highlight the tensions within these social worlds to provide a better portrait of their dynamic nature. With the exception of the three chapters describing the engineering school (chapters 7–9), I dedicate two chapters to each social world. One chapter provides rich description of the social world itself and the other chapter highlights a narrative of a student with a unique relationship to that particular social world.

The rich descriptions of the social worlds shape a mosaic of WSU life. In the chapters dedicated to single students, however, I delve into their histories prior to college. A student's background, or as Bourdieu would say, *habitus,* also shapes one's practices and experiences on campus. I use these individual narratives and experiences of four students to make better sense of the intersection of social worlds, campus life, and student backgrounds. These narratives also serve a practical purpose—through the many pages of ethnographies, or presentation of qualitative data, it is easy to get lost in concepts, forgetting participants' unique identities. These individual portraits, serve as rich, streamlined examples of how Black students in the same engineering school experience the same campus in different ways.

The goal of *Black Campus Life,* was not simply to enumerate how Black students are either thriving or struggling. The goal was not to identify a culture of deficits or assets. Rather, the goal was to examine Black engineering majors' campus lives and culture as they were. In learning more about Black student engagement at an HWI we might develop pragmatic strategies of increasing Black students' persistence in engineering and higher education in general. The research begins with the acknowledgment that racism exists in the United States. Given these conditions, however, my assumption is that individuals and postsecondary organizations are able to work against disabling structures—but one must first understand them. When we learn what is happening we can better identify problems and potential solutions. Hence, I am suggesting that we need to know more about Black student life in order to bring about change.

2

Understanding the Past and Present
of West Side University

West Side University (WSU) is a world of its own. The gate spanning the boundary of campus with sharp, spearlike tops, and spaces too small to squeeze through would be an eyesore if it was not partially shrouded by magnolia trees, aloe, and other shrubbery. The cast iron rods, almost like a wall surrounding an old castle, create a physical boundary between the campus and the neighborhood.

WSU's reputation as a selective university with an international network precedes itself, beckoning hopeful students from across the globe. Tours begin near the student union, a central point of university activity. In this area, one can find ATMs, a food court, and the WSU Black Cultural Center. The guides, current WSU students, wear khakis and signature polo shirts with the school's colors. They lead throngs of guests around WSU, backpedaling at a leisurely pace, sharing bits of campus history and rehearsed stories and facts about campus life.

History is always present, providing the foundation for current contexts and how people understand their conditions. In much higher education research, however, campuses are constructed as universities without histories. Taking my cues from university tour guides, Critical Race Theorists, as well as the sociologist Pierre Bourdieu, I buck this trend and provide temporal context. Part of a Critical Race Theorist's work is excavating histories of racially marginalized people to better understand the racial realities of the present (Patton 2016).

The racist and sexist history of engineering culture in America is no secret (e.g., Bix 2004; Slaton 2010). WSU is no different, representing

19

a microcosm of the historical trends in engineering culture. I show how WSU's construction of engineers changed over time—from White men, to the inclusion of White women, to the inclusion of other racial groups in the construction of possible engineering students. I make the case that WSU engineering school—a progressive, majority-minority school—is uniquely situated as the site of study to tell us more about campus life, modern-day race relations, and life as a Black engineering major. I finish setting the stage for the remainder of the book by previewing the social worlds I highlight in the subsequent chapters.

Campus Life and Shifting Campus Color Lines

College life, upon the inception of higher education in America, was decidedly for White men. Up until the mid-twentieth century, with the exception of Historically Black Colleges and Universities and few other cases, students, faculty, and administrators were, for the most part, White men. Black people, however, were inextricably bound to the inception and expansion of American higher education—not as students, but as enslaved people.[1] The founding fathers of the first colleges and universities sold Black people as property and used enslaved Black people as a free labor source to build university buildings, effectively using chattel slavery to subsidize the beginnings of higher education (Wilder 2014).

The question of Black campus life at predominantly White universities, in particular, came to the fore during the Black Campus Movement of the 1960s. Black social worlds on nonblack campuses were forged through student protest and other manifestations of Black student agency. In the swell of the Civil Rights and Black Power Movements, Black student activists advocated for resources to create and support student organizations centering on the needs and interests of their specific culture and race (Rogers 2012). The Black Campus Movement similarly shaped Black students' lives at WSU. Only after concerted Black student activism and demands did WSU create a Black Cultural Center. Concerning the need for the center, one of the Black Student Union (BSU) leaders said, "Black students are unwelcome here and are not receiving needed services. We need to focus to ensure their retention." Through higher recruitment of Black students as well as the creation of Black Cultural Centers, Black-affinity residence halls, and Black studies programs, a more distinct Black campus life emerged.

A similar tenor can be found in the voices of Black students in more recent times. Mirroring the walkouts and protests of the Black Campus Movement (Biondi 2012), 2015 and 2016 in particular saw numerous protests concerning racial justice and antiblack racism on campuses (Dache et al. 2019; Hailu and Sarubbi 2019; Morgan and Davis 2019; Racial Tension 2015). The resurgence of Black student protests, however, did not take place in a vacuum. Rather, Black campus activism is tied to #BlackLivesMatter, a movement for Black lives and liberation that came about in response to highly publicized extrajudicial murders of Black people as well the justice system's inability to find their killers guilty of any crime. Students protesting the extrajudicial murders of Black people outside of the institution were also fighting for racial justice inside of their institutions. Students across the nation protested inequitable campus experiences, demanding more Black representation of students, staff, and faculty, the removal of racist campus monuments, and other changes that might foster a more inclusive campus racial climate. From the Black Campus Movement, to the nationwide protests between 2015–16, to the racial uprisings and subsequent student demands during the summer of 2020, how students experience the campus racial climate will remain a perennial issue.

Demographics in the United States have also shifted, making the study of race in higher education at this moment unique. WSU serves as an ideal location to learn more about what the historically White and majority-minority institutional context means for Black students. WSU's school of engineering, Caldwell, is also a majority-minority school (refer to Table 1.1). It is important to note, that in both the school in general and the school of engineering, a classification of majority-minority is not synonymous with a majority Black student population.

Caldwell School of Engineering promotional folders, brochures, and web site headlines boast the relatively high representation of women in the school at 40 percent. The percentage of Black students in Caldwell was harder to find and unavailable on the school website. After requesting data from WSU, I found that fifty-eight total Black undergraduates were majoring in engineering or computer science at the beginning of my fieldwork. At first blush, one might rightly think Black students make up a small fraction of the engineering school. In the coming chapters, students give pointed examples of how their small numbers shaped their experiences at WSU and in Caldwell. Despite marginal Black representation, Black students and staff often spoke highly of Caldwell's diversity efforts. How is this possible? The answer, in part, begins with the history of Caldwell.

The History of Caldwell School of Engineering

WSU awarded its first engineering degree in 1910. A developing program, engineering classes were held in an old building on campus. WSU engineering students complained about the poor conditions at the school, joking that they had to hold umbrellas over their head when sitting through lectures if it was raining. The roof of the building was notoriously leaky. One student jokingly recalled his professors trying in vain to write formulas on a wet blackboard. The engineering department moved into a new building in 1928 and continued to grow. In 1967, the first buildings surrounding the Engineering Field, affectionately known as the E-Field by current students, were constructed.

In the early 1960s, an Asian American WSU engineering student who served as editor of the engineering section of the university magazine, *The West Side,* described the section as the "voice of the WSU School of Engineering. It is read nationally, by other students, companies, alumni, and visitors." I scoured volumes of *The West Side* in the university archives, each edition from 1950 to its discontinuation in 1985, flipping pages, scanning for Black faces, any reference to Black people, and how engineering intersected with identity. I rely on the engineering section of *The West Side* magazines and the WSU daily newspaper,[2] to: (1) describe how White men were constructed as the prototypical engineer, and (2) examine the history of Black students in relation to WSU engineering.

WHEN WSU ENGINEERS WERE WHITE AND ASIAN MEN

"Who is truly representative of the engineering student body?" the WSU engineering dean asked in the March 1963 issue. He went through a litany of categories including the "fraternity man," or "the quiet and industrious scholar who shuns publicity while devoting most of his waking hours to his education." The dean celebrated the different typologies of engineering students, boasting, "The engineering student body at WSU is probably the most diversified of any major university." The dean, however, was referring to diversity within a rather homogenous group comprised of White and a few East Asian men. Women engineers and engineers of other races were not considered within the realm of possibility.

Because of racist, sexist, and classist societal structures, engineering was a profession almost exclusively for middle-class White men (e.g., Beddoes 2017; Secules 2019). *The West Side's* engineering section was similarly geared toward White men, the prototypical engineers. In the same 1954 Letters to the Editor section, one note expressed gratitude about a piece on U.S. air defense, while another read, "Forget the magazine. Sell pin-up pictures." The magazine's audience were engineers, and thereby men who would presumably enjoy "pin-up" photographs. Editors, enrolled Caldwell students, were not so bold as to have a labeled "pin-up pictures" section. Up until the late 1970s, however, they did dedicate a one-page, sometimes two, spread to a monthly "Girl to Watch." While later editions were focused on the woman's interests, earlier editions featured women in bathing suits, with crass commentary.

Early editions of the magazine had a section called Curves, with an illustration of a White woman in a bikini. Perhaps risqué for the time, this section was "old boys club" in nature, including jokes about engineering culture and life as an engineer, which meant life as a White man. Most jokes objectified women or attempted to describe the relationships between awkward engineers (i.e., men) and women. Consider the misogynistic "joke" from a 1963 issue:

The girl greeted her boyfriend with the question, "Notice anything different?"

"New dress?"

"No."

"New Shoes?"

"No"

"New hat?"

"No."

"I give up."

"I'm wearing a gas mask."

Within the very same issue, an article covered the Women in Engineering conference held at WSU. During a keynote speech, the WSU engineering dean emphasized the need for women in engineering, suggesting that women's proclivity toward organization would be useful. He also pointed to how women in Russia, a competitor in the space race, were becoming engineers. The dean's sentiments toward women were certainly sexist and patronizing. Yet, considering the time period, his support for women in engineering might also be considered somewhat progressive. The misogynistic jokes in the very same issue of *The West Side* demonstrates the tensions and failings of advocating inclusivity in an otherwise discriminatory context.

The societal construction of engineers was gendered—everything related to an engineer was referred to as "he," "him," or "his." Women were seen as "co-eds," dates, or objects to lust after. Although the *The West Side* began advertising for the Society of Women Engineers in 1966, there was little doubt about who were the prototypical engineers. In a student column in a 1972 issue, a man majoring in engineering recounted his surprise upon seeing over a dozen women in an electrical engineering class. The author mentioned that all of the men looked confused at the sight of women in the class. The professor, confused as well, learned that the women were actually in the wrong class. Reflecting, the author, said:

> I had witnessed the engineer's reaction to the female—and it paralleled exactly our approach to an electric circuit: the safest course is to stay away all together, that way no mistakes are made and we can keep our GPA up.

Women did not fit the engineering image and, if *The West Side* is any indication, were actively made to feel unwelcome in Caldwell. The misogynistic culture apparent in this university-sponsored periodical provides insight to the history shaping the male-dominated tech and engineering fields today (e.g., Margolis and Fisher 2002; Seymour and Hewitt 1997; Stitt and Happel-Parkins 2019). Black people, however, faced uniquely racialized barriers to engineering education at predominantly White institutions across the nation (see Slaton 2010). The history of WSU engineering is similarly fraught with racism and a pronounced absence of Black people in the role of engineering students.

THE SHORT HISTORY OF BLACK PEOPLE IN ENGINEERING AT WSU

"The scene is darkest Africa. But Africa is lightening," reads the first two sentences of an advertisement for a global engineering company. The advertisement pictures an illustration of two African men with short hair and black skin reflecting light from their bare backs, carrying boxes out of a jungle. Below them is a construction site. Featured in a 1952 issue, this advertisement was the first reference, of any sort, to Black people in the periodical. The company, much like other engineering companies during the time, touted its diversity. Ironically, diversification was often used to describe the range of products an engineering company specialized in building—not diversity in racial representation. The next appearance of a Black person was in a Kodak advertisement—a shirtless dark-skinned African man wearing a headdress, drinking a Pepsi. In the late 1960s, however, Black people began to be pictured in the roles of college students, soldiers, scientists, and engineers. Advertisements in *The West Side* tell a story. While first pictured as unskilled laborers and images in advertisements divorced from technology, by the 1970s Black people could be identified as possible engineers and scientists in the magazine.

The West Side addressed Black people in engineering for the first time in 1968—fifty-eight years after the first person graduated with an WSU engineering degree, fifty-nine years after the first Black student earned a WSU undergraduate degree, and forty-seven years after the first known Black student enrolled in engineering at WSU. The dean of the engineering school at the time, Dean Thomas, was shaken by the assassination of Dr. Martin Luther King Jr. and penned a two-page piece about Black people in engineering. The number of Black engineers at WSU, according to the dean, was "a straight zero." In reference to other groups, he noted, "Our society has done a relatively good job of integrating Orientals and Jews throughout the entire fabric of industrial and professional life." Lamenting the limited Black and Latinx representation, Dean Thomas continued, "Our student body is so deficient in Negro and Mexican-American students that the casual observer would surely think that we had a segregationist in the admissions office, while nothing could be farther from the truth." The "sad fact" concerning the lack of representation was that "we simply don't have, across the nation as a whole, more than the tiniest trickle of Negroes and Latin-Americans coming into engineering schools, and this has been true for a very long time."

Dean Thomas's move to blame the lack of Black representation, however, is questionable, considering the critical role of Historically Black Colleges and Universities (HBCUs) in the wider context of the production of Black engineers. Before the Civil Rights Act of 1964 for example, most Black engineers graduated from six HBCUs (McNeely and Frehill 2011). Even after 1964, nearly a full decade later, these six institutions continued to graduate almost half of new Black engineers (Blackwell 1987). While the representation of Black engineers at schools like WSU increased, their numbers were marginal.

Relative to the times, Dean Thomas seemed to take a progressive stance concerning racial diversity in engineering, describing the opportunity to increase the number of Black engineers at WSU as a "great opportunity." The dean also applauded a trustee who, within hours after Dr. King's assassination, established a $50,000 endowment for a Martin Luther King Jr. scholarship specifically for Black students. Addressing economic constraints of Black people, the dean also suggested that additional scholarships be given to Black engineering students. As if anticipating negative responses, he entitled one section, "Implications for White Students," assuring readers that White students would neither be affected nor would admission standards be lowered. He concludes with a rallying cry, "It is all up to us—employers, teachers and parents—in this point and time in history to do our part in fulfilling this dream for a better world."

The engineering school later created a Multicultural Engineering Office in 1975—two years prior to WSU's creation of the Black Cultural Center—to assist in the recruitment, retention, and graduation of historically underrepresented students pursuing degrees in engineering. Considering that the Multicultural Engineering Office was created prior to the Black Cultural Center, it is possible that WSU's school of engineering was more progressive or more easily convinced of the importance of inclusivity than WSU in general. Their relatively progressive stance on racial diversity, however, should not be confused with racial equity.

The pages of *The West Side* did not carry many clues related to what life was like for Black Caldwell students. Black students were rarely pictured prior to the mid-1970s. The absence of Black people in images and in discourse, however, is important. *The West Side* provides insight into the social idea of who engineers were—White or Asian American men. As such, the social idea of a White or Asian American man as an engineer becomes a controlling image (e.g., Collins 2000; Golash-Boza 2016). Controlling images "are designed to make racism, sexism, poverty, and other forms of social injustice appear to be natural, normal, and inevitable parts of everyday life" (Collins 2000, 69). The controlling image of typical engineers defines both who was associated with engineering and who was not.

A CRT analysis of higher education holds that "[t]he establishment of U.S. higher education is deeply rooted in racism/White supremacy, the vestiges of which remain palatable" (e.g., Patton 2016, 317). The same is true for engineering education. Evidence of an engineering culture subscribing to racist and sexist logics littered the pages of *The West Side* engineering section—from images of Black people as laborers divorced from the creation of technology to the absence of any mention, reference, or picture of Black engineers prior to the assassination of Dr. Martin Luther King Jr. WSU's complex history, both of structural identity-based exclusion and relative progressive stances on diversity, is the foundation for campus life as experienced by participants in the present study.

Diversity and Caldwell

WSU's school of engineering, Caldwell, has continued its progressive tendencies in terms of equity. Aside from the 2 percent Black undergraduate engineering population, Caldwell might even be considered a model school for diversity efforts. The administration and staff view racial representation and equity-based issues as engineering problems and engage with them in a scientific fashion.

The director of admissions explained the difficulty of increasing the racial representation of Black students in Caldwell. Almost echoing Dean Thomas's sentiments over fifty years earlier, the director sighed, "It's our biggest problem in historically underrepresented populations. The majority of the applicants are not prepared. There's nothing we can do about it other than continue to talk about it." I asked, "So, what's your biggest issue in getting more Black students here?" After pausing for a moment he replied, "I think that, my personal opinion is that the fully prepared Black students can literally go wherever they want. Because there are not many fully prepared Black students." The director conveyed that it was not for a lack of trying that the Black population was low. He gave an example of the institution's problem-solving approach to recruitment and admissions. Admissions identified that, on average, 4–6 percent of underrepresented racial minorities would "melt," or commit to enrolling but fail to matriculate into WSU. The following year, they used consistent and intentional communication with this population with the help of WSU's Multicultural Engineering Office over the summer prior to the new class's enrollment. With a smile, he told me the result, "Last year, zero percent melt in our underrepresented populations." While I do not know how much of this fraction were Black students, this example is indicative of Caldwell's efforts toward increasing diversity.

As Nina, an executive board member[3] of the National Society of Black Engineers (NSBE) at WSU told me, "Caldwell literally leads the way. We do something and the rest of WSU follows. . . . We hired a Diversity and

Equity Officer first. So it goes for diversity too." In 2015, during what the Black Student Union president referred to as "the campus climate era," WSU implemented a diversity action plan, requiring every department to name a "Diversity Liaison." Most departments at WSU simply entrusted an existing faculty member with added Diversity Liaison duties. While WSU did not make a hire specifically to deal with issues of diversity and equity for the school in general, Caldwell did.

"We decided to reformulate what we do here. And so, we created a new office for the Director of Equity and Inclusion," the dean of Caldwell told me. Reflecting on their efforts to increase diversity and equity at Caldwell, the dean said, "I look at all this with very much an engineering mindset." He also was involved in a nationwide pledge to increase diversity in engineering schools across the nation. In addition to the social justice and ethical component of increasing diversity he finds diversity beneficial to the field. In a twist of irony, the dean of Caldwell used Charles Darwin's thought, once used to justify racism and exclusion, to explain the benefits of racial diversity in engineering:

> [J]ust like in Darwin's evolution, only the good ideas or what-ever, survive and then becomes the new thing. The same thing is with knowledge and ideas. And so, the more diversity you have in this, the more possibilities you can have, better ideas coming.

Engineering schools are often characterized as "chilly" environments, conservative in terms of diversity and inclusion (e.g., McGee and Martin 2011; Rincón and George-Jackson 2016). Caldwell, at first blush, seems to buck that trend. During an annual luncheon celebrating graduating underrepresented racial minorities in engineering, the new director of equity and inclusion, a Black woman, applauded Caldwell, noting that WSU was among the first institutions to fund an office dedicated to engineering diversity. She punctuated the fact, laughing, "That's when you applaud."

This text studies campus racial climate and the campus experience through the lens of Black Caldwell students. The findings I present are specific to the temporal moment, on the heels of the "campus climate era," as well as within the context of an HWI that, by many regards, leads the way in terms of diversity in the school of engineering. United by a Caldwell engineering major, participants were uniquely positioned to speak about their niche community of Black engineering as well as other communities, or campus social worlds.

Introducing Four Social Worlds and Four Students

Black Campus Life, as I mentioned earlier, is divided into four parts. Each part provides a portrait of a particular campus community or social world. In order to vividly portray each social world, I dedicate at least one chapter to describing the characteristics, unique membership practices, boundaries, and tensions students face in navigating the social world. Social boundaries exist in each world, signifying who does and does not belong to a community. Following the lead of other scholars (Carter 2006; Cohen 1999), I also use the idea of boundaries to provide a vivid depiction of the complex and multifarious nature of Black student life. In each part, I also dedicate a chapter to one student with a unique relationship to that particular social world. The four students I spotlight tell us not only about the social world they are especially enmeshed in, but also about how the same student can feel both included and alienated on the same campus (Table 2.1). These portraits provide rich description of the interplay between social worlds and individual experiences.

Table 2.1. Introducing Four Students

Name	Major	GPA	Class Year*	Socioeconomic background	Ethnicity
Johnson	Industrial & Systems Engineering	2.7	Junior	Working Class	Caribbean American
Jasmine	Math & Electrical Engineering	3.4	Junior	Working Class	Caribbean American
Nina	Mechanical Engineering	3.05	Junior	Upper Middle Class	Black American**
Martin	Electrical Engineering	3.0	Sophomore	Upper Middle Class	Black American***

* I listed a participant's class year based on when I first met the student during fieldwork.

** Nina's father is White and mother is Black. In her demographic survey, however, she did not list her father's ethnicity.

*** I use the term Black American to refer to Black people who are descendants of enslaved people in America. I employ this term, Black American, not as a point of divisiveness but to clarify a distinct ethnicity.

My attempt to classify actions or practices in relation to specific worlds is, to an extent, imprecise, as social worlds are dynamic and overlapping. In my research, however, I identified four distinct campus worlds: (1) the Black WSU community, (2) the WSU NSBE community, (3) the Caldwell Engineering School community, and (4) the mainstream WSU community (Table 2.2).

THE BLACK WSU SOCIAL WORLD

Involvement in the Black community is not a given based on one's identity. At historically and predominantly White institutions, Black students could very well spend the bulk of their cultural and social lives in homogeneously Black social worlds such as the Black community. Black students can avoid racial microaggressions within this community, but tensions still exist. While engagement or attachment to the Black community can offer friends, belonging, and a place of respite—membership comes at the cost of time. For engineers, time is hard to come by. The NSBE community, while not completely distinct from the Black community, often better suits the specific needs of Black engineers.

Table 2.2. Different Worlds, Different Practices

Community	Membership/Engagement Practices
Black	1. Attending BSU meetings and BSU sponsored events
	2. "Hanging out" with other Black students
Black Engineering	1. Attending NSBE meetings and events regularly and holding leadership positions
	2. Attending NSBE conferences/conventions
Engineering School	1. Membership in engineering society
	2. Membership in Caldwell Student Association
	3. Attending Caldwell sponsored events/lectures
Mainstream WSU	1. Membership in a fraternity/sorority on Fraternity Row
	2. Membership in campus groups other than ethnic specific organizations

THE BLACK ENGINEERING SOCIAL WORLD

I understood the WSU NSBE chapter as the center of the Black engineering community's social world. I met all but two of the undergraduate Black engineers in my sample through NSBE meetings. While most Black engineers were NSBE members, the regularity and intensity of their participation varied. Engagement in the NSBE social world included attending weekly general body meetings, coming to NSBE events, volunteering with NSBE committees, and coming to NSBE-led leisure activities (e.g., movie nights or parties). NSBE also provides networking with engineering professionals, regional and national conferences with recruiters coming with the express interest of hiring Black engineers, informal and formal tutoring, and workshops at general body meetings related to the job application process (e.g., constructing cover letters, formatting resumes, and preparing for interviews).

THE ENGINEERING SCHOOL SOCIAL WORLD

Black engineers in the school of engineering are often the only person of their race in their class. This fact, along with the culture of their major, influences how students perceive and experience the engineering racial climate. Black engineers' responses to being the only ones, however, are varied. While all Black undergraduate engineers technically were part of Caldwell, the school of engineering, they were not necessarily part of Caldwell, the community. Students involved in the Caldwell community partake in Caldwell-sponsored organizations that are not centered on race. Groups included Caldwell Student Ambassadors, Caldwell periodicals, engineering interest groups, or engineering fraternities. Students involved in the Caldwell community were often in contact with students across racial lines.

THE MAINSTREAM WSU SOCIAL WORLD

I defined participation in the mainstream WSU community simply as having membership in a historically White fraternity/sorority or involvement in a student group on campus that was not centered on race. Beyond group involvement, students took part in the mainstream community for school-wide events such as sporting events, tailgates, or WSU-sponsored concerts. To an extent, all participants are involved with the WSU community given their status as WSU students. Yet, as I show in chapter 10, the minority of participants were actively engaged in this social world. In what follows, I take the reader on a tour of WSU. This tour, however, begins where some scholars have not observed, and many have taken for granted—the Black campus community.

THE BLACK COMMUNITY

3

The Time and Space to Engage in the
Black Community

Olivia loves being Black. She wears her hair natural, once commenting, "There's so much beauty in the curl." The once president of the WSU National Society of Black Engineers (NSBE) chapter reflected upon a gendered and racialized interaction, unsure if the offense could be considered a microaggression, saying, "People always want to dilute my Blackness . . . I've had it as a pickup line. Like, 'What are you mixed with?' Nigga . . . nothing. That always happens to me because I'm more fair skinned." She giggles, "I'm Black and Blacker." During that same interview, Olivia mentions, "I'm not integrated into the Black community here." How is it possible for someone like Olivia, who is comfortable in and proud of her racial identity, to feel like an outsider to the Black community? Simply identifying as Black does not grant one access into the Black community at WSU. Four WSU Black engineers, for example, expressed in some fashion that they did not feel connected to the Black community. The complexity and dynamism of campus communities and cultures are often taken for granted. Students spoke of the WSU Black community as an identifiable community with boundaries and unique qualities.

How are racially affirming campus spaces sustained? Do campus communities simply exist or are they made and remade? What makes an affinity-based organization such as a Black Student Union (BSU) invaluable to some but unnecessary to others? Such questions remain underexplored when scholars neglect to examine the interplay between the structure and agency of students' campus lives. As I show in this chapter and throughout the book, Black students are not simply acted upon by external factors. Campus cultures, environments, and racial climates are not discrete external forces that singularly shape students' experiences. Students themselves have a hand in shaping the campus.

Research on Black students' campus lives, however, is limited. Work supposedly about the general campus experience or work intending to provide insight into the social lives of undergraduates at four-year institutions, whether intentionally or unintentionally, revolve around White students (e.g., Armstrong and Hamilton 2013; Boyer 1987; Chambliss and Takacs 2014; Horowitz 1987; Moffatt 1989). In other words, campus life is given a white face. Consider Rebekah Nathan's *My Freshman Year* (2006), a widely cited ethnography of contemporary campus culture. Noting the absence of Black students in her study and in the university's cafeteria, Nathan secretly followed a Black woman grabbing lunch "to-go" in a failed attempt to see where the woman took her meal. In a like manner, research on campus life stops short of seriously interrogating the fullness of Black student life, rendering Black students' experiences beyond racism underexplored. Black student life is implicitly understood as existing on the periphery of campus life.

In this book, however, I begin the "tour" of WSU campus life within the racially homogenous Black WSU community social worlds. Critical Race Scholars center the voices and experiential knowledge of students of color (Parker and Lynn 2002). In line with a CRT approach, I center not just Black students' knowledge, but also their worlds. The WSU Black community, for example, is a world of its own with its own rules and practices, or what Bourdieu (1984) would call, *illusio*. The social worlds of *fields*, Bourdieu suggested, have unique *illusio* that people buy into, characterized by actors' investment in a *field*'s distinct traditions and symbols.

My decision to start the "tour" of WSU campus life within the Black WSU community was purposeful. The work of Black scholars studying Black social worlds (e.g., Anderson 2000; Baldridge 2019; Brooms 2015; Cox 2015; Jackson 2001; Pattillo 2010; Posey-Maddox 2017) informed how I understood this project. At base, such work demonstrates the fact that Black social worlds are sociologically interesting, vibrant, and necessary to study. Marcus Hunter and Zandria Robinson (2018), in their work studying predominantly Black cities, for example, analyzed the dynamism of Black life in the city, exploring "how Black people made and live within their own maps, whether in response to or in spite of institutional discrimination" (19). Black students attending HWIs such as WSU are similar—they create communities in response to or in spite of university structures and contexts. This chapter illustrates the characteristics of the Black community; how it serves as an anchor for engagement for some students and facilitates a sense of belonging. I also explore why Black engineers might struggle to feel like a part of the Black WSU social world, facing unique time restraints from their coursework. In doing so, I provide a portrait of the Black WSU community, centering a community often rendered tangential by scholars and student affairs leaders concerned with student life.

Black Places on Campus

Campus tour guides meet visitors in the student union building before taking them outside to begin the walking tour. The tour I am leading you, the reader, on is different—we'll start in the Diversity and Equity Building, where all of the racial and cultural affinity spaces are housed, and enter the Black Cultural Center (BCC). Four rooms make up the BCC—a lounge with a couple of sofas, offices for the BCC's directors, and a small computer lab. Students' art hangs on the walls. Hundreds of pictures of Black WSU students doing everything from dancing, to lounging in the BCC, to protesting, to doing step shows cover what would have been empty wall space. Most students in the photos have long since graduated. You can estimate when pictures were taken by the fashion styles—men casually sporting headbands, wearing tall T-shirts, and rocking intricate cornrow designs in their hair, for example, suggest an early 2000s photograph. The photos tell a story of the temporality and loose connectedness of the Black WSU community. While no longer present, Black alumni fashioned lives here that, perhaps in subtle ways, shape how students experience the WSU Black social world now.

Walking into the BCC, during the early stages of my fieldwork, I noticed a glossy, hardback book propped up on the front desk, *We Are the Ship: The Story of Negro League Baseball.* Tae, the assistant director of the BCC, purchased the book during a trip to Kansas City, Missouri. When chatting about his trip, he mentioned his experience in the Negro Leagues Baseball Museum. With a somber laugh he said, "I feel like the Black community doesn't really exist anymore." Tae quoted statistics about the Negro League, describing how Black businesses thrived during this time of exclusive Black patronage. He spoke with a melancholy pride of a past he never experienced but seemingly longed to remember. Among many

Black engineers, Black administrative leaders such as Tae and Catherine, and other Black WSU students, the idea of a Black community, its status, its strength, its flaws, and who was "in" the community often emerged as a topic of discussion.

Students considered to be part of the Black WSU community engage in various membership practices. For example, these students are noticeably present in spaces and events related to Black affinity groups. They attend BSU meetings, go to BSU-sanctioned events, frequent the BCC, and are known, at least by face, by other Black students. Also, as I explain later, membership in the Black community also entailed an aversion to or avoidance of historically White fraternity and sorority events. Another avenue to involvement in the Black community and membership practice included living in the residence hall specifically for Black first years. Through events, discussions, and places, a Black community is fostered, made, and maintained. For students like Johnson and Dajuan, who were integrated into the Black WSU community, involvement in this social world facilitated engagement and a sense of belonging. Similarly, students who mainly surround themselves with their Black peers, often experienced a positive campus racial climate. When asked how his race impacted his experience at WSU, Dajuan, for example, said, "It definitely makes up my entire experience here. Because the majority of my friends are like Black, so that's all I hang out with. I mean, it's been pretty positive."

Dajuan's sentiment of associating his Blackness with the entirety of his campus experience, which was shared by many participants, has important implications. Black communities, as some scholars have shown (e.g., Foster 2003; Gilkes Borr 2019; Guiffrida 2003; Patton 2006), are not tangential to some primary or generic campus experience. As the educational anthropologist, Kevin Foster (2003) points out in his research, taking seriously Black campus communities, "is also a precursor to effective student life programming and policy development" (265). By neglecting to study, engage, and support Black communities on campus, scholars and institutional administrators are potentially neglecting some students' entire campus social lives.

THE BLACK COMMUNITY AND A SENSE OF PLACE

The places, or lack thereof, designated for Black students shaped how students fostered a sense of engagement. For students attempting to integrate into the Black community, some entry points were easier than others. One reason Payton, for example, said she did not feel very attached to the Black community was that she did not live in the Black residence hall for first years: "A lot of friends became close that way . . . but I had to like find Black people other ways." Her words echo the scholarship of Tamara Gilkes Borr (2019), who found that Black students at HWIs often go to great lengths, expending time, energy, and comfort, simply to be around and build relationships with other Black people. Dajuan, on the other hand, lived in the residence hall "with the Black people floor," so he could easily make friends with other Black people in his class. This residence hall served as a conduit into the Black community.

Black places are important to the socialization and engagement of Black students at HWIs (Patton 2006). While residence halls can be sites of racial friction (Hotchkins and Dancy 2017), Black-affinity residence halls can be sites of belonging for Black students who might otherwise feel ostracized. Many Black students, however, did not have the luxury of living in the Black-affinity residence hall. Only about thirty Black first-years could live in this hall at a time.

The BCC is the only other brick and mortar place dedicated to Black students (see Figure 3.1). BCCs play a dynamic role on campuses,

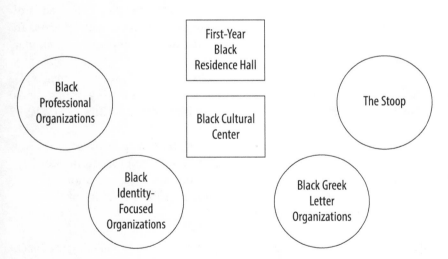

Note: Circles represent Black organizations and/or events. Rectangles represent brick and mortar places on campus dedicated to Black students.

Figure 3.1. This figure represents the Black places on campus. The brick and mortar places are depicted in rectangles, and circles represent the other spaces (e.g., student group meetings).

facilitating connections, offering professional development, programming events, and providing a place of reprieve on otherwise racist campuses (Hypolite 2020; Keels 2020; Patton 2006). Three administrators lead the BCC. Catherine works as the director, with two assistant co-directors, Tae and Lilly. In addition to holding events for WSU, but specifically the Black WSU community, the BCC serves as a place where all Black students are welcome. On a slow day, R&B or hip hop can be heard from Tae's desktop. A stream of Black WSU students flow in and out of the BCC throughout the day—stopping by to eat between classes, studying, lying down on the couches, and meeting up with friends. Black students do not need a reason to come to the BCC, a welcoming space. At base, I think many students ventured to the BCC to feel seen.

The BCC also provided a space for Black students to discuss topics directly related to the Black community and provided a space of healing. Outside of organic conversations, the BCC sponsored Real Talk Tuesday—a venue for Black students to talk about different topics in a "safe space." Catherine noted, "I feel like this year has been particularly challenging, obviously with elections and Black Lives Matter and everything so I definitely feel like the community is more tight knit." The BCC was an important space after tragic murders of Black people at the hands of police officers and the legal system's failure to punish such officers. In the BCC, students shed tears, expressed frustration, and shared a similar feeling of loss.

Despite the limited institutionalized space for Black students, WSU students and staff sustained a vibrant Black community. My observations echo Foster's (2003) findings concerning Black communities at HWIs:

> Black students maintain their own system of fraternities and sororities, have favorite gathering spaces on campus, coordinate extra-curricular activities designed to appeal to one another, and in other ways operate as a distinct subcommunity of the student body at large. (265)

Student-led Black-affinity groups played a central role in shaping the Black community. Events ranged from scheduled networking opportunities, panels with professionals from various fields, discussion forums, socials, movie nights, game nights, and, of course, parties. A number of Black-affinity groups exist on the WSU campus including the BSU, the Brotherhood (an organization for Black men), and the African Student Association. Students were also involved in Black-specific professional organizations such as a pre-law group, African Americans in Health, Blacks in Business Association, and NSBE. A smaller population, consisting of fewer than fifteen students, were members of Black Greek Letter Organizations. Most prominent, serving as the umbrella organization for all of the Black-affinity groups, however, was the BSU. Given BSU's status as the overarching Black student group, the BSU might be considered foundational to the WSU Black community.

The social world of the Black community becomes more complex when one considers the varying manifestations of Black places on campus. Similar to the sociologist Thomas Gieryn (2000), I understand *place* as a "space filled up by people, practices, objects, and representations" (465). Members of Black student organizations create Black places on campus. Organizations such as NSBE and the BSU, for example, have regular general body and executive board meetings, hold curated events for Black students, do community service, and throw parties. The spaces holding these events—anywhere from residence hall common rooms, to houses off campus, to lecture halls in the business school, to a reception hall in the campus center, are made into Black places, if only for an hour. Given the transience of Black places on campus, the visual I provide (see Figure 3.1) is necessarily simplistic. This visual cannot capture the numerous Black organizations on campus or the flickering constellations of Black events in the universe of campus life. Perhaps the best example of the ephemeral nature of Black places at WSU is The Stoop.

THE STOOP

Outside of the student union, students eat their lunches and chat on the steps spanning the length of the building. During the first couple weeks of school, Panhellenic Sororities, majority White, sit on the steps during the busy lunch hours wearing the letters of their organizations. Student groups do not have to schedule times with the university to use the space; the steps have organically turned into a space of visibility for student groups. On certain, BSU-sanctioned Wednesdays, from 11a.m. to 2p.m., these same steps become The Stoop. The day before leading up to Wednesday at lunch, BSU members post flyers advertising the fact that Black WSU students will be congregating on the steps outside of the student union. This gathering is The Stoop.

For example, after leaving his music class, Johnson saw six Black students sitting on the steps. Joining them, he said, "This is The Stoop, right? I'm on the flyer for it and that was the only time I went. Spencer was on it too and he's not even in the Black community anymore." "Who's Spencer?" Mustafa asked. "Exactly," Johnson chuckled. Spencer's absence from the WSU Black community's events and spaces rendered him an outsider to the Black community's social world. The Black community is, of course, not gated, sectioned off from the rest of WSU, yet, as Johnson alludes, the Black community has boundaries and membership practices.

Tae, who went to WSU as an undergrad, made a concerted effort as a staff member to "bring back The Stoop." He explained that "[i]t was almost like our porch. We'd talk, we'd gossip, we'd see what's going on." Tae explained that Black students congregating felt more organic back then: "[Now] I think there needs to be a reason for people to get together or it needs to be scheduled. But I don't think that there's an inherent value with the students right now of just being together."

Catherine, however, noted that students connect in different ways with the advent of social media: "There's all these other ways to connect. I feel like students are still getting The Stoop but in a different form." The different forms of The Stoop included digital spaces such as GroupMe, Instagram, and Facebook. Catherine's words suggest that community building and placemaking takes different forms in this era. Throughout my fieldwork, however, I wondered if something was lost in the digital shuffle by relying on social media to connect. How, for example, might the Black community's practices or reliance on digital platforms and affinity groups be altered with a creation of a larger WSU Black residence hall?

Place is central to the campus experience. Place facilitates belonging, attachment, and the potential for collegians to build social worlds. How does the Black WSU community remain recognizable with limited designated spaces (i.e., the BCC)? Concerted effort and labor. Through creative, agentic processes, Black students repurpose a set of rounded concrete steps outside of a building into The Stoop, a Black place. By studying Black places such as The Stoop, scholars and student affairs administrators stand to learn about the relationship between structure and Black students' collective agency (Hunter et al. 2016; Posey-Maddox 2017; Tichavakunda 2020). One notices both the lack of institutionalized Black places but also the creative and collective agency of Black students to create an affirming site of belonging on a set of steps. On top of the standard duties of a student—going to class and doing homework—Black students in the WSU Black community create and sustain places for themselves through planned meetings and other events. In other words, the WSU Black community does not simply exist—it is intentionally made and remade through the labor of students and BCC staff.

Engaging in the Black Community

Catherine has worked at WSU for two years in the BCC. She is often out of her office, speaking on panels, attending student affairs meetings, or advocating for Black WSU students in some fashion with campus administration. Since the "campus climate era" she has been in high demand, pulled in many directions, from different departments or offices seeking to engage more with diversity. When Catherine is in her office—ornamented with elephant statuettes in honor of her sorority and pictures of friends and students—she is responding to e-mails, scheduling appointments, or answering the phone. After a "Hey, Cathy!" or a friendly knock on her door, without fail she turns around from her computer, and greets the guest with a smile. The only time the door to her office is closed is when she is holding a meeting.

In our interview, Catherine reiterated the sentiment that students could simultaneously identify as Black but not be part of the Black WSU community. At base, membership in the Black community was demonstrated through active involvement with other Black students and participation in BSU-related events. I asked one student what it meant to be part of the Black WSU community—she responded, "It means that you hang out with Black people, you go to Black events, maybe BSU, and you don't fuck with Frat Row." Frat Row, as I explain in greater detail in chapter 10, is a street close to the main campus lined with historically White fraternity and sorority houses. Neither students nor staff felt that active involvement in the Black community, however, was incumbent upon Black students. Catherine explained, given the diversity of backgrounds of Black students, that she did not expect all Black students to necessarily participate in or need the WSU Black community. I asked Catherine, "What does it mean to be a Black student, but not part of the Black community?" She replied,

> We have such a diverse range of Black students. Black students who are used to being around other Black people and then we have Black students who have been the one of only in the classroom, right? They don't have to be around Black people. Those students, they may get my e-mails; because I do send touch point e-mails to everybody. They may ignore them. Because they don't feel like they need to connect into the Black community and for me, I'm like, that's cool. Do what you need to do.

Similarly, Tae said, "I'm not necessarily saying that [the BCC] is necessary for everyone but I do want people to know that it's available."

Some Black students, who previously were not involved in the Black community, started participating in BSU events and coming to the BCC after a racist incident. Catherine has seen this story play out many times. She recalled a story of a student who became more active in the Black community after her first year:

> Some of those students, I do see after they may have an incident. Whether that's with faculty or another peer. I know that happened a couple years ago with a student. She was kind of, sort of, not really involved [in the Black community] until she went and tried to go to a party on Frat Row. They wouldn't let her in. Then she came in here the next Monday in tears. I was like, "Oh, welcome. You're Black. You're Black!" You know?

As mentioned, Frat Row is understood as a White space, inhabited by predominantly White WSU students. Catherine's response suggested that, as a Black person, one should not be surprised by an act of racism in that context. Racial realism (Bell 1992), the idea that racism is permanent, shapes the contours of the Black student community. After perceived racist events or encounters, the BCC and other Black places take on the role of counterspaces, or sites "where those of a similar social identity gather to validate and critique their experiences with the larger institution" (Keels 2020, 11). For students who feel uncomfortable or invalidated in WSU spaces where they are the only one, being around other Black students and rooting themselves in the Black community is not only a way to experience a more positive climate, but also a way to foster a greater sense of engagement (Guiffrida 2003; Harper and Quaye 2007; Patton 2006). Students can seek membership in one of the ethnic student organizations under the umbrella of the BSU, go to BSU-sponsored events, or even take leadership in these organizations. Regardless of their prior involvement in Black student organizations or Black places, students were welcomed into the Black community as a resource when they needed the support or camaraderie.

Social worlds—their practices, characteristics, and boundaries—are dynamic. Similarly, counterspaces, which can be thought of as worlds of their own, do not simply exist—they are made, sustained, and intentionally cultivated. As Foster (2003) points out, Black campus communities are often wrongly given an a priori status. While having the space for the BCC is important, for example, the space is not automatically culturally validating or racially affirming. The BCC and other sites in the WSU Black community become vibrant Black places only through the actions of Black students and administrators. A senior student even described the Black WSU community as "coming in waves," portraying how some years the community seemed more cohesive and more visible than in other years. The tectonics of campus social worlds are continuously in flux, thereby under tension. I focus on these tensions to highlight the social worlds' characteristics. In the Black community, one tension came to fore in my analysis—the tension between collective and individual interests.

Tensions between Collective and Individual Interests

Membership practices in the Black community require active participation in Black events and presence in Black places. Yet, being an active member in the Black community as well as other campus communities can prove difficult. Aliyah, the Black Student Union (BSU) president, for example, argued that participation in the Black community, in some ways, was "hindering," explaining: "For us it's like either you are in the Black community and then you are not in any other community and you can't fully exist there." During my time shadowing Black engineering students, I witnessed potential difficulties of "fully existing" in the WSU Black community. A challenge of engaging with the Black community existed within participants' tension of mediating their personal and professional interests with what was understood to be the WSU Black community's interests. WSU's School of Engineering involvement fair provides a useful example of this tension.

WSU's NSBE chapter relies on the engineering school's involvement fairs to recruit Black students. At these fairs, engineering students walk around the school of engineering, check out the posters of different organizations and list their contact information for newsletters. Black engineering majors' work of recruiting students makes it worth occupying their NSBE table for two hours. During the hours of the fair, however, the BSU held a large event commemorating the life of Dr. Martin Luther King Jr. Certainly, students could do both by planning ahead, leaving one event midway and walking across campus to attend the other. My point here, however, is that Black students, especially Black engineers interested in participating in the Black community, balance more niche, professional passions with their participation in the larger Black community.

Extracurricular student organizations play a central role in campus life (Kuh 1995b). Organizational involvement provides opportunities to form relationships, stoke diverse interests, and build a résumé (e.g., Astin 1984; Keels 2020; Museus 2008; Roulin and Bangerter 2013). Involvement fairs and decisions to join organizations can be overwhelming—does one join the breakdancing club or try out for a hip hop dance team? Do they meet on the same day? Does one have enough time to dedicate to the electrical engineering society, a sorority, and course work? Like every college student, Black students have multiple interests and identities and are tugged in different directions in terms of organizational involvement. Yet, unlike every college student, Black students' participation is both complicated and bolstered by a sense of linked fate.

Linked fate is a political science concept used to describe the belief held by many Black people that their individual life outcomes and well-being are inextricably linked to the larger Black community (Dawson 1994). In other words, what is good for the Black community, economically or politically, for example, is good for the Black individual. The collective nature of linked fate emerges from a shared sense of oppression and the continued understanding that racism plays a formative role in society. Linked fate in the HWI context compels students who might have little in common with each other beyond their Blackness and student status to attend BSU meetings or visit the BCC. As such, involvement in Black affinity organizations seems to feel more consequential—they are not *just* extracurricular organizations or something to do outside of studying. The stakes, I believe, are higher because students understand themselves to be actively participating in and sustaining the Black community.

Aliyah, the BSU president, described the tension between collective and individual interests for Black students, stating in a matter of fact tone that the typical WSU students are, "prioritizing their academics and being involved in a bunch of different clubs . . . that is what WSU is about." Prioritizing involvement in the Black community at WSU, in her opinion, was placed on the back burner for the average Black student. Aliyah did not fault students for prioritizing their academics, it made sense to her: "It's like, 'Oh, I need to hold onto my scholarship. I need to be in the library.' So they are not prioritizing something that, little do they know, can make this whole experience twenty times better." Similarly, Tae articulated a change in the values of Black WSU students, saying, "I don't know where that shift kind of took place but I definitely think there's a shift between the collective 'this is us' versus like 'I'm going to be out here for me.'" One might find Tae's words curious given the individualistic nature of college. College is often understood as a path for individual self-exploration and personal fulfillment. The metrics scholars often use to judge educational outcomes—such as graduation, grade point average, postgraduate employment—are likewise individualistic. Tae, like Aliyah, however, is not finding fault in students prioritizing personal academic or professional development. Rather, Tae is operating out of a sense of linked fate, questioning how Black students might both achieve and serve the larger Black community.

Involvement in the Black community necessitates an element of service to the community. For example, the BCC worked with the admissions office to coordinate an initiative of recruiting Black WSU students by calling Black high school seniors admitted to WSU. The purpose of this initiative was to increase the subsequent enrollment of Black students to WSU. Even with the added incentive of free pizza, few people showed up to make calls. On the day I volunteered to call, four other people showed up to help. Catherine said some students even asked, "What do I get paid?" when she tried to get Black WSU students to participate. "You have to do your part, you can't just complain," Catherine continued, referring to students' complaints of a small Black community.

A common sentiment, as Payton explained, was that the WSU Black community was "very clique-y." Olivia, for example, reflected on her lack of involvement in BSU, saying, "BSU could be a place where I would meet more Black people, but it seems like cliques naturally form. It seems like if you didn't start there, you can't penetrate it." Despite the BSU leadership's efforts to foster an inclusive environment—the practice of BSU leaders and presenters mentioning gender pronouns before introducing themselves, instituting liaisons for different Black communities (e.g., athletics liaison and Black Greek Letter Organization liaison), and starting a mentoring system between the more senior students and first-years—few engineers were involved in the BSU. Students feeling unwelcome to the BSU was not a fault of the organization but, rather, the near-impossible and undefined expectations placed upon the BSU and Black community in general. Participants did, however, notice boundaries to engineering students' full participation in the BSU and other facets of the Black community.

Commenting on the fragmentation in the Black community and among Black engineers, Aliyah said, "It's very divided because you have

Black career folks who, honestly, probably don't even feel they are part of the Black community most of the time." Catherine shared the sentiment explaining that engineers are "balancing a very rigorous course load. Some of those students still want to be involved with the Black community . . . and I feel like maybe, at times, it's hard to juggle." The strict scholastic requirements of engineering can prove to be a boundary to actively participating in the WSU Black community.

Social worlds are defined both by what participants share in common and by boundaries signifying who does and does not belong (Carter 2006). For Black engineering students, the most pronounced boundary to active participation in the Black community is time. Payton, for example, frequented the BCC, but as a junior, between work and more intensive classes, she did not have much time: "Like if I don't have to go to NSBE [meetings], I definitely don't have time to just walk over to the BCC." In order for Black engineering students to maintain a presence in BSU and in NSBE, they would have to dedicate at least two straight hours every Monday to general body meetings. For engineering students with limited free time, hanging out in the BCC, attending BSU meetings or their events, and other ways of serving the Black community at WSU often proved challenging. Of note is the fact that limited time outside of studying creates the boundary—not alienation from Black students who are not engineers. While engagement with the Black community can offer friends, belonging, and a place of respite—membership comes at the price of time in Black community spaces. For engineers, time is hard to come by. Despite complaints of a tension between a collective and individualist culture as well as symbolic boundaries, the Black community at WSU was vibrant. Shows of the Black social world's collective agency, such as the bi-annual Midnight Brunch, facilitate a more welcoming environment for many Black collegians.

The Midnight Brunch

"Is it possible to write an 8-page research paper in 4 hours?" Johnson's text bubble appeared on my phone. I asked if he needed help thinking his paper through and he replied, "It's due tomorrow, yes please!" I was planning on coming to WSU to attend the Midnight Brunch with the Black men's group, The Brotherhood, either way, so I told him I would meet him beforehand. WSU opens a cafeteria for a Midnight Brunch for two nights during finals. The Brotherhood created a tradition of "mobbing out," or showing up as a large group, to Midnight Brunch.

We met in the common room of a residence hall near the cafeteria where Midnight Brunch would occur. He was wearing his customary black hoodie and black hat, with Beats headphones draping his neck. After Johnson complained about the co-president of The Brotherhood's hesitancy to show up for the brunch, I asked if he thought he should go to the library instead. He told me that he felt like somebody in leadership had to be there. Johnson was a co-president and founder of the group. Then, motioning to his Bluetooth speakers, "Who else would play the music?" Seeing that he was dead set on going to the breakfast we started talking about his paper.

I chided him, asking why he was just now asking for help.[1] "I completely forgot, bruh," he told me. "I woke up early, ran to the gym and worked out . . . you know it's a natural stimulant, releasing endorphins, you know." When he got back to his residence hall, however, he was tired. Between stressing about his classes, battling fatigue, and self-loathing for working at the last minute, he failed to write more than a paragraph during the entire day. We talked through his ideas and by the end of our work session, he had more than a page double-spaced and an outline.

"You sure you just don't want to work on your stuff, bro?" I asked as he packed up his laptop, preparing to go to the cafeteria. "I'll just separate myself from everyone and work. I want to at least swipe people [into the cafeteria] though." As we walked toward the cafeteria we ran into Amari, a Black man studying film. "Johnson, how are you, man?" Amari asked, dapping Johnson up. "It's coming to a seventy-two-hour stretch where I either fail or pass my classes," Johnson replied with a chuckle. Amari corrected him, "*When* you pass your classes. When." "True . . . my advisors definitely gave me the 'anything is possible' speech," Johnson replied.

Johnson is dynamic. He's smarter than he gives himself credit for, but struggles prioritizing his time. Part of this is the validation he receives from the general WSU Black community in which he thrives—a validation he does not receive in other social worlds. While writing the paper, he checked his phone often, calculating how much he would have to write to meet his goal, and seemingly looked for small distractions. This avoidance and discomfort, however, dissipated as he neared the cafeteria.

At not even quarter to midnight, Johnson, Amari, and I walked to the front of the already snaking line to the cafeteria. I told them I felt guilty for cutting the line. "What they gonna say to us? Be real?" Johnson said. I became acutely aware of our status as Black men on a historically White campus. Johnson, of course, was right and no one objected. We shared a laugh and met the mass of seventeen students at the front of the line. Thirty-one more Black students, also aware of the fact that students of other races would not dare object to their jumping the line, joined us at the front. Busying ourselves while waiting for the cafeteria to open, an organic circle formed. A couple of students took turns freestyling. After finishing a rhyme, one student motioned to Johnson to take a turn at freestyling. "Too much pressure. I'm not Black enough," he said, throwing his hands up, to a laugh from the onlookers.

The doors opened promptly at midnight and Johnson stood next to the cashier swiping students' IDs for entry. "Everyone who needs a swipe, get on my right. But only if you need it," Johnson instructed. In almost assembly line efficiency, students benefiting from Johnson's generosity waited for the cashier to swipe them into the cafeteria, one by one. He swiped twelve students in that night. "How do you have thirty-two swipes left?" a student asked Johnson. "I really care about this event so . . . ," Johnson responded with a shrug. Throughout the semester, Johnson would intentionally go to events with free food so he could conserve meal swipes for this specific event.

I was impressed with the spread of food—sushi, cheese blintzes, pancakes, fluffy biscuits and gravy, French toast, and more. The food, however, was secondary to the event of Black students coming together and having fun in the cafeteria during the height of final exams. Black students, for a variety of reasons such as small numbers, busy schedules, organizational commitments, studying, or disparate friend groups, did not often show up en masse to events. Eighty-two Black students occupying a large fraction of a cafeteria was special. While the one section of the cafeteria was dense with Black students, more Black students were peppered throughout the rest of the space. Of the Black students, I saw seven Black engineers including Johnson. Understanding the rarity of the occasion, the brunch had a sacred air—so much so that Anasa, the co-president of the Black men's group, asked, "So are we going to pray?" Around the cafeteria, the Black students joined hands and bowed heads. Anasa, wearing his old gold and black fraternity hoodie, bowed his head and said grace.

Johnson DJ'd from his phone on his Bluetooth speaker, moving with and directing the mood of the students. From sing-along songs like Shai's "If I Ever Fall in Love" to popular, more current hip hop, Johnson curated a party. Unedited songs with the n-word blared in the alcove of Blackness, adjacent to the rest of the cafeteria for all to hear without apology. Plates of food cooled off as students, enraptured in the moment, rapped along with lyrics, stood up to sing along with songs, or danced in between tables. Every student who hopped up to dance, even those more rhythmically challenged, were celebrated and encouraged with claps and "aaaayyye's" from students. The group of Black students, while occupying a side on the edge of the cafeteria, was the center of attention. It was a spectacle. Students of all races outside of the section looked on and nodded along with the music.

When Johnson played the song "Milly Rock," he left his post of DJ and did his own Milly Rock. "The key is in the footwork," he once told me. For almost thirty seconds the spotlight was on him as he expertly Milly Rocked, whirling his arms, and rotating his body with speed, precision, and an improvisation that had a hypnotic effect. For that moment, he was supremely confident. The students roared with like excitement. For that moment, he was in control—in control of himself, and in control of the community which he so cared about.

I left at 12:25 a.m. I wondered, while he was DJ'ing or dancing, if Johnson was thinking about the final paper that was due the next day, or the final exam he would take in less than ten hours.

I wished Johnson good luck on his exam in the morning. He responded that afternoon:

JOHNSON: I fucked up big time. Missed the exam. Didn't finish the essay.

ME: I'm so sorry. What happened bro?

JOHNSON: I don't wanna talk about it.

ME: Make sure you forgive yourself about the test stuff. If you want to talk or anything, lemme know.

JOHNSON: I can't right now. I really can't.

The Black Community Social World: In Summary

The sociologist Pierre Bourdieu (1984) reminds us that people are not automatons engaging in cost-benefit analyses for every decision they make. Most college students, regardless of race, might relate to the tug of a social event while studying, or shirking academics for social engagements or fun. Johnson's experience—neglecting his coursework to spend time supporting the WSU Black community—is extreme and not indicative of most Black collegians I met. Johnson, however, as we'll learn more in the next chapter, is far from irresponsible. A microanalysis of his background and experience in different social worlds at WSU helps us better understand his academic challenges and overextension to the Black social world. I included his story, however, to show how participation and avid involvement requires time. For college students, especially engineers, time is a commodity; a commodity that can be used to help co-create a joyful, validating experience for Black students at an HWI or to finish up a final essay and study for an exam.

The Midnight Brunch serves as an example of the interplay between the historically White institutional structures and Black students' collective agency. Structurally, the congregation of Black students was made possible because of the institution-sanctioned event. Further, the Midnight Brunch likely would not hold the same sacred air if more Black students attended WSU or if WSU had more spaces dedicated for Black students. The breakfast, while a tradition for all WSU students, became a Black place through the collective labor and creative agency of Black students (Hunter et al. 2016; Tichavakunda 2020). Despite their numbers, Black students collectively carved out their own space within the breakfast, fashioning the event to their needs. Eighty-two Black students interspersed throughout the cafeteria would not do. For it to be a Black event, for their presence to be felt—by each other and by onlookers—they had to be together. So Black students arrived early, cut lines, and swiped each other into the cafeteria to ensure they could create a Black place for themselves. What was intended by WSU to be a treat during the stress of finals for all students became a moment for the WSU Black community to fellowship.

CENTERING BLACK CAMPUS COMMUNITIES

Education stakeholders continue to wrestle with how to create environments where students can meaningfully engage across racial difference (e.g., Chambers 2011; Chang 1999; Hurtado et al. 2012; Warikoo 2016). Similarly, as microaggressions research, and other research on Black students demonstrate, much cross-racial interaction ends up being negative for Black students (e.g., Ogunyemi et al. 2020; Solórzano et al. 2000). The benefits of racial diversity are known and commonly accepted as valuable to education. An unintended consequence of education's preoccupation with cross-racial interactions, however, is the largely underinvestigated nature of Black communities at HWIs. Black students, as I demonstrate throughout this book, have lives beyond racial conflict and are oftentimes more than content with a predominantly Black social circle. One way of learning about Black students' multifaceted campus lives is by centering Black communities in research. To ignore Black communities at HWIs is to potentially ignore the core of Black collegians' social lives.

The WSU Black community is a world of its own, informed by and overlapping other social worlds, but identifiable and unique. Other HWIs have distinct Black communities of their own, with distinct traditions, histories, and cultures. Black communities, to be sure, are not utopic. Boundaries distinguish the Black campus community. For example, access to the time necessary to participate in Black events and be present in Black places acted as a boundary to engaging in the Black community. While not the focus of this text, oppression and alienation also exist within Black communities (e.g., Austin 1991; Cohen 1999; Harris and Patton 2017; Jourian and McCloud 2020). In order to examine marginalization and potential divides within Black communities, however, one needs to center the study of Black communities.

W. E. B. Du Bois, again, offers insight here. In reflecting upon his time as one of the few Black students at Harvard University in the late nineteenth century, he said, "The Harvard of which most White students conceived I knew little" (Du Bois 2013, 353). Yet, Du Bois was not clamoring to join White student life. Rather, Du Bois was "voluntarily and willingly outside its social life," explaining that he was "encased in a completely colored world, self-sufficient and provincial, and ignoring just as far as possible the White world which conditioned it" (2013, 355). Du Bois at Harvard in the end of the nineteenth century and Johnson at WSU in the twenty-first century both experienced the bulk of their campus lives within the social worlds of Black campus communities.

Black students create places of belonging for themselves, with or in spite of their institutions on otherwise racially hostile and/or on majority nonblack campuses. A set of steps, a midnight breakfast, an area of the library, Wednesdays in a cafeteria, or a lesser-used campus green space might all prove fertile ground for repurposing into a Black place and site of belonging. Black places are best understood when higher education stakeholders center Black communities, rather than view them as on the periphery of campus life. Important research highlights the centrality of

Black places on campus (e.g., Brooms 2018a, 2018b; Patton 2006; Winkle-Wagner 2009). Yet, as this book demonstrates, and other research supports (Foster 2003; Gilkes Borr 2019), Black communities are the result of continued collective labor. Institutions can either support or stand in the way of vibrant Black campus communities. By better understanding how Black students support themselves, higher education stakeholders will be in a better position to support Black students.

Most studies concerning Black students' experiences in HWIs or race relations begin in racially diverse or predominantly nonblack social worlds—similar to the Caldwell and WSU social worlds we explore in the latter sections. The cross-racial interactions, coalitions, tensions, misunderstandings, and microaggressions are logical starting points of study. By starting at sites of racial friction, however, we miss the instrumental role of NSBE, the dynamism of the Black community, and the labor Black students expend to maintain these communities. We miss Black students' joy in Black places. We miss Black students' lives and worlds they make either because or in spite of institutional structures.

4

Johnson's Story

Johnson was raised in the Bronx, New York, and attended a majority Black and Latinx public high school. He is a first-generation U.S. citizen and his parents are from the Caribbean. He has dark brown skin and sports a high-top fade hair style. Instead of combing his hair out however, he keeps it curly. On more than one occasion, I observed Black women jokingly ask him for his hair routine. Johnson, a DJ and producer, often wears Beats headphones around his neck and carries a Bluetooth speaker box with him just in case a gathering or organic meeting of his peers can benefit from background music.

"I feel like every Black person I've met, I've met through you," Chukwu, a sophomore, reflected with a chuckle. Johnson replied, "I started a lot of the initiatives to kinda bridge that divide between the Black community and the Black engineering community because engineers don't really be out there like that." A similar logic guided his decision to major in industrial and systems engineering. He describes the work as a systems engineer similarly: "I'm pretty much the bridge between like, regular people and engineers. I know a little bit about engineering, but I also know about people." Johnson connects the Black community to the NSBE community, but struggles to assimilate in other social worlds. "I can have all of the work in the world to do, but I'll stop it if someone needs something. That fills me. My mom says I have a savior complex," Johnson lamented with an air of inevitability. His father is not as patient, and once told Johnson, "You didn't come to college to be Martin Luther King."

The Black Community

The Black community at WSU is different from the Bronx. "WSU is the first place where I met people that were just Black," he chuckled. His parents warned him about Black Americans, but he actively tried to change their views on people who are "just Black," helping them understand the legacy of slavery in America. Johnson "discovered" he was Black, in part, when he came to WSU. By that, he meant he realized what it meant to be Black in White spaces.

During one of his first BSU meetings he recalled the BSU president saying something like, "You all probably have to deal with being the only Black person in class." Johnson sat in the front row in class so he never noticed. After hearing the words from the BSU president, he began making a conscious effort to turn around in his classes after seating himself to test this hypothesis and noticed, "I really am the only Black dude here."

He is most at home in the Black WSU community and feeds off of supporting fellow Black students. While hosting an NSBE study night, for example, he once groaned, frustrated that he was missing another Black organization's forum on cultural appropriation occurring at the same time. "That topic is dope too," he sighed, accepting the fact that he would have to miss the event.

Being a bridge between communities is demanding work. Johnson sometimes spreads himself thin. While I knew him, he served on the e-board for NSBE, founded an organization for Black men at WSU, and cohosted a WSU radio show. Outside of school-sanctioned organizations, he also served as a mercenary photographer for students wanting graduation photos. He even co-curated an exhibit of his photographs of Black women on campus. In addition to being a DJ for hire, he also founded a group dedicated to enhancing the experiences of college students through curated/engaging social events for the Black WSU community. As I mentioned earlier, for engineers, time is precious. Hours spent planning an event could be hours spent prepping for an exam. More organizational involvement meant less attention to engineering work. Johnson often battled this tension: "I'm not home, 'cause I'm out being a leader and shit."

During the Fall semester of his senior year, he told me, "I'd be happy right now if I didn't have the [Black] community . . . and these are the stressors that nonblack people don't have to deal with." A perceived linked fate adds gravitas to Johnson's social life, which he suggested is unique to the Black community. What events he attends, and what organization he is involved with, is not just dictated by personal interests, but also a sense of obligation to the WSU Black community. Johnson finds purpose within the Black community. While his involvement in the Black community anchors him to the campus, fostering a sense of engagement and belonging, his involvement also burdens him.

His obligation to the WSU Black community is both admirable and frustrating. "I've been the 'yes-man' of this community," he told me once with a dry laugh. His attitude concerning involvement in the Black community fluctuates. Sometimes he's "ghost"—absent from social media, meetings, and the social scene—in an attempt to prioritize his studies. Other times, he rationalizes his involvement, once saying, "If I'ma do bad in school, I might as well do something for the community." The Black community provides a sense of validation he does not feel anywhere else, so he never ghosts the community for too long.

One of the things he did for the community was found The Brotherhood, a WSU organization for Black men to come together. The group boasts a regular meeting attendance of more than forty Black men as well as campus notoriety of being the place for Black men to network with other Black men on campus. One of the reasons he wanted to start The Brotherhood was because he was tired of being the go-to WSU Black guy asked to sit on panels, volunteer to talk to high schoolers, and do other service. Through The Brotherhood, the responsibility was spread. Other scholars have found that Black masculinity is sometimes expressed through campus leadership (e.g., Harper 2004; Harries et al. 2011). The same can be said of Johnson.

Saying "no" is a challenge for him. His therapist and his family expressed that he needs to stop being so giving and be more selfish with his time. His engagement in the Black community pulls him in one direction, his studies in another, and he struggles to find a balance. During the Spring semester, for example, BSU requested him to film and take pictures of an event featuring a prominent Black intellectual giving a talk on campus. While he said no to that particular event, he already had plans for another engagement DJing a party the next day. He had three midterms the following week.

As I highlighted in chapter 3, the Black community itself was neither anti-intellectual nor a distraction for Black students. Rather, similar to someone spending excess time in sorority activities, partying with friends, leading a student group, or even participating in an engineering society—mismanagement of time will always adversely affect one's studies.

The Black Engineering Community

During my fieldwork, Johnson held and stepped down from two positions in NSBE. For the WSU chapter, he held the Academic Excellence position of the executive board, attending e-board meetings and holding weekly study nights. NSBE, he explained, can be a bit of a popularity contest, and he cites his popularity among Black students and his passion for earning the position with a 1.8 GPA.[1] His competitor had a 3.8.

He ran for another NSBE position on the regional level. His speech was powerful enough to sway his opponent to urge members to vote for Johnson. Olivia, a past WSU NSBE president who knew of Johnson's academic struggles, however, was against his campaign. She pointed out that Johnson had just stepped down as Academic Excellence chair for his local chapter and she asked how he expected to hold this position at an even greater level. Unmoved by Olivia and inspired by the new role, Johnson did not withdraw. A little over two months into his tenure, during the summer, however, he stepped down from the regional role to focus on his two classes from the Spring semester marked as "Incomplete."

Johnson is one of the more involved members of NSBE. Hearing about Black WSU engineers who were not avid members of the NSBE community but came to the National NSBE conference and received job offers, Johnson said, "I be doing all these [NSBE] jobs, but it be the niggas who don't even show up to general body meetings getting all the [engineering industry] jobs." Despite his engagement with NSBE, he lacked the *career capital* that would grant him many jobs.

Capital, in a Bourdieusian sense, works as a toolkit of resources, skills, or characteristics that result in success or distinction in a specific context (Edgerton and Roberts 2014), specifically the social and cultural repertoires/competencies, and knowledge of pertinent information to a given *field* or social world (Bourdieu and Passeron, 1990). I understood *career capital* broadly as the tools and repertoires necessary to manage the obligations of being an engineering student and securing employment in engineering. Examples of *career capital* include research experience, high GPAs, engineering-related internships, and connections with representatives from various engineering and tech companies,[2] which I explain in greater depth in later chapters.

The Engineering School Community

JOHNSON: Am I still invited to study with you guys for the midterm?

BRIDGETTE: Of course haven't started yet though haha

JOHNSON: Do you know what time you guys will be starting?

The midterm was the next day. No one replied to Johnson's last text that night. The text thread included three other students, all of whom were nonblack, in the same class. The thread continued the next day after the test as if Johnson had never texted them, and his message was never acknowledged. "This is my Caldwell experience in a nutshell," he texted me. Johnson, however, describes the racial climate in the school of engineering as neutral and doubts that Caldwell, the school of engineering, could or should do more for diversity. Two interrelated factors, however, make his experience in Caldwell a struggle—a shaky math foundation and interpersonal connections with classmates.

Johnson went to a school where the emphasis was passing, not achieving. He parroted his high school teachers, saying in a happy-go-lucky voice, " 'Nobody is good at math, don't sweat it! All you need is a sixty-five to pass.' " He continued saying, "You're hearing that from your professors so it's like, 'Fuck math, I don't need this.' " In addition to not taking algebra until high school, he was further disadvantaged in that his high school first instituted Advanced Placement (AP) classes his senior year. Johnson's mom made him take them all: "She kept me at a higher standard than my education system."

"It's always grind time. I wasn't built ready so I always got to get ready," Johnson texted me once in response to asking if he was studying. While not explicitly, Johnson was referring to the *habitus* he developed toward academics and engineering prior to college. *Habitus*, a core concept in Pierre Bourdieu's (Bourdieu and Passeron 1990) Theory of Practice, can be described as the dispositions people learn from their backgrounds, including their unique cultures, class, high schools, and family. *Habitus* gives one a feel for the customs and practices in a social world, or *"le sens pratique,"* which is roughly translated as "a mode of knowledge that does not necessarily contain knowledge of its own principles" (Bourdieu 1990, as cited in Reay 2004). In this case, his *habitus* was not aligned with the practices, rules, and modes of engagement in the engineering school's social world.

"My case is pretty much like, well, have you heard of the 'Doubly Disadvantaged?'" he asked me once while we took a break from studying. Referring to Anthony Jack's (2014) sociological research, he identified with the Doubly Disadvantaged in that he identifies as intellectually gifted yet low-income and a product of an underresourced public school. "If it wasn't for my photographic memory and last minute study skills I wouldn't even be here," Johnson once told me after he did better on a quiz than he expected.

In his engineering classes, he feels like he is perpetually playing catch up. Johnson sits in the front row and participates in all of his classes, but struggles in Caldwell. Professors move through material too quickly, assuming everyone had the same scholastic background. Because of the class's speed, Johnson would often find himself two or three weeks behind, spending time reading the textbook, working at a pace that worked for him. Johnson, however, is exceptional. He casually brings up sociological concepts, has a photographic memory, learned piano without formal training, and thinks deeply. He is a leader, and his peers are drawn to his personality. How many people can sway a crowd and even their opponents to vote for them in an election? Despite his strengths, his background of attending an underresourced high school with an inept math program haunts him. Solely because of his K–12 background, he feels like engineering may not be for him, but at this stage in his studies, with only two semesters left of required classes, graduating without with an engineering degree is out of the question.

His educational background influences his interpersonal interactions in Caldwell, ultimately impacting the social capital (Bourdieu 1984), or potential resourceful networks, he has in Caldwell. "I don't have friends in my major because I'm the struggling student . . . and if I do have friends, they're struggling too. . . . I can try to work with people with A's but they just don't get back to you in time," Johnson explained. Even Alexis—same year, same major, same race—gave him similar treatment. "She'll be like, 'Oh it's not that hard,' but not actually help me out," Johnson said, concerning his relationship with Alexis. He did not harbor any ill-will toward people who opted not to work with him because, in his words, he is an "anchor" slowing classmates down. Johnson's experience, however, demonstrates the relational nature of social capital and networking in classes. Advisors and professors offer similar proverbs for academic success, suggesting that students view their classmates as resources. "Get the contact information of a few people from each class." "Form study groups with classmates."

This familiar advice, however, is flawed, making the assumption that students welcome working with other classmates, regardless of their race or educational background. Johnson's example shows that a student can contact classmates, attempt to join study groups, and attempt to build working relationships with the highest achievers in the class, but still have no one willing to work with him. As I show throughout this book, higher education stakeholders cannot assume that students will happily collaborate with all students in their class.

"I thought I was going to come to WSU and be Iron Man," Johnson reflected, thinking about his first visit to Caldwell. An engineering society caught his eye as a prospective student. It seemed like an extension of his robotics team work. Engineering societies are Caldwell-sponsored organizations specifically related to engineering that range from groups designing cars, to rockets, to cement boats. As a first-year WSU student, Johnson went to an engineering society meeting but felt in the way; none of the students were welcoming. One student, he remembered, said, as if waving him off, "You can just watch what I'm doing." Upon further prodding, I learned Johnson was the only Black person present. While he did not attribute his feeling of alienation solely to his race, that meeting was his first and last.

Johnson has grown more disenchanted with Caldwell. Growing up, he told me, "that academic integrity shit, I took serious." In college, however, academic integrity is "out the window." He understands why people cheat on exams or use Adderall for added focus: "It's people's future at the end of the day . . . people will do whatever it takes to finish the class. I know for a fact that certain fraternities have test banks. That's illegal." Thinking back to Johnson's successful campaign for Academic Excellence chair, he commented that people were put off by his opponent's idea of starting a test bank. No one in NSBE wanted culpability.

Surprisingly, given his negative experiences within Caldwell, Johnson describes the school as "pretty neutral." He cites the programs Caldwell has for Black students, saying, "[The Multicultural Engineering Office] tries to do a good job of taking care of Black students and really trying to foster community." Johnson continued, "I feel like being Black, you don't feel out of place at Caldwell, unless you're like someone who isn't used to seeing White people." Despite the supports Caldwell provides institutionally and the support of other Black engineers in NSBE, Johnson still feels "small" in Caldwell: "I felt small but it didn't have to do with me being Black. It mostly had to do with my foundation in math and science and coming from a different socioeconomic background." His background, or habitus, shapes how he navigates Caldwell and even his potential to make friends in his major.

Among his Black engineering peers, Johnson was of the minority. Only eight students, making up less than 20 percent of the Black undergraduate engineers I interviewed, listed that their parents did not attend college. Further, almost 70 percent of the students described their upbringing as middle-class or higher. Additionally, the majority of the students I interviewed attended schools where they felt academically prepared for classes at WSU. Johnson, who was underprepared academically, a first-generation college student, and from a working-class background, was different.

Johnson saw little else Caldwell could do to support Black students, arguing, "[Caldwell is] pushing the right campaigns, but if they did anything else it would be a little overkill-y." His attitude toward being Black in an HWI is, in his words, "very unpopular," arguing, "It's like [some Black people] come to a [HWI] and they want an HBCU experience and it's like, you can't do both, you know?" Johnson was clear about why he enrolled in WSU and attempted to make the most of his courses. The fact that he was often the only Black student in his classes did not necessarily bother him:

> I wasn't like at orientation like, "Damn, where the Black people at?" . . . And it's crazy because you would think that would be my reaction just because I come from a predominantly Black neighborhood, but it's like, nah. That was not the case. I was definitely at WSU for the resources.

He came to WSU, and Caldwell in particular, for the resources—to feel like Iron Man, to work in engineering societies, and to build cars and rockets with his peers. He did not come to WSU to feel like "a happy Black person." Yet, his ability to make use of the resources, to build social capital with classmates, or even join an engineering society, was limited by his educational background and, likely, his Blackness.

Considering how he was made to feel in the Caldwell community, his heavy participation in Black communities makes sense. Caldwell was a constant letdown—unanswered texts from classmates, unwelcoming engineering society members, professors' incorrect assumption that every student had the same high school pedigree, and constant reminders of his working-class background. In the Black communities on campus, he was welcome to take center stage. In Caldwell, he was made to feel small.

The Mainstream WSU Community

Between classes, Johnson greeted an Asian American guy, "Let's hang soon, man. Seriously." Johnson, laughing, anticipating my question after seeing the unlikely greeting, said, "Yeah that's the day one homie—before the Black community scooped me up." Johnson, finding his engagement in the Black and NSBE communities, has little attachment to the general WSU community. In the mainstream WSU community, Johnson felt out of place. The WSU culture, predominantly White and rich, was unlike his roots. During a walk between his classes, Johnson, feeling particularly frustrated with his grades, said, "If I could do it all over I wouldn't have come here."

"I feel like I spend so much time adapting, keeping up with the Joneses that it hurts. I'm tired of trying to play the game," Johnson said with a sigh. Thinking about his experience at WSU, he expressed that if he went to a school that matched his culture, he would have fared better academically. His eloquent description is saddening. Outside of the sentiment, however, the same words seem an easy fit for a Bourdieusian analysis. One thinks of habitus, or more specifically, a "destabilized habitus, torn by contradiction and internal division, generating suffering" (Bourdieu 2000, 159). In near-perfect alignment with Bourdieu's Theory of Practice, Johnson also likens the WSU culture to a game. Bourdieu, in describing his concept of field, compares field to *le champ*, a literal football field and space for a sporting competition. Yet, Johnson's experience is much more complex than a habitus misaligned with the cultural field of WSU.

Recall, during chapter 3, my description of the Midnight Brunch and Johnson taking center stage—what are we to make of this? While a mainstream WSU event, the dinner was simultaneously important for the Black community. He was not simply someone on the outside struggling to fit in the mainstream culture. It was precisely because of his heavy participation in the Black community that he, at that moment, was comfortable in a culture that otherwise "hurt." At the same institution, depending on the social world, he could feel both at home and alienated.

Because his out-of-class experiences were often mediated through NSBE or the Black communities, Johnson did not have many negative racialized encounters he could recall at WSU. After leaving a general body meeting at the end of the Spring semester, Johnson and I saw headlights shine from behind us. It was a campus security vehicle. "Wait, are we getting profiled right now?" Johnson snickered. Moving to the side of the road, the car drove by and a Black and Latina officer waved to us. I felt myself exhale after they passed. Black people's encounters with police, whether on or off campus, can result in racial profiling, violence, wrongful arrest, or even death. The knowledge of police violence shapes how Black people, especially Black men, navigate spaces, campuses included (Brooms and Perry 2016; Jenkins et al. 2020; Smith et al. 2016). "I've been pressed[3] three times since I've been out here," Johnson mentioned. Only one time was by WSU police. While meditating outside of the music building around noon, using his meditation mobile app, a couple of WSU officers asked if he went to WSU. After he provided a WSU school ID, their tone changed.

Meditation and mindfulness are important to Johnson. He sometimes struggles with his mental health, especially when he feels as if he is not performing well academically. Johnson once texted me, responding to me asking how he was feeling, "Mental health just getting worse and worse with each late morning wake up." While I was in the field, Johnson had switched therapists and also the prescription medicine he takes for his mental health. Attending a school with a culture with which he felt misaligned at times added another layer to his mental health struggles. With a new therapist and prescription regimen during the summer, he hoped that he would be able to reach his "full potential."

During that summer, we once studied together in a lounge in his residence hall. Upset about where he was, a rising senior without an internship and two Incomplete classes from the previous semester, he vented, "It makes me feel like shit, the WSU family. People back home look up to me . . . the WSU family is good and bad." Attending an elite school such as WSU made him an inspiration to his peers and friends back in the Bronx. Yet, he also felt inadequate comparing himself to his peers in NSBE, saying, "You have people who have internships everywhere—one girl had an internship at Facebook her freshman year and she's at Google this summer." A short silence, filled with my inability to find the right reply, ensued. "I'ma do something," Johnson said, to himself more than to me. He could have been referring to a number of things—grades, the semester, his career, or just the demands of the day. "I'ma do something," he said again, putting his headphones on, directing his attention to his work.

THE BLACK ENGINEERING
COMMUNITY

5

Examining NSBE

How Black Engineers Do It for the Culture

Without NSBE, we'd probably have two Black students.

—Carmen, the Multicultural Engineering Office director

Migos, the rap group, dropped *Culture* during the beginning of my field-work. Students sometimes quoted lyrics from the album in conversation, and one line in particular, "Do it for the culture." On a Friday night in March, I heard of two parties thrown by Black WSU students, both with the same name—"For the Culture." Johnson was DJ'ing one party that benefited the East African Student Association, while the other party benefited a campus mentoring organization. On some occasions, partici-pants would encourage attendance for National Society of Black Engineers (NSBE) events by punctuating their requests with a "Do it for the culture." During an NSBE game night I asked Ayana, the NSBE president, "What do you mean when you say, 'for the culture'?" She laughed, saying,

> It depends on the context. So like, if you ain't going to be an engineer who going to be an engineer? Who's going to put up with the BS? So you just do it for the culture. And then there's NSBE traditions, so you just do it for the culture.

The "BS," or bullshit, Ayana referred to, included the daily trials of being the only Black woman majoring in mechanical engineering in her year.

Beyond the NSBE culture, however, students seemed to be alluding to the larger Black community. At the crux of Ayana's statement of doing something for the culture are two interrelated theoretical issues that I continue to explore throughout this book—linked fate and racial essentialism.

A sense of linked fate (Dawson 1994) underlies Ayana's words. Shouldering the racialized and gendered stress of being the only Black woman in her major was not simply for her benefit, but for the benefit of the larger Black community in America. Linked fate connects the micro to the macro. For Ayana, her individual success as a student and her efficacy as a leader of NSBE is tied to the well-being of the Black community. Less apparent in her statement, however, is a notion of racial essentialism, or the belief that a singular experience for a racial group exists (e.g., The Black Experience) and that specific social behaviors and dispositions are linked to the essence of the race (Austin 1991; Chao et al. 2013; Harris 1990).

Ayana, a Haitian American who grew up in New York, was keenly aware, of course, of cultural differences within Blackness. She knew race was a social construct without a biological foundation. Yet she also knew that race had real life consequences, shaping her experiences at WSU. "Do it for the culture" became a rallying cry for strategic essentialism—a reminder that while the fifty-eight Black engineering majors at WSU were indeed diverse, they might be stronger together under the banner of NSBE. Critical Race Theorists themselves similarly walk the tightrope of acknowledging the diversity within Blackness, while also essentializing Blackness. As the Critical Race Theorists Delgado and Stefancic (2012) note, CRT adopts a form of racial essentialism both for the purposes of political solidarity and in the assumption that all People of Color are positioned to provide valuable experiential knowledge about racism. As I show in this chapter, racial essentialism arises as a boundary within the Black engineering social world.[1]

In this chapter, I highlight NSBE—the Black engineering social world—its culture and its instrumental role in creating a welcoming community for Black engineering majors. Despite the potentially central role NSBE chapters play in the persistence of Black engineering majors, scholars often only mention NSBE or use this group for participant recruitment. In other words, sometimes NSBE is referred to, others times NSBE is used, but rarely is NSBE studied. The same can be said of other ethnic student organizations. Daisy Reyes's (2018) work serves as an example of what scholars stand to gain from centering ethnic student organizations in their research. By focusing on Latinx student organizations, Reyes's scholarship engages with campus racial climate as well as how institutional context shapes students' racial and political development. Neglecting to examine student groups' role in shaping the campus experience for members is a missed opportunity to learn more about how to support students in a meaningful way.

Through NSBE events and meetings, NSBE provides a mechanism for engagement. Similar to the Black community's social world, students heavily involved in the NSBE social world display agency, co-creating the campus racial climate to better suit their needs. Within the NSBE social world three primary tensions exist: (1) a tension between engagement and responsibility to the maintenance of the NSBE social world; (2) a tension between strategic essentialism and antiessentialism within NSBE; and (3) a tension between a family and engineering focus.

The NSBE Community at a Glance

At the end of the 2016–17 school year, The Caldwell School of Engineering's Multicultural Engineering Office (MEO) held a "Celebration of Excellence" banquet for all of the organizations under the MEO umbrella, that is, NSBE, the Society of Women Engineers (SWE), LGBTQ Professionals in Engineering, and the Society of Hispanic Professional Engineers (SHPE). Students arrived in business casual attire. In prime time for final exam studying, four tables in the hotel ballroom were empty. Students sat with their respective organizations, Black students with NSBE, Latinx students with SHPE, White women with SWE,[2] and a small, albeit racially diverse group with the LGBTQ Professionals in Engineering.

Graduating seniors received recognition and a gift bag from the MEO representatives—Carmen and Keith from the MEO office, Dr. August, and Dr. Pittman—and walked to the stage to shake their hands. Embraces varied from hugs to handshakes depending on the relationship between students and the staff. While giving a formal handshake to most students, Professor August, a Black man and professor of engineering, emphatically dapped up Robert, Thomas, and the other Black men graduating. More than a formal handshake, giving dap or dapping someone up has a level of intricacy—slapping hands, hooking at the thumbs, with a crisp clapping sound.

Presidents from each MEO organization recognized members with awards for their academic excellence and/or service. Ayana, similarly, represented NSBE at the front of the ballroom and awarded students who were not present, studying for finals elsewhere. Ayana's presentation, however, was different. She wore her hair natural. Her gold, elephant earrings—an homage to her sorority—were almost hidden behind the curls of her hair, more defined after being uncoiled from braids. She concluded her speech about NSBE and the awardees the same way she concluded NSBE meetings, saying, ". . . and in true NSBE fashion . . ."

Reflexively, every NSBE member, sixteen people, and myself, stood from our seats. Students in other organizations looked up from their seats, some visibly confused, furrowing their brows and others smiling. In unison, with more exuberance than the routine recitation at the end of NSBE meetings on Monday nights, we said the NSBE mission: "To increase the number of culturally responsible Black engineers who excel academically, succeed professionally, and positively impact the community."

"You saw how I stunted on 'em?" Ayana said to me after, referring to our collective show of the NSBE mission. I asked her if she had planned to do that with the chapter beforehand and she laughed, shaking her head, "I knew y'all would know what to do. Y'all would know to do it for the culture." Dr. Pittman walked toward us, put her hand on Ayana's shoulder, and said, "You know, I really wish the Dean could have seen that. I mean, wow."

Far from fading into the background, far from feeling alienated, NSBE members made their presence felt. Ayana's organic orchestration of the recitation of their mission tells us a bit about the interwoven nature of culture and structure. NSBE—like SHPE, LGBTQ Professionals in Engineering, and SWE—are supported by Caldwell under the MEO umbrella. In turn, NSBE is shaped by Caldwell structures, yet NSBE works upon Caldwell structures themselves. In other words, while Caldwell and other external forces shape NSBE, the students creating the NSBE social world are not passive agents. Although constricted, Black engineering students work to shape the campus environments they traverse.

NSBE STRUCTURE

NSBE was founded in 1975 at Purdue University. The founders started NSBE with the intent of recruiting and retaining Black engineers while also working to facilitate their acquisition of jobs in the engineering industry. With more than three hundred collegiate chapters, NSBE is one of the largest college student-led organizations in America. Without a dedicated room or office, NSBE is not spatially bound (see Figure 5.1).

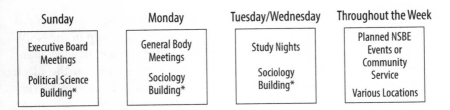

Sunday	Monday	Tuesday/Wednesday	Throughout the Week
Executive Board Meetings Political Science Building*	General Body Meetings Sociology Building*	Study Nights Sociology Building*	Planned NSBE Events or Community Service Various Locations

Note: Students reserved rooms in these buildings ahead of time.

Figure 5.1. The Black Engineering Social World.

Yet, Black engineers create places in reserved classrooms across campus. WSU's NSBE chapter meets almost weekly for general body meetings on Monday evenings. For a little over an hour, NSBE members turn Room 129 in the sociology building into a welcoming place for themselves, Black engineers. On any given general body meeting, anywhere from eleven to fifty-eight Black undergraduate and graduate engineers would be present. The NSBE executive board (e-board) meets Sunday evenings. On Tuesday or Wednesday evenings, they reserve a room for NSBE study nights. Once a month they hold a community service event, teaching middle and high school students the basics of engineering. Similar to the WSU Black community social world, events and meetings, rather than dedicated brick and mortar spaces, serve as Black places for the Black engineering social world.

NSBE, as an organization, does not exist in a world isolated from others, but dynamically takes its shape in relation to other organizations and the institutional context. In this chapter, however, I only focus on tensions within NSBE. In doing so, I intend to provide a snippet of how NSBE served as a mechanism for student engagement.

Tension between the Engagement
and Burdens of Being an NSBE Member

Similar to the Black community, the participants who are heavily involved in the NSBE community mediate a tension between individual engagement and a broader responsibility to the Black engineering community. Involvement in NSBE yields various benefits, including a sense of engagement, networking opportunities, jobs, tutoring, and, more fundamentally, friendship. Yet, as I demonstrate later, such engagement might manifest in unfair responsibilities tasked to Black undergraduates.

The majority of Black engineers at WSU are in some way involved in NSBE. Similar to the Black WSU community, membership in the NSBE community was granted through presence and involvement. In a like manner, it was possible to be a Black engineer but not be part of the Black engineering community. Membership practices of the Black engineering community's social world involved regular attendance at NSBE-sponsored events and meetings. Students who were part of the Black engineering social world engaged with NSBE through various processes: attending weekly meetings, joining the NSBE e-board, supporting NSBE events, and helping fundraise for conferences. Participants involved in NSBE have a pride in their organization, rivaling that of fraternities or sororities. Some members even purchased glossy, black NSBE jackets, reminiscent of line/crossing jackets worn by members of Black Greek Letter Organizations.

As a member of the first Black Greek Letter Organization myself, I noticed similarities within the NSBE culture. Similar to fraternities and sororities, NSBE regions have different call and response chants. WSU NSBE even had their own chapter-specific chant and won the Best Chant Award for the video they submitted to the national NSBE conference. Ayana's words encapsulate the attitude of the WSU NSBE chapter: "We like to win. That's it." The chapter is a regular awardee at regional and national conferences. Olivia, a past president of the chapter, described how the WSU NSBE culture was shaped by the WSU culture, saying, "We're just weird." After pausing for two seconds with a smile, she continued, laughing,

> We're arrogant. We literally think that we're the best. But that happens at WSU, they kinda train us as any [WSU student], like, we are trained to be the best. It's just like a thing . . . we're tight, come at us! And engineers—we're naturally a little more stuck up, because we're the problem solvers, we think we can do everything. So you put it together, we're obnoxious as hell.

The wider WSU culture shapes the NSBE and engineering culture. While Olivia suggested that NSBE members are "obnoxious as hell" in jest, her words show how Black WSU students neither exist in a vacuum nor consider themselves perennial victims.

More than a pride in NSBE, many students became friends through organizational involvement. For some students, their entire friendship networks came from NSBE. William, for example, explained, "Most of my friends outside of engineering, I was introduced to from my NSBE friends." Having friends within the organization was a draw to keep coming to meetings as well. Joseph, for example, said,

> I liked hanging out with them . . . they were pretty good with just being like, "Hey, how are you doing?" And like, especially freshman year they try to like keep the people that do show up. So I like that, and I like that space just to be with other Black engineers.

Bianca reiterated friendship as a catalyst for continued involvement: "Once you start getting to know people, it's more fun to go and talk to people, so I think that's when I got more involved."

Four months into fieldwork, I interviewed Chantelle. She told me in March that she would not have time to chat with me for an interview until May. Even at NSBE meetings, while present, she was working on her computer science homework. In describing NSBE she said, "You get to relate. Although they're in different fields and all that stuff, they're Black. So. It's a place that I feel comfortable—like a breath of fresh air." I pushed further, asking, "You come to meetings and just do homework sometimes, so why even come, you know?" Chantelle and many other students showed up to NSBE meetings with their laptops open, coding, or heads down staring at notes, working out problem sets. Splitting attention between course work and whatever presentation or activity was occurring in the meeting was an unspoken norm of NSBE culture. Chantelle gave insight as to why students would sacrifice prime studying time and divide their attention between an NSBE meeting and halfway working on a homework assignment. Nodding, she explained, "Just being in the comfort zone, like yeah, just feeling like I belong. 'Cause a lot of times I feel like I don't belong in [Computer Science]." Students received from NSBE what they could not receive anywhere else at WSU—the warm embrace of other Black engineers. During NSBE meetings, students felt a feeling, typical of counterspaces, that they could exhale. For just an hour and some change on Monday nights, Black engineering students could exist within the comfort and affirmation of their Black engineering community.

Students were united in their shared racial identity, engineering workloads, and responsibilities for event planning and participation in events through NSBE. Olivia discussed the benefit of planning events with other members saying that "if we're trying to plan an event, there's a lot of other things we have to think about. So those challenges, it just makes us work together. . . . I don't know. I love them." Organizing events such as their study nights/days, fundraisers, parties, a Black History Month debate, Halloween movie nights, and others, further requires NSBE members to work with each other toward a common goal. Leaving students to their own devices is necessary and part of the college experience, yet how much responsibility is too much?

Nina, the president during the latter half of my research, said, "We want to make it normalized that Black engineers exist" during the first NSBE general body meeting of the school year. NSBE, to an extent, does just that. They attempt to engage with the Black community at WSU by working, on occasion, with the BSU and sending two NSBE representatives to weekly general body meetings. They engage with the neighborhood community, holding almost monthly NSBE Jr. events, dedicating at least half a Saturday to leading engineering-related activities to middle and high school students from public schools in the WSU area. They show up and help staff Caldwell events for the annual STEM Week. They lead tours for prospective students for admissions events. Active NSBE members at WSU are engaged with the campus through NSBE in many ways, yet such engagement can prove to be an added burden for students.

THE POTENTIAL BURDENS

Volunteering at Caldwell events is normal for student organizations. Through volunteering, organizations receive supplemental funding and recognition within the school. Ayana, however, told me that in order to get funding from Caldwell or WSU in general, she or another e-board member would sometimes have to skip class to present their proposals. A computer science professor mentioned in an interview that he was worried that students may spend too much time with their organizations—even at the cost of academics. While he was speaking of instances with Latinx students involved within the Society of Hispanic Professional Engineers, he wondered aloud if Black students similarly prioritized NSBE duties over academic duties. The majority of Black engineers I interviewed, however, did not seem to have this issue. Yet, Black students' work for NSBE or simply being Black in Caldwell did, at times, seem burdensome compared to nonblack students.

NSBE played a central role in Black engineers' experience because of intentional, concerted effort by Black students themselves. The presence of NSBE and other student groups on campus is not a given. Rather, the strength, relevance, and usefulness of NSBE was contingent upon students' labor. NSBE members find and recruit Black students to join the chapter. Robert, a senior, for example, was often cited as the reason people became involved in NSBE. He would stop Black people in libraries, cafeterias, or hallways if he saw them with a computer science book or leaving an engineering class.

For Black engineers, engagement in the Black community or Black engineering community is not a given. Similar to the WSU Black community's social world, students intentionally sought out the Black social world of NSBE. As I mentioned in chapter 3, the phenomenon of Black homophily, or the process of finding and maintaining relationships with other Black people, on historically White campuses is taken for granted. Given the small numbers of Black students and limited structured opportunities to form relationships with their same-race peers, Black students are agentic in joining Black affinity groups and attempting to meet other Black WSU students. In other words, as Tamara Gilkes Borr (2018) points out, Black homophily on predominantly nonblack campuses cannot be explained by structure alone. Black communities such as the Black engineering community are often made through the labor and creativity of Black students themselves. NSBE members are active in the maintenance of their community either by way of searching for a Black engineering community or by informally recruiting students to join NSBE. Consider how Hanna, who made friends in NSBE and found a place of belonging, only discovered the group as a junior. A member of the NSBE e-board, Nina, happened to take a writing class with Hanna and pushed her to come to a meeting. Unsure of how she could have not heard of NSBE as an organization, she jokingly said, referring to the Whiteness of WSU, "I live under a very White rock, apparently." Hanna's case demonstrates the dynamism and relational nature of campus communities.

Students' gender also shaped how they interacted with NSBE. The labor of students to sustain NSBE was not equally spread across members and often fell on the shoulders of women. While men participated in NSBE leadership, women held the president and vice-president roles during the two years of my data collection as well as the year prior. In the one NSBE election I observed, no men expressed interest in running for the position of NSBE president. Further, as I show later, it was a woman who spearheaded efforts to reactivate NSBE at WSU. Black women were the face of NSBE at WSU. I would venture to say that NSBE and its success as a student organization is largely because of women. Their visibility, their high standing in the Black engineering community, and their leadership in NSBE, I believe, was inspiring. Yet, I also wondered if there was an implicit assumption that a woman would take the greatest responsibility in leadership. While the women in leadership did not complain about their positions, examining how gendered responsibility plays out in Black student organizations is worth exploring in future work.

The head of the MEO, Carmen, felt as if Black engineering majors, regardless of gender, were unfairly burdened with responsibilities that the university should carry. Carmen expressed that NSBE was invaluable, suggesting, "Without NSBE, we'd probably have two Black students." NSBE at WSU grew in size, largely because of a few core Black students, and one in particular, Naa Koshie—a Black woman. Only seven years prior to my fieldwork, NSBE on WSU's campus was dormant. Naa Koshie changed that. She graduated more than three years prior to my fieldwork, but more senior students and MEO staff would speak of Naa Koshie and her successful revitalization of NSBE as part of chapter lore. Going through university red tape to reactivate student organizations involved collecting signatures from students and staff alike and attending meetings. Without an equivalent to NSBE, Naa Koshie also led efforts to find other Black Caldwell students, tell them about NSBE, and build a culture within the organization that made people want to remain members. Given what I knew about her, she was indeed worthy of her legendary status.

Carmen recalled, however, that Naa Koshie would vent to her when feeling discouraged, explaining, "There are less of us but yet we have this expectation to be at every admission event . . . SWE [Society of Women Engineers] can do it because they have a large number of members . . . I'm at everything because who else is going to do it." To be clear, I never spoke to Naa Koshie, but consider what I learned about her: as an undergraduate student she simultaneously navigated the school of engineering as a Black woman, reactivated NSBE, and represented NSBE across campus, and she did all of this while also completing course work and attempting to have a social life. In reflecting upon her foundational leadership and the continued leadership of Black women in NSBE, I wondered if Black engineering students had, to an extent, potentially internalized the Strong Black Woman stereotype. This stereotype suggests that Black women are inherently strong, self-sacrificing caregivers, and independent (Donovan and West 2015). The glorification of the Strong Black Woman image is a response to the gendered racial oppression Black women have historically faced and continue to endure. While research shows that Black college women often endorse the Strong Black Woman ideal as part of their identity, adopting this ideal is also associated with negative mental health outcomes such as stress and depression (West et al. 2016).

Speaking about Caldwell's view of Black students in general, Carmen expressed, "You have a different expectation for them on their engagement. They did not commit to attending WSU and Caldwell in order to help us recruit more students." Beyond being engineering students, Black students were implicitly tasked with creating a welcoming environment and support system for each other and future Black students. Carmen provided a concrete example of the unfair expectations placed on Black engineering students. A couple of years prior to my fieldwork, NSBE's regional conference occurred at the same time as a Caldwell admissions event. The NSBE conference was not a surprise to the university because Caldwell helped subsidize NSBE members' costs for travel. Of an already small NSBE membership, only two students were staying at WSU and missing the conference. Caldwell student affairs and admissions representatives requested NSBE members to report to the event. One student e-mailed the night before saying, "I can't make it," and the other did not show. The Caldwell staff holding the event did not take NSBE's absence kindly and the staff member "kind of lost it." Carmen was showed the exchange. The organizing staff looked to Carmen incredulously saying, "Carmen can you believe this?"

After pointing out that Caldwell was aware of the regional conference and conflicting dates, she also said, "Your engineering societies—they're mostly White male. You would not have talked to them like that. And why is it that?" They're like, "Well, you know . . . one of the things is that if we don't have a community already existing, it's hard for other under-represented students to come." She agreed about the necessity of having a visible Black community in the engineering school to attract prospective Black engineers to WSU. Yet, she diverged with the Caldwell staff:

> We want them to stick with engineering, [that is] their primary job . . . that sense of entitlement that I feel like Caldwell has in like, "Come on." Sometimes it's even guilt, like, "Come on, if you aren't at these events how can you expect Black students to come here?" It kills me. And that's [from] people in student affairs and in admissions.

Caldwell placed unique and unfair expectations upon Black students. As Carmen points out, viewing Black engineering majors as more than students, but also as unpaid ambassadors for the school's diversity efforts, is added labor for students. What is striking is Caldwell staff's entitlement to Black students' labor and time. This expectation of Black students' labor and the callous disregard for Black students' primary status as students is a pointed way of othering and marginalizing Black students. This insensitive approach and failure to see Black students simply as students is racist. A similar phenomenon occurs for Black faculty. Cohen (1998), for example, refers to the added service, mentorship, and labor Black faculty do to support students of color and institutional diversity efforts as the "Black tax." Black students are likewise taxed. Caldwell administrators attempted to relieve themselves of any responsibility for the small Black Caldwell population by pointing to Black Caldwell students themselves, suggesting that their limited involvement in recruitment was a cause of marginal Black enrollment. To blame Black engineers for a small incoming number of Black engineers is racist. To assume that Black students should leap at opportunities to do diversity work for Caldwell is likewise racist.

When does a sense of engagement turn into a sense of obligation? Through an assumed linked fate (Dawson 1994), students active in the Black community, Black engineering community, or other organizations seem to feel a duty to the well-being of their groups. Some of this duty is of their own volition, and can provide leadership skills, lasting friendships, academic advising or tutoring, networking opportunities, a sense of belonging and engagement, as well as attachment to their university. Time, however, is currency. Every hour spent fundraising for an event, attending and planning meetings, giving tours to new students, or speaking on panels is an hour spent away from studying or involvement in career preparation. Striking a balance is difficult. The obligation students feel to NSBE, however, is not a feeling of its own creation. As Carmen demonstrated, this responsibility is in some ways socialized by staff and administrators. Yet, for some members, NSBE duties—the service, the challenges, the time spent for the betterment of the NSBE chapter or promoting the visibility of Black engineers—are responsibilities that give meaning and joy to their engineering experience.

Tension between Strategic Essentialism and Antiessentialism

From ethnicity to socioeconomic status to gender to general interests and more, NSBE was diverse. Yet students sometimes messaged ideas about how

Black people were supposed to act or be. During a game night, the group played heads-up on an iPhone, a guessing game where people give clues to someone without using the word/phrase on the phone. Maahka held the phone to her head and "surfing" popped up on the screen. Thomas, trying to give a clue and make a joke said, "Shit White people do." "Skydiving" came up during Maahka's turn as well, to which Thomas said, again, "Shit White people do." Charlie looked up from his chemistry problem set and said, "Shit, do niggas do anything?" In this playful interaction, Thomas's jokes are underscored by racial essentialism—the belief that a singular Black experience exists and Black people, by virtue of their race, have the same likes and dislikes. Students never seriously suggested that Black people were a monolith, yet some participants seemed to understand there to be some shared essence to Blackness. An essentialized idea of Blackness, or how Blackness should be done, created a symbolic boundary within NSBE.

This boundary, however, did not create strife or any clear division within NSBE. Rather, the boundary of racial essentialism is perhaps most apparent to participants who felt outside of Blackness or who had only recently begun to reflect upon their Black racial identity. Research demonstrates that counterspaces such as Black student organizations are beneficial, in part, because they provide members with a sense of cultural familiarity and validation (Guiffrida 2003; Harper and Quaye 2007; Museus 2008). While true for some, as I highlight in this chapter, other students joined NSBE precisely because of their cultural unfamiliarity with what is understood as Black American culture. For these students, NSBE served as a mechanism to become more acquainted with Blackness. This feeling, as I show throughout this section, however, assumes that an essence to Blackness exists.

Chukwu, the newly appointed membership chair on the e-board, led the packed room of forty-two students in an icebreaker for the first NSBE meeting of the Fall semester. "So for an icebreaker, I want you to say your name, where you're from, your major, and your favorite rapper." Because of his baritone voice, his request sounded more like a command. "What if I don't listen to rap . . . are you trying to stereotype me?" Johnson asked in feigned outrage. "Well you shouldn't be here," Chukwu retorted. His joke might have been lost within his monotone response.

J. Cole. Kendrick Lamar. Joey Bada$$. Migos. The big names were called upon by most students. I made the mistake of saying Tupac, to which Johnson replied, "See . . . you're dating yourself, bro," to collective laughter. Nina commented during one of the earlier introductions, "Take notes of who's in your major so you can get notes in your classes." Alexis, whom I had not seen at a meeting during the semester prior, introduced herself and said, "I don't even listen to rap." Dayo commented from the other side of the room, "See. Inclusion." I chatted with Alexis a week later and she brought up that icebreaker saying, "I don't listen to rap. That's the wrong question. That was the first one, too." Johnson also commented on the icebreaker in a separate conversation with me: "That kinda narrative infiltrates everything." "For Black engineers," he explained, "you have to represent the culture and be a nerd. Thomas and Robert pull it off. They're both geniuses but mad cool. But that's so much harder to do. . . . White America? They can be nerdy . . . they don't have the extra baggage." Johnson alludes to a unique "baggage" of performing Blackness in a certain way to feel like part of the Black community. The tension between a contested idea of what Black culture should or should not be comes to fore when examining the diversity within NSBE.

"Not every Black engineer feels comfortable in NSBE," Laurie told me. She continued,

> I know a couple people who are just, they just don't feel as comfortable, probably because of where they come from. So like, we don't hate them. Like if you feel uncomfortable, that's fine. But we, of course, try to recruit them. Because we don't know what they're comfortable with so it's like, "Hey, try it out." If it isn't something you're into, then, "Okay, fine." At least we tried to make you all feel comfortable.

While Laurie did not specify, one can assume that she was referring to students' backgrounds or habitus (Bourdieu 1984). Where students come from, whether they were most comfortable spending time with Black students in K–12 settings, their country of origin, and other factors shaped students' habitus and their comfort in NSBE. Charlie, a product of a predominantly White private school for most of his K–12 experience, similarly pointed to the role background plays in one's comfort in NSBE, explaining that some might feel like "they aren't welcomed by Black people." To his estimation, he identified three reasons why Black engineers would not join NSBE:

> One—they don't know about it. Or two—they have no time management. Or three—they feel as though they don't need it or they feel slighted. It's a very weird world. That don't make

no sense. Like why wouldn't you be part of something that can help you get a job?

Robert pointed out how, logistically, it can be difficult to make everyone who comes to an NSBE meeting feel welcome. He explained, "The e-board is close to each other so we sit next to each other and talk with each other a lot. And then you'll have underclassmen who aren't sitting with anyone." Robert even considered the idea of pushing the e-board to sit next to new members every general body meeting. Yet for college students on a Monday evening, such intentionality and discipline in a place of reprieve can be difficult. Similar to Laurie, concerning Black engineers who do not come to NSBE, he said, "I always encourage it but you know, I don't have any beef with them."

Alexis, a senior, was critical of NSBE, saying, "I just feel like the only thing that connected all of us was the fact that we were Black." Addressing the heterogeneity within Blackness she continued, saying, "Within that, there's just so many variables. For example, just because you're Black doesn't mean you're first-gen. It doesn't mean that you're poor." Alexis herself is a first-generation college student and grew up in a low-income household. She felt that socioeconomic status and upbringing was not recognized in NSBE:

[B]eing Black, yeah, it's a mark against you. However, it's not your deciding factor. If you have a family who's gonna protect you and your life has been great other than the fact that maybe somebody says one racist comment every blue moon . . .

She implicitly provided an intersectional critique of NSBE, suggesting that it was not just race that was a "mark against" her, but also her class status. While most NSBE members, she believed, were marginalized because of their race, she was doubly marginalized by both her race and class (Crenshaw 1989). Interestingly, she made no mention of her gender. This may be because NSBE was largely led by women. I say more about gender in chapter 9.

Some students joined NSBE to meet more Black people at WSU and, in some ways, learn more about and be closer to the proverbial Black community. Despite her critique of NSBE, Alexis spoke with regret about not knowing many Black students as a senior, saying, "I just feel like I kind of missed out on that part of WSU." Growing up in a predominantly Latinx area, going to a majority Latinx high school, she feels most comfortable around Latinx people and also joined a predominantly Latina sorority:

> [T]he other reason why I chose [a Latina] one as opposed to like a Black sorority, was for the same reason. I feel like I can vibe with [Latinxs] on a deeper level. Probably, because I grew up with a lot of Hispanic/Latino people.

Given her background and her critique of NSBE, I asked why she still wanted to make connections with Black folk in Caldwell and WSU. She replied, "I don't know. I feel like, even though I love my Hispanic friends . . . at the same time there's a part of me that always wanted to be a part of the Black crowd."

Four other students expressed a similar sentiment of learning about Blackness. Willis, for example, is biracial—his mother is Black and father is White. His mother grew up in low-income housing in Chicago and, wanting to shield him from that experience, raised him with his father in a White suburb in Minnesota. "I know some things about Black culture, but I feel bad because I'm not like . . . I don't know too much. And I wanted to join NSBE so I could be around Black people," Willis explained. There is something familiar about NSBE that he cannot quite articulate, but that reminds him of his mother's family: "I'll go to family reunions and then, that's kinda what I see in NSBE. Those same things, like, 'Oh I know what this is.'" What he recognized, but could not put his finger on was, perhaps, a learned idea of Black American culture.

NSBE, like the larger WSU Black community, is comprised of, for the most part, only Black students. Yet the group is ethnically diverse. Black folks raised in Barbados, Nigeria, and Ethiopia. Black folks born in New York City but whose parents were from Jamaica or Trinidad. Black American folks whose known ancestry was fractured by the Transatlantic Slave Trade, so they trace their roots to Chicago, Mississippi, or Virginia. Other Black students identified as biracial or multiracial. Their racial identity, their Blackness, and their status as engineering students at WSU, however, united them. The strategic essentialism (Chadderton 2013; Delgado and Stefancic 2012) of uniting under the shared Black engineering identity did not mute the inherent diversity of the community. Difference, however, can lead to tensions.

Ethnicity, for example, is often taken for granted in research on Black students (Agyepong 2017; Fries-Britt et al. 2014). Black students themselves wrestle with the diversity within Blackness and with understanding their racial identity. First or second generation African and Caribbean NSBE members often expressed a desire to learn more about Black American culture. Funke, who was born in Nigeria, said she started coming to NSBE to "get more in touch with my culture and meet more African Americans and get to know more about what it's like." A Habesha student, Hanna, also said having Black friends was new for her, explaining, "I don't know, I guess I wasn't raised with it." NSBE provided a more intimate space than the larger WSU Black community for participants to construct ideas about what it means to be Black.

While not the goal of this book, predominantly Black spaces are furtive ground to study the racialization of Black students. Ethnic background and immigrant status can become more pronounced in a group of Black people. In extending the work of other scholars (e.g., Mwangi and Fries-Britt 2015; Mwangi et al. 2017), the diversity within this particular group of Black engineers at the same institution is a critical reminder of the heterogeneity within Blackness. Consider, for example, how Dayo and Timothy, who are both Nigerian, understood "roasting." Dayo used to get in trouble in high school when he hung out with Black students and felt like they did not value education like he did. Within NSBE, however, he found, "educated, not as roasting African Americans. I mean, they still roast you but it's like a little better. They're not going to roast you for being smart." Timothy, who went to a top high school in Nigeria with the children of diplomats, doctors, and politicians, was unfamiliar with being "roasted" prior to NSBE. He missed an NSBE group picture during a trip to Disneyland and grew mildly irritated at NSBE members continually saying that he got lost at the park. He said, "They never really let that down for like, for a year. They're always like, 'Oh, where is Timothy?' If you don't see me in the picture you're like, 'Oh, where is Timothy? Is he lost again?'" This playful teasing or "roasting," rubbed him the wrong way at first, but after some time, he started finding it funny and making jokes about himself.

Initially, Timothy was hesitant to join NSBE. He knew the stereotype that "African American students on campus might not necessarily be the most academically focused." After attending NSBE however, as if putting the stereotype to rest with one example, Timothy bragged, "But . . . last semester [NSBE] had the valedictorian of Caldwell Engineering School." It is worth mentioning that upon first meeting Timothy, he had a 3.94 GPA in his engineering courses.

Like any group, NSBE works through the tension of being inclusive with a diverse group, attempting the impossible task of making all members feel comfortable. As young adults, they work through this tension on top of their engineering courses. NSBE battles against stereotypes and deficit-based assumptions about Black students from the outside, and faces the monumental task of creating community for the expansive construct and culture of Blackness on the inside.

The reality of a small number of Black engineers and an even smaller number of Black students in specific majors plays a central role in their experience. Oftentimes, they are the only ones in their classes. Some students speak enviously of students in computer science (CS) who have more than one Black person in their classes. A few students specifically pointed to Laurie and De'Lante, who were both Civil Engineering majors in the same year, and had nearly all the same classes.

Active NSBE members shoulder the burden of recruitment, visibility, and community building in addition to regular organizational work and school work. For some, however, the burden is simply a part of life and provides meaning—something difficult to describe. As Olivia said, she loved the challenges and struggles she faced with NSBE in planning events and in reviving the organization at WSU. While students took time away from their studies to sell churros for NSBE fundraising, or do homework in a loud NSBE meeting as opposed to a library, or skip a class to ensure funding for NSBE events, they gained something that could not be achieved in a course—belonging, engagement, purpose, friendships, and leadership. As Carmen asked, however, how much responsibility is too much, and how much of their engagement is unfairly placed on them by the institution?

Outside of learning about Black culture, facilitating connections, and fostering a sense of engagement and belonging, there is something else about NSBE—the something that neither the participants nor myself could pin down. Before moving on to discuss the tension between a family focus and an engineering focus in NSBE, I include a short scene about Elsie—a Black Caldwell graduate student and self-proclaimed introvert—that might provide insight to the "something else" of NSBE and inclusion.

At WSU, NSBE usually does fundraising to subsidize their expenses for travel to the NSBE conferences. One fundraiser was a raffle drawing—NSBE members sold tickets to other students or just bought some themselves. At the end of the general body meeting, Ayana led the raffle drawing, Robert picked out tickets and read out the names. She asked for a drumroll prior to each name being called. The drumroll died after the first drawing for the most part, with the exception of four people. For the last drawing, Elsie, with her knuckles, was the only one still providing a drumroll while she looked off into space. Robert read, "Elsie Miller?" A look of happy surprise overcame her. She got up, wearing a Black NSBE polo tucked into her jeans, and walked toward Robert to retrieve her prize. For some reason, whether because she was the last winner, or something else, everyone clapped.

Elsie did not know many people in NSBE and usually keeps to herself. Social interactions, she told me, can sometimes be tough for her. Math, engineering, and clubs for her other interests, such as Anime, are her places of comfort. Maybe the NSBE members who applauded recognized part of themselves in her. Maybe they knew she felt like an outsider even among her own. Dealing with diversity is a challenge for any organization. Such moments, however difficult describe, I think, make NSBE feel more like a family and a home—even for those who are used to feeling out of place.

Tension between a Family Focus and an Engineering Career Focus

GRACE: "Imma be at the stoop from 11–12:30 tryna do some work if anyone wants to join." [Sent at 10:13 a.m.]

PAYTON: "I'm at [the stoop] until 1:50 if anyone wants to come hang out with me." [Sent at 12:37 p.m.]

The above messages are from the NSBE GroupMe, a virtual space. NSBE, while distinct, overlaps with the Black community, uses similar spaces, and deals with some of the same tensions as the Black community. NSBE e-board members, for example, made a concerted effort to build community among Black engineers. This included holding more meetings dedicated toward community building (e.g., game nights), leisure activities like movie nights, or reaching out to others in the NSBE GroupMe and making themselves available for other members to join. "We have fun, we have parties together, we study together, that sort of thing. So it's more than an organization. It's a community," William explained. When asked to describe NSBE, the majority of participants used either the word "family" or "community." Erving, for example, said he loves the family atmosphere of NSBE and suggested that Caldwell in general has a different atmosphere: "When I think about Caldwell, I think about academics and just tryin' to get good grades. But NSBE . . . NSBE for sure I see as kinda . . . it balances out that shift." For him, the shared struggle of being Black and "in the trenches" of engineering was important. Saul, speaking about the introverted personalities of many engineers and their busy schedules, said, "It's just nice to have a place where you're connected beyond just what you guys do. I think it's a lot easier to, like, connect and try to associate. And you can also make new friends."

Friendships were often facilitated through their similarities of simply being Black engineers at WSU. Speaking about NSBE, Payton said, "I could just tell they were of kin." Laurie and many other participants shared the sentiment, "It's where you can fit in." A big part of fitting in was being able to relate to their rigorous workloads. Laurie provided an example of how she shared more in common with the NSBE community than the Black community:

> [Like], even in the Black community and you're an engineer they still won't understand the struggles at school. So having people who are like, "That test? Wow that was rough." They get it. So when you're like stressed out, it's a different type of stressed than, "I have this paper due [for my] ethnic studies major." It's a different type of stressed. Having people understand what you're going through is different. You can talk about it and relate. It's just nice to have people understand what you're going through. Because they understand they wanna help out . . .

Part of NSBE's smaller size makes it feel more like a family, Laurie implied, comparing NSBE to the Society of Women Engineers (SWE): "You have the SWE culture, but it's just so big. But NSBE, I think it's like a family." Continuing her thought process, she illustrated how the NSBE community is nested within different communities, likening NSBE to her "own little family within this huge place. Not just WSU but inside Caldwell because there's a lot of us in there." Through NSBE, members created fictive kinship—relationships, despite being unrelated by blood or marriage, that adopt a deep, familial nature (Fordham 1996). This is not to say that Black engineers were unable to build deep bonds with people outside of the NSBE social world—many did just that. However, through the shared overlapping identities of being both Black and engineering majors, NSBE facilitated fictive kinship and support for Black engineers.

Beyond family and friends, students made useful connections with other NSBE members. When asked if they had any mentors on campus, students often cited other people within NSBE. Dajuan, for example, said

"Yeah I guess like Nina—she's pretty cool. She kinda helped me with research." Through this connection, Dajuan was directed to a staff member who put him in touch with the professor with whom he is now doing research. Gary, who transferred from a community college, offered, "For someone who's just figuring everything out for himself, it's good that I can ask somebody. . . . I talked to Akari after the last meeting about how was it getting a PhD, because he went straight from undergrad to PhD." Such stories are common within NSBE.

Engineering jobs, often referred to simply as "the industry," also play a central role in NSBE. Members can travel to annual regional and national NSBE conferences, where students network with industry representatives. At the same conferences, companies interview, recruit, and extend offers to Black engineers. A good portion of e-board meetings are dedicated toward methods of fundraising for these conferences. NSBE meetings also are often centered on the industry in other ways too, such as covering how to construct a resume or prepare for technical or behavioral interviews. Sometimes, these workshops are led by companies such as Intel or Microsoft. Other times, these companies come to meetings to tell NSBE members about their careers and to pique students' interest in working for them.

In this manner, NSBE provides career capital that better positions members in their effort to secure a career in the engineering industry. Career capital for engineers includes anything that might aid in landing an engineering job—high GPAs, summer internships, research experience, and relationships with recruiters from companies of interest. Without NSBE, Gary said, "I would have a lot less exposure to companies, because it's a professional organization." Students inevitably mentioned the job opportunities and face time they received with recruiters when reflecting on NSBE. Outside of planning for conferences, elections, game nights, or panels, most NSBE general body meetings featured recruiters from companies looking for Black engineers. In addition to highlighting their companies and describing the experience of working there, representatives also provided professional socialization. The professional component included resume workshops, interview practice, technical interview advice, or cover letter feedback.[3] From these meetings, students met recruiters, met current employees at prospective companies, learned more about the industry, and received tangible skills they could apply to the job or interview application process.

Joseph told me that he did not know many Black engineers outside of NSBE. "It makes sense too," he explained. "There's always companies that come out and if you're engineering, you try to get an internship over the summer. So it's very useful, in addition to community . . . NSBE takes the school resources and channels, organizes it for Black engineers." Erving expressed a similar sentiment:

> Having these companies come on campus and talk to us, and even having Faculty Night so we get to know the faculty more so we're not that intimidated . . . we do things like this so it's not as uncomfortable for us to get into the working field [and] meet these people.

The professional aspect of NSBE was beneficial for students. Nubia, for example, explained, "I had a chance to actually act like a professional engineer, because that's not something I would've known how to do . . . this was at the career fair at [NSBE] nationals." Thus, attending conferences, speaking with people from the industry, and interning helps socialize NSBE participants for the engineering work force.

Dr. Pittman, the Caldwell Director of Equity and Inclusion spoke to NSBE during one general body meeting, demonstrating both the familial and professional nature of NSBE at WSU. She mentioned, during her speech to the NSBE members, more than thirty in the audience: "I'm excited to work with you, because they tell me you're one of the premier chapters in the nation. . . . Is that true? That's what the streets say." Her answer to her own question was met with a chorus of "aaaayyee's," "yups," and "gang gang's." Excited with the reaction, Dr. Pittman looked at the president, saying, "Now Ayana, we need uniforms." Ayana looking less than excited, gave a nervous laugh, "Uh, I don't know about that." Some students chuckled, and Dr. Pittman continued with a smile.

"I will say, Caldwell has been a leader in diversity in that," she paused before delivering the punch line with a hair flip, "they hired me." She said, "I clown sometimes, but on a serious note, some schools just named a faculty member as a diversity chair. But to recruit someone, that's pretty serious." After her speech, introducing herself and her role in Caldwell, she opened the floor for questions, clarifying, "You don't have to be polite, you don't have to be nice . . . we family. The doors are closed."

Lisa asked a question about how she might get an internship without any experience as a first-year. Dr. Pittman recommended she attend NSBE's national conference saying, "I have never seen someplace where students walk away with so many opportunities." She paused, and with a laugh, clarified her position, "Now if you leave there without a job don't be, like, 'Well Dr. Pittman said you would hire me.'"

Despite the familial environment, it is easy to attend an NSBE general body meeting and not meet anyone. Chukwu, after the third meeting of Fall semester, spoke with Johnson, expressing his worry that freshmen only associated NSBE with jobs and not about community. Johnson agreed saying that was part of the Black engineering culture: "It's like NSBE folk are just like, 'They gon' have jobs?!' It should be more than that." Johnson continued, "It's hard to get to know people when jobs are the focus and that's it. It's very job focused." Some Black engineers, while dues-paying members of NSBE, do not necessarily participate in the NSBE community until conferences for job fairs. That particular conversation occurred after a meeting featuring a presentation from Accenture consulting representatives. The next day, Microsoft came to campus, and Goldman Sachs the following day. The following week, Caldwell sponsored the engineering fair. Ernst and Young, an accounting firm, presented at the next NSBE general body meeting. Events related to jobs and postsecondary engineering opportunities are simply part of their daily undergraduate life.

Timothy's first experience with NSBE during his first year at WSU highlights the tension between a family and career focus. He wanted to see if NSBE had old tests that he could use to study. He came to a meeting, and realized that NSBE did not have a test bank. In his mind, he told me, he thought, "Oh, my God. I probably just need to walk out of here," but he did not want to be rude and leave the meeting that had just started. He recounted his experience:

> We were watching . . . I don't really remember what it was. It was like a Christmas movie that was just fucking hilarious . . . everybody was just laughing and having conversations. I was like, "Oh, this is pretty cool. This is a pretty nice atmosphere" . . . one of the things that . . . has attracted me to NSBE is that even with our small numbers, I mean it's a small proportion of the Caldwell school, we are very tight . . .

NSBE did not have everything Timothy expected. Yet NSBE provided something else—fictive kinship and belonging. NSBE fulfills different purposes for different students. Given the many roles this organization must play for its members, a singular focus on either career capital or belonging would fundamentally alter the organization. I conclude this chapter with a scene highlighting the interplay of structure, culture, and the agency of NSBE members at WSU.

Brown Sugar

The e-board met a little over two weeks prior to their second annual party, Brown Sugar. Ayana had called the meeting to order promptly at six. They held the meeting in a classroom on campus. On the drop-down screen, members could see the minutes being typed up by Laurie, the secretary at the time, on Google Docs. She wrote down the names of everyone who had an unexcused absence or tardy. "Oh we're making money today," Johnson said upon seeing how many people were absent. Earlier in the year, Ayana, who was discouraged by seeing so many e-board members come late to meetings instituted a $2 late fee and a $5 unexcused absence fee. All funds went to WSU NSBE's account. NSBE e-board meetings loosely follow Robert's Rules of Order. Agendas are set prior. Meetings are called to order. The secretary takes minutes on the Google Doc. The rest of the e-board meeting flows without Robert's Rules of Order slowing them down.

"Are we doing anything for STEM Week? Is anyone going to the STEM Ball?" Ayana asked, later in the meeting. "[It is] always double booked with like some better event for Black people." Johnson responded. "Robert, didn't you go?" Ayana asked. "It's trash," Robert replied. "But you don't drink [really]?" Nina said, clarifying for the other e-board members, who laughed. "But it's still trash." Robert said, "They be drunk as hell. I've never seen Caldwell students so fucked up. Like, they're kids. It's annoying." Ayana commented, "They do have an open bar though. Do we encourage this?" Without an answer she said, "Maybe we'll raffle a couple of tickets, add some diversity." With a chuckle, she moved on to the next topic.

Science, Technology, Engineering and Medicine week, or STEM Week, has been held annually for more than fifty years. Explaining why he had no intention of going, Thomas said, "It's like, eighty percent guys, twenty percent girls. Everyone is just White and drunk so . . ." The party was not his scene, or for many other people in NSBE, for that matter. Ayana ended the meeting, making a motion to adjourn, and Thomas and Anthony raced to "second" the motion—yelling "seconded" at nearly the same time.

NSBE served Mexican food at the general body meeting on the Monday before their party on Friday. Charlie led the meeting at the podium giving announcements, saying, "If you come to meetings and eat this food, you should probably come to the party."

The party, slated to begin at 10, was still empty at 10:15 p.m., Friday night. The Black engineers held the party at an e-board member's house. Prior to entering the party, students paid a $5 entry fee and got a mark on their hand. Instead of the typical "x" some groups might use, Robert used a marker to write the Japanese symbol for Mo on people's hand. The house, affectionately called The Yard, had been the spot for multiple parties throughout the semester for Black student groups at WSU. It was certainly a college house party. The living room, dining room, and kitchen were partially cleared out for dancing. The white tile floor was hazardous and became more slippery throughout the night as more people arrived. Comically, a few people slipped and fell while dancing. The room had an extremely large poster of a Black woman, donning an Afro, on the wall.

As the party progressed, a line formed around the bathroom, frighteningly close to the refrigerator. On top of the fridge were a couple of boxes of cereal. On the counter were some six-packs of beer and a tub of their jungle juice, affectionately called Brown Sugar. The jungle juice was a mix of vodka, Bacardi, and brown sugar—a hangover in a red cup.

Johnson was seated as he DJ'd. He wore a New York Knicks starter jacket, metallic blue, and puffy with the signature Knicks' orange decal. He seemed a bit flustered. "I can't even mix," he told me. He did not have headphones that he could use for the speaker system. "These are Bluetooth speakers, so I can't really do anything," he explained.

The music skipped for a momentary period of silence at least once per song. It sounded as if Johnson was purposely silencing the song, like a DJ stopping the audio for people to sing in the familiar words of a chorus or hook. After every skip, he would shake his head, adorned with his baseball cap facing forward. For longer skips, he would laugh a defeated laugh. As matters with the speaker got worse, he asked Thomas for help. Thomas hunched over the speakers. "It's only going to get worse," Johnson sighed. Thomas brought out his phone, appearing to look up a way to stop the speakers from skipping.

More WSU students arrived. A little after 11, a friend of Johnson's who ran on the track team, Javon, walked in with large, satisfactory speakers. He set up the new speakers next to Johnson's computer. Three people near the DJ booth turned the lights on their phones toward Javon and Johnson as they fixed the DJ equipment. Javon waited just until Johnson faded into a new song. With new, louder, clearer, music with a deeper bass—it worked. Javon dapped up Johnson and left.

Johnson's confidence soared with the new speakers. Confident in his equipment, his DJ'ing changed. He abandoned his chair, stood upright, with headphones over his head, but only covering one ear. He put on a song by YG and the growing crowd ate it up—mouthing, rapping, and yelling the lyrics in unison over the bass.

Undergraduate house parties are objectively nasty. The floor was wet. Walls were sweating. Standing by the door outside, I could feel a wall of heat inside the house, heavy with young adults in drunken revelry. Yet, something was beautiful about the scene. No negativity. Just fun.

By the end of the party, Johnson was in form. Mixing in club music with current jams, West Coast music, and dancehall, the crowd loved his musical curation. At the peak of the party, the inside carried at least eighty people. I saw mostly Black students, many familiar WSU faces. Some students of other races were there as well. But the party was very much Black.

Ayana thanked me for coming, saying, "I told you we get lit." Engineers were dancing. William, a computer science/gaming major, wore an Eddie Bauer shirt and had little regard for the beat. But after his cup of Brown Sugar, his inhibitions let him feel the music in his own way. The combination of the drink, the music, and a positive crowd egging him on, pushed him to dance even harder. He fell on the slippery floor at one point, but the crowd was forgiving and cheered him on. For many of the engineers I interviewed, including William, Brown Sugar was the only party at WSU they would attend the entire year. At the close of the party the house mates and NSBE members were left to clean up. The GroupMe was rife with a recap of the party—who lost what, who broke a screen on their phone, who was missing a set of keys, and who was dancing with whom.

The next week, NSBE members volunteered for events in Caldwell, which also helped the standing of their organization. I jokingly asked Laurie if she was running for STEM Queen for the upcoming STEM Ball while we volunteered for a STEM-Week event. She gave me a deadpan look saying, "You have to go to the Ball to run." Students were neither fighting to go to the STEM Ball nor feeling left out from the Caldwell-sponsored party. For many Black engineers, they had had their own, more appealing celebration in Brown Sugar only a week before the STEM Ball. Within the NSBE community, they created a space and party for themselves and other Black WSU students. Without any institutional support from the school, they created a joyful event for themselves and raised money in the process.

The Black Engineering Social World: In Summary

NSBE is a social world of its own, overlapping, informed, and shaped by the campus and other communities at WSU. Students use the community in different ways. For many, NSBE is how they foster a sense of engagement with the university outside of class. For some, NSBE is a conduit into learning about their racial identity and understanding more about Blackness. For all, NSBE provides networking, interview practice, and conferences that may lead to a job. For most Black engineering students, NSBE plays a central role in their WSU experience.

NSBE and other Black student groups provide examples of the tension between essentialism and antiessentialism. This tension is not unique to NSBE. CRT scholars, themselves (Cabrera 2018; Chadderton 2013; Delgado and Stefancic 2012) as well as leaders of various Black Cultural Centers (Harris and Patton 2017) continue to wrestle with the tensions of strategic essentialism. In galvanizing the support of members, NSBE used strategic essentialism. Recall the mantra of "do it for the culture." To what extent can "the culture" be intersectional along the lines of class, ethnicity, and gender? The sustained leadership of Black women in NSBE, for example, is inspiring and important. Similar to the Black community, however, a tension exists between engagement and undue responsibility, in this case, for Black women.

How NSBE members understood Blackness, whether they felt like a member of the proverbial Black community, or if they felt like they were part of Black culture, varied. As Alexis pointed out, "the culture" or view of Blackness in NSBE, did not seem to include her reality as a first-generation student from a low-income background. Of course, race is a social construct. Blackness is expansive. Yet, participants referred to an identifiable, essentialized view of Black culture. Some longed to understand or be part of this culture. Others were steeped in the culture. In this way, participants engaged with the tension of essentialism, recognizing their unique identities, identifying as Black, but also identifying a prototypical Black experience. Examining such tensions can provide insight into how racial identity develops and how Blackness is performed.

Scholars studying student organizations such as NSBE tend to engage with the same central question—how does involvement in a student organization affect collegians? Yet, such examinations mischaracterize the group as acting upon the student. NSBE is made, remade, and sustained through concerted student and staff effort. Consider how NSBE was defunct prior to the effort of a few students like Naa Koshie. Because stakeholders in higher education tend to understand Black communities and student groups in an a priori manner, Black students' labor to upkeep, or even create, the very social worlds that welcome, engage, and support other Black collegians either goes unnoticed or is taken for granted. Lerma and colleagues (2020), for example, examined how student activists engage in what they term racialized equity labor, or the "the struggle of organizational actors, from a variety of positions, to address race-based marginalization and inequality" (287). While student activists continue to play an integral role in creating more equitable campuses (Dache et al. 2019; Linder et al. 2019), the labor to create a better campus racial climate is not solely enacted through student protests and petitions. Participants in NSBE show how the labor to create a more racially affirming and welcoming campus racial climate takes various, no less important, manifestations.

Black engineering students aid in the enrollment of future Black engineering majors by showing up for events held for high school seniors visiting Caldwell. Black engineering students aid in student affairs by creating events through NSBE. Black engineering students aid in diversity work by creating a welcoming climate for Black engineers through NSBE's events and meetings. Simply put, the university and school of engineering profit off of the unpaid labor of Black engineering students. Given the immense time commitments necessary to achieve an engineering major, the hours participants invested in sustaining NSBE is remarkable. Yet Black engineering students were not coerced into this work.

At the end of every NSBE meeting, students stand and recite the NSBE mission in unison: "to increase the number of culturally responsible Black Engineers who excel academically, succeed professionally and positively impact the community." As can be seen in the mission and throughout the chapter, students' sense of linked fate served as a motivating force in their dedication to NSBE. The university, however, seems to play upon students' sense of linked fate. The assumption that Black students should want to invest their time laboring to create an affirming environment for themselves and other Black engineers is inequitable.

I asked Olivia, who expressed that she felt disconnected from the Black, Caldwell, and WSU communities, "How are you making it then?" She replied, "NSBE." Similarly, recall Carmen's statement—"Without NSBE, we'd probably have two Black students." These statements about NSBE serve as both an inspiration and an indictment. The collective agency of NSBE members is worth applauding and appreciating. The fact that a student-led organization is seen as more valuable than institutional offices or services in Black student retention, however, is a problem. Indeed, Caldwell subsidizes some of NSBE's functions. Students, however, breathe life into NSBE, sustaining the chapter and its practices. Institutions might work with organizations such as NSBE to learn how universities might provide better support for such integral groups.

6

Jasmine's Story

Jasmine usually wears a WSU cap with the bill facing forward. Sometimes her ponytail neatly hangs out of the space above the adjustable band at the back of her hat. The only Black electrical engineer in her year, Jasmine always sits at the front of her classes. Monday evenings, she attends BSU and NSBE meetings. Hunching over her computer or a notebook full of equations, her homework competes for her attention during meetings. Most of the time, homework wins. Less often, she looks up with a smile or quizzical look in reaction to something said in the meeting before focusing on her work again. She keeps to herself. Yet, between classes or meetings, the iPhone headphones hanging from her ears connect her to her family. During more stressful periods, usually around finals, her dad or sister accompany her from across the country, staying on the phone with her while she studies. Jasmine, a transfer student, finds meaning and engagement primarily through NSBE, and while she achieves in her Caldwell courses, she feels ostracized in the engineering school.

Growing up with her sister and father, Jasmine knew both comfort and poverty. After her father lost his government job, they "went from the top of the top to the bottom of the bottom." Her family's experience struggling economically shaped her attitude toward education as well as her decision to major in engineering:

> I always knew that I needed to go hard and do the best that I could and I knew that even that is not always enough. Because my dad went to [an Ivy League school] so like, why should somebody who is Black and Ivy League be struggling—it's

like, damn, is there anything I can really do at this point? I
told myself that I wouldn't pick one of those majors where I
would be struggling to find a job. But I also didn't want to
put it in my head that if I got this major, my life would be
set automatically. . . . So I was like, I might as well do what I
wanna do and something I can get paid for.

Jasmine speaks glowingly about her father: "He's literally the smartest person I know." He came from Barbados, graduated from college,
earned a postgraduate degree from an Ivy League institution, and cared
for Jasmine and her sister without the help of their mother. She credits
her father for her academic success, explaining, "He busted his ass so me
and my sister could be where we're at today. We've been evicted, we've
been homeless, we've been through mad stuff. But he's like if you work
hard things will work out."

Jasmine was born and raised in Brooklyn—a fact she mentions
whenever possible. During conversations she often says, "Maybe it's
because I'm from Brooklyn . . ." or, "I mean, I'm from Brooklyn . . ." Her
experience prior to WSU was Black. "[I attended an] All Black middle
school. All Black high school. All Black college. And then I came here!
Like I was Blacked up and Blacked out, then I came here," she explained
with resignation. She came to WSU as a part of a "three-two program,"
where she completed three years at her original school, a historically Black
college, and two at WSU to graduate with an engineering degree. I met
Jasmine during her first year at WSU.

She often used the historically Black college she attended as a foil to
interpret WSU campus life. She described the "aura" at WSU as "weird."
As a junior transfer student, Jasmine expected hurdles meeting people,
but was surprised by the heavily segmented nature of WSU. For Jasmine,
WSU did not have the social or physical conditions necessary to forge
relationships between Black students. Consider how she describes the
communities within the WSU Black community:

It's like the Black athletes, then there's the BSU, then it's like
Black Greek[s], then it's like Black STEM, then it's like those
Black people who hang out with the Whites, and shit it's
like. . . . There's no central place for like . . . I don't know
where to go . . . who do I want to hang out with?

Without a central space for forging relationships in the Black community, she found her place in NSBE.

The Black Engineering Community

Three months into fieldwork, I heard Jasmine, a math and electrical engineering double major, speak for the first time. She gave a speech in front of the more than thirty NSBE members in the meeting, running for an executive board position for the following year. Given her reserved nature, her speech held added significance. "And no shade, but, you know, I'm an introvert and it takes a lot for me to talk to people, so as programs chair I want to make a better effort to reach people like me," Jasmine said during her speech. One other person ran for the same position, but Jasmine won. With added confidence, Jasmine posed questions to people running for different positions. I joked with her a few weeks later about her going from one extreme of not talking to giving her opinion on every candidate. We shared a laugh and she explained, "I mean; I saw people nodding when I gave my speech. I won. So I knew everyone fucked with me. So hey, why not?" After the meeting, Thomas approached Jasmine saying, "I swear to God, I never heard you talk before that." Jasmine smiled with a hint of discomfort, almost as if she were holding on to the version of herself she had just discarded.

NSBE was her entry point and anchor to the campus. Her involvement could be seen from her consistent attendance of NSBE as a general body member and her last year, as an e-board member attending executive board meetings and general body meetings. Most meetings, Jasmine was working on some type of assignment, but her work load did not dissuade her from coming to the meeting. Even if she did not participate in the meeting, even if her focus was squarely on her homework, she was there. Sometimes, just being around her fellow Black engineers was enough to keep her going.

At her prior school, she did not attend NSBE meetings often, but at WSU the climate called for her participation: "I feel like here, it's so essential." She continued saying:

I just feel like it's the only place here where people understand what you're going through. Like they don't think like it's an

excuse. They don't take it like, "Oh well, you just saying that."
They actually . . . they experienced it. Like tryna explain to
like my White friend what I'm going through, they don't get it.
They don't. . . . But if I go to NSBE, they get it. They probably
experienced it. . . . So the support there is real because they
know where I'm coming from. . . . They understand.

What NSBE members could understand, more specifically, were the
unique racialized experiences of being among the few Black students in
an engineering class and feeling unwelcome. Similarly, she connects with
NSBE members because they understand the rigor of an engineering
course. She explained that comparing experiences outside of the school
of engineering was difficult, explaining that someone might say, " 'It's hard
being a poli sci major, too.' And it's just like, 'I'm sure it might be, but
girl . . . but you ain't going through what I'm going through.' " While she
found relationships and comfort in NSBE, she also ventured out of her
comfort zone and grew. Perhaps because of the familial nature of NSBE,
she felt more comfortable running for an executive board position, leading,
and speaking in front of the NSBE members.

The Black Community

Jasmine initially started attending BSU meetings to meet more Black people
and make friends but felt uneasy. BSU felt "clique-ish." In explaining the
vibe of BSU she spoke of how it felt exclusive:

[Y]ou have to prove yourself in a way. You can't just be you. You
gotta be like super Black Lives Matter, you gotta be so woke,[1]
and all. And I don't got time to be woke. Like I got fucking
shit to do. . . . You gotta be wanting to do protests, you gotta
be Black to the bone. And I'm just not—that's not who I am.

Jasmine, of course, was not renouncing her Blackness. Rather, she identified a performance of Black racial identity within the BSU that she did
not identify with. Her words also demonstrate how racial essentialism
creates a boundary, making students like Jasmine feel like they did not
exhibit their Blackness in a way that would be appreciated by the group.

Similar to other students, Jasmine was surprised by the lack of participation in events held by Black-affinity organizations. Comparing her life at WSU to her Black college experience she said, "It makes me very sad. I used to go to events for no reason. [At WSU] They be in the group chat, promoting shit like twenty times to get five people." Jasmine joined the BSU e-board for the duration of her last year at WSU. I asked why she joined the board even after she expressed that she felt less than comfortable in BSU meetings and she shrugged it off saying, "My dad always tells me to be the change and not complain and all that. If I see something I don't like I should change it, so . . ."

The Engineering School Community

She always remembers being good at math and speaks of her time in high school calculus as her "prime." In college, Jasmine even helped her dad study for the math section of the GRE while he was preparing to apply to a PhD program. While she has a propensity for excelling in math and a work ethic to match, engineering at WSU still proved difficult. Her challenges, however, were due to the campus climate—not the curriculum.

Like other Black students in Caldwell, group work was a perennial challenge for Jasmine. Her first semester at WSU was a struggle. While dealing with the fact that she was the only Black person, let alone Black woman, in her classes, her classmates brought added attention to her race. "There has been instances when people have come up to me, like, 'Oh, hey, like why'd you decide to do electrical engineering?'" Jasmine recounted, continuing, "Or like, 'Oh, like you're the only Black girl I've seen [in the major], like no offense.' But it's like, that's offensive. But you know, 'no offense!'" She punctuated the latter "no offense" with a sarcastic tone and a laugh. She even did group work by herself, explaining in a conversation with me:

JASMINE: Like last semester, I didn't work with anybody. Like no homework, no studying, like I literally was just out here sticking it by myself. But I mean, this semester I've been talking to more people. But yeah, last semester I did everything by myself. Like labs by myself, group projects by myself, I did everything . . .

ANTAR: Wow. Group projects by yourself?

JASMINE: I did everything by myself. Nobody wants to work with me. They don't want to work with that Black girl over there. I did everything by myself. Yeah.

Later in the semester she found a group to work with, a Spanish woman who transferred the same year, as well as two other students. Groups were invaluable for her. While she used to do homework and labs by herself, with a group she could split sections with her working group and reconvene to discuss their approaches.

For Jasmine, cheating posed another challenge. Not only did she refuse to cheat on exams, she also did not have access to past exams or study materials available to other students. Jasmine saw people cheating during exams. She also overheard a student saying a friend in an earlier period had texted him a picture of the exam prior to taking the test. It is difficult to know for sure to what extent students had added supports within electrical engineering, but Jasmine was convinced: "I feel like they got everything. Like I've met this guy, who I think he graduated last semester and he was electrical engineering. He's like, 'I have like a Dropbox full of stuff from like other semesters.'" The student, however, did not share the resources with Jasmine. Comparing her grades to other students, Jasmine said, "When you see people's grades, you're like . . . yeah, I got that seventy-five, but I earned that seventy-five." This posed a problem for her relationships with professors, Jasmine explained, saying, as if to a hypothetical classmate, "You got that ninety and you cheated for that ninety, but the teacher don't care . . . the teacher's like, 'Well, I'm gonna work with that smart student.' Not the one who didn't fuckin' cheat."

Her relationships with professors also informed her campus experience. Jasmine, after her first semester at WSU, went to a professor for advice about research related to the electrical engineering class he taught. She earned a B in the class. She felt disheartened after his response, and spoke with another student, a White woman, who earned an A and also asked the same professor for advice about research, finding out that

he literally gave her way more permission than he gave me. But like I knew because we talked about it after. He told her what internships to apply for, what not to take. . . . He ain't giving me that shit. He told me to look it up.

Jasmine was not brushed off by the professor because she was a woman, but because she was a Black woman. Black women face a unique gendered racism in engineering fields (Ireland et al. 2018; Leath and Chavous 2018). Gendered racism refers to how sexism and racism intersect to create unique forms of oppression and stereotypes impacting women of color (Essed 1991). Such interactions can have major consequences. As a Black woman, relevant research opportunities and positive faculty interactions can aid in student success (Cole 2007; Espinosa 2011; Hurtado et al. 2009; Newman 2015). The professor, however, did the opposite of what would have helped Jasmine—he signaled his disinterest in working with her and did not provide guidance in research experiences.

Jasmine also noticed a difference in how professors took interest in certain students and not in others. Comparing the "vibe" of her conversations with professors and others, she said, "You hear [the professors] ask someone, 'Oh what are you interested in?' . . . And then when you talk to them, you don't get that same kinda conversation. Like do you not care what my interests are?'" After a pause, somewhere between sarcasm and hurt, she said, "I'm interested in stuff, too, like if you want to know like. . . . But yeah." She never finished her thought but told me more about her experience in Caldwell. "People been here since their freshman year, so they're used to it, but I'm not used to none of that. Like I'm not used to teachers not caring," Jasmine said, comparing WSU to her old school. Concerning her professors at WSU, Jasmine did not mince words and said it plain: "They don't give a fuck about us." Whether a show of favoritism for other students or a stark indifference toward Jasmine, such examples shape her experience of the racial climate at WSU.

Jasmine's relationship to and perception of the Multicultural Engineering Office (MEO) also shaped how she viewed the Caldwell climate. The MEO is a Caldwell-institutionalized support dedicated to underrepresented racial minorities in engineering. In addition to staff managing different diversity-related events, the MEO, as a space, is open twenty-four hours to underrepresented minorities in Caldwell. Despite the goals of the MEO, Jasmine did not often use the space. Jasmine visited MEO a few times but did not study there. "I tried, but MEO also rubs me the wrong way," she said. Part of the reason, is because she still felt "like an outsider" because Latinx, predominantly Chicanx, students mainly use the space. Jasmine mentioned that the students in the MEO often spoke Spanish, which she did not take umbrage with, but mentioned that in some ways she still felt "singled out." She continued:

I be seeing like White boys in there, and I'm just like, "What
are y'all . . . why are y'all in here?" And it's like, you know,
people just invite their friends and to me, this became like
another study hangout where like other people invite their
other friends. Not like, strictly for minorities. So I just go in
for the free prints and I appreciate it.

Despite her challenges dealing with the racial climate, Jasmine had a
3.4 GPA and landed an internship after her first year at WSU. Her success
at WSU holds an air of gravitas. Jasmine and her sister were the only ones,
among all the cousins in their family, to attend college. Further, Jasmine
was the only engineering major. She felt an added pressure, saying, "I
don't want to let anybody down so I feel like I have to thug it out. I can't
give up because they gonna be like, 'You're the only hope. If it ain't you,
what are we gonna do?'"

She has a resolute nature. Because Jasmine felt like she was not
holding to her commitments and giving up on her endeavors, she became
a vegetarian—partly for health and partly to prove to herself that she
could do it. Jasmine studied for her electrical engineering courses with a
focused ferocity. This may not come as a surprise considering who she is,
her experiences, and where she is from. She saw her father, the smartest
person she knows, accomplished by most measures, lose his job without
good reason. She saw students of other races receive favorable treatment
from professors. She saw students working together on tests and inheriting
study materials. After already earning a degree in math, students asked
her why she would major in electrical engineering. She was the only Black
electrical engineering major in her class. In some ways, her supreme focus
might be understood as a logical response, but those same conditions
might be too much for other students to endure.

For Jasmine, her work ethic and academic success is not an option
but a requirement:

I don't have a choice but to keep going. Because they want you
to not be here. So it's just kinda like, "You're not going to run
me out just so you can cheat your way to a job. You're not
going to run my ass out. . . . I'm going to be here and get you
mad here every single day because I know you do not want
me here. Every single day. And I'm going to sit in the front
[of class] every day."

Similar to other Black women in Caldwell, I wondered how she dealt with such blatant inequities and continued to achieve. As I wrote this book, however, I realized I, unfortunately, did not ask how she coped with such stressors. Future work might examine the self-care practices of Black women in predominantly nonblack universities.

Jasmine's achievements, indeed, have the backdrop of adversity. So when she earned the second-highest grade on an electrical engineering exam or when she received a lucrative full-time job offer less than two months into her last year at WSU, her accomplishments, from where I stood, mattered that much more.

The Mainstream WSU Community

Life as an engineer, anywhere, is regimented. Jasmine's experience as an electrical engineer might be similar to others of different races in reference to her busy schedule. She explained her bleak social life, saying,

> I don't go nowhere. Like I don't go out. I don't get to like go out and party, like–I'll just literally be in my room like twenty-four/seven like in my books. I don't have time to like enjoy parties, go to outings. . . . I went out maybe like three times last semester. I went out maybe twice this semester.

Beyond the stressors of an engineering degree, however, she also is burdened with racism.

WSU made a poor first impression on Jasmine. At an orientation event for transfer students, Jasmine recalled that she walked to the reception desk to check in and get a name tag. A White woman also walked up to the desk next to her. The greeters at the desk, as if they could not see Jasmine, asked the White woman for her last name to check her in and give her a name tag. "Do you not see me standing here?" Jasmine asked them. The greeters apologized. To herself, Jasmine thought, "There's no way you did not see my Black ass standing here. Like there is no way you didn't see me." After that initial event, she said, "From then, I was like, 'You know, fuck this school.' "

Jasmine emphasized that the incident was "such a small thing," but that exchange, she felt, was the representative attitude of the school. She had difficulty adjusting to the campus racial climate at WSU and dealing with microaggressions. She used to get "bothered by everything." Yet, in time, she became numb to the slights: "After a while it's just kinda like, whatever, like, what's she gonna say that I ain't already hear. . . . Like there's nothing . . . you're going to do it in a different form, but it's going to be the same thing." Dealing with racial slights became less about the microaggression, and more about her response. Explaining her mindset, she said, "Aight, you don't like me 'cause I'm Black. I like me 'cause I'm Black, so. Like, you don't think I'm smart cause I'm Black. I know you cheating, so I know you ain't smart." She was no longer shocked by racism and adopted a racial realist mindset (Bell 1992), understanding racism as the status quo on campus. Her racial realism, however, was coupled with something else, love for herself and pride in her Blackness. By coupling racial realism with racial pride, she was equipped to navigate hostile spaces and experiences in Caldwell without being completely demoralized.

In a conversation with Laurie, during Jasmine's senior year, Laurie asked why she decided to run for an e-board position in NSBE. Similar to what she told me about her involvement in the BSU, Jasmine responded saying that once, when complaining to her dad about NSBE, he suggested running, saying, "If you wanna change something, be part of it." And so Jasmine became a part of NSBE. She was only connected to WSU through her involvement in Black social worlds on campus. Through NSBE she found friends, a sense of belonging, momentary peace, and the courage to use her voice.

THE ENGINEERING SCHOOL COMMUNITY

7

Organizational Involvement

Diversity Dilution and Antiblackness

The Caldwell School of Engineering social world encompasses the practices and cultures surrounding engineering coursework and Caldwell-specific organizations. To understand Black engineers' experiences in Caldwell, one must reckon with their unique minority status. One must reckon with the fact that only fifty-eight total Black undergraduates are in Caldwell. This means that more Asian American students can be found in the first-year class *alone* than Black students across years (see Table 7.1). The same is true for first-year White and Latinx students in comparison to Black engineering majors.

Table 7.1. Number of Full-Time Undergraduate Caldwell Engineers 2016–17

Identification	First Year	Sophomore	Junior	Senior	Total
Black	14	11	17	16	58
White	166	165	251	292	874
Asian-American	96	102	203	249	650
Latinx *	63	56	104	117	340
Native American	0	1	0	0	1
International *	79	121	125	122	447
2 or more races*	26	20	49	31	126

*race not listed

Source: Data compiled from the *American Society for Engineering Education*

This chapter begins the conversation about how Black students experience a predominantly nonblack, but majority-minority space. How, if at all, does race matter in a space where most students are considered "people of color" but Black people are of the stark minority? What do these racial demographics mean in the Caldwell school of engineering? Robert and Noelle, two high-achieving Caldwell students, provide useful examples of how Blackness shapes engagement with the Caldwell social world.

◆ ◆ ◆

The professor waited until the rest of Robert's group had left the courtyard. With the stern affection of a coach speaking to the team's best player, the professor lectured Robert. "Come on Robert, step up. You've got to get this group together. I'm being serious man, come on," the middle-aged, White professor said, clapping his hand on Robert's shoulder, "You all aren't going to get this project done if you don't start pushing them. It has to be you." Robert had already TA'd for two computer science (CS) classes and excels academically.

Robert is often mistaken for a grad student. He stands at 6'2" and, at the time, had a five o'clock shadow instead of his usual full beard. Almost a head taller than the professor, Robert bowed his head, displaying the well-trimmed, vigorously brushed, wavy texture of his short hair. He looked at his feet with a bashful smile, as the ankh pendant on his gold necklace hung off of his chest. Looking back at the professor, he agreed, sounding mildly irritated, "I got it. You're right. You're right." Many students might be able to relate—being a CS student is hard enough and his professor was asking even more of him.

On another occasion, I saw Robert using one of the rooms slated for a NSBE study night, for his cyber security class's group meeting. He already set up the room, orienting the tables in a large rectangle. Robert also wrote an agenda on the chalkboard. Nine people including Robert were in the group. Only one White person, a man, was in the group. The majority of the members were Asian and two were Latinx. They were tasked with creating a server that would mimic a banking system and hacking another group's server. "We're basically playing a version of capture the flag," Robert explained to me. Robert facilitated the working group meeting. "I guess we should figure out how to divide this," he started. "Should we try to get a sense on everyone's background?" an Asian American man suggested. After a couple seconds of silence, Robert jumped in, reporting the programming languages he was familiar with, "I guess I'll start . . . HTML . . . Javascript . . . I guess that's most pertaining to what we're doing. Javascript." Everyone then went around the circle saying their relevant programming experience. "Does this time work for everyone?" Robert asked after they went around the room listing their skills. They came up with meeting times and began research for their project. The next time I saw Robert, I asked if he was the group leader. He laughed, "Nah. It just needed to be done, so yeah . . ."

Robert, in most of his interactions with others, seems well adjusted and at ease. One of his closest friends, and a fellow CS major, Thomas, described Robert, saying, "Robert involves himself with Latinos, Black people, and is a very sociable guy. Talks to everyone. Everyone." Based on his sociable nature and the above descriptions, the conversation I had with him during the summer may come as a surprise.

While he was summer interning at a credit card company, I asked Robert if his race impacted his time at Caldwell. "I feel like race here has forced me to act a certain way," Robert started with a labored sigh. After a second of collecting his thoughts, he continued:

> Essentially you get the vibe that, especially since I'm tall, and like I look older—I have a beard and stuff—you kinda get the feeling that people look at you and they're like, "He's kinda intimidating." So I always feel pressured to be the nice guy. I'm always the one to initiate conversations. Like, "Hey, how's it going? How are you doing on this assignment?"

Without a pause his stream of consciousness took a turn, as he continued, saying,

> But like sometimes I'll also embrace that perception of me. Like, "Okay you all think I'm intimidating." But they also get the sense that I'm not that smart, right? So a lot of times like, I notice people looking at me, so I just have a stare down with them, just to reinforce it.

He chuckled, his ironic laughter juxtaposing the seriousness of his reflection. Flitting back to a somber tone, he said:

> "Don't underestimate me." . . . "Don't think you can fuck around with me," kinda thing. And it kinda sucks, like I really hate that, but I feel compelled to. I just feel like I have to like, put up this image that I'm not one to fuck with.

After a brief pause he concluded his thought, laughing, "But I'll really talk with anybody."

"Why you stare back, though?" I asked. "I feel like they're questioning my being here and I feel like they're not used to seeing me. I stare them down because I know who I am. I'm not gonna back off. Like I'm gonna go hard, right?" Robert replied.

Other students, like Noelle, had less to say about being Black in Caldwell: "I feel like being a student in the classes, race isn't a factor unless it's because you noticed you're the only one in the class. Otherwise, I don't think my Caldwell experience is different than someone else's Caldwell experience." Noelle and Robert are both in CS. Both are high-achieving. Both are involved in NSBE and seem well adjusted in the Caldwell social world. Why, then, would these two seemingly similar students feel so differently about being Black in Caldwell? Were Robert's classmates frightened by his tall stature, identity as a Black man, coupled with his golden brown complexion and features rendering him unmistakably Black? Part of the answer may lie in a student's habitus, a sociological concept used to analyze the dispositions one learns at a young age as a result of class, culture, and family upbringing (Bourdieu 1984). In Caldwell, for example, a student's habitus are the implicit signals that demonstrate to others in Caldwell whether that student seems like they belong. Perhaps something about Robert's mannerisms gave away his low socioeconomic background or his pedigree from a majority Black public high school in Chicago. Could Noelle's classmates tell she'd grown up in a higher-income household and attended an elite, predominantly White private school? Is Noelle's neutral, if not positive, experience with Caldwell mediated by her comfort around White and Asian American students and the fact that she spent her first year in the honors' residence hall at WSU? Their perceptions of the campus climate and understanding of Caldwell, I argue, are shaped by their social positioning on campus as well as their unique histories, or habitus.

In this chapter, I first introduce the reader to the Caldwell social world, offering two points about life for Black students in Caldwell. The first point is that is that engineering is a broad discipline—different majors within engineering have diverse cultures. While students are often grouped under the broad category of engineering for ease, the difference between a biomedical engineer and a mechanical engineer are stark. I mention this to both qualify my findings, but also to point out that even broader categories such as Science Technology Engineering and Mathematics (STEM) can be unwieldy in generalizing student experiences. Secondly, while students' perceptions of Caldwell's racial climate were generally positive or neutral, a deeper analysis into their words told a more complex story shaped by antiblackness. As Dumas and Ross (2016) explain, "[A]ntiblackness is not simply racism against Black people. Rather, antiblackness refers to a broader antagonistic relationship between blackness and (the possibility of) humanity" (429). Drawing from this definition, I understand antiblackness in the WSU and Caldwell context as both racism directed toward Black people as well as the antagonistic relationship between Blackness and the possibility of being viewed as an engineering student. After providing context for Caldwell as a social world, I analyze two tensions related to how formal Caldwell organizations and programs influence students' experiences: the tension between (1) diversity and invisibility, and (2) membership in NSBE and other engineering organizations.

Caldwell at a Glance

"I wanted to be an [Caldwell Student] ambassador because I really love going here and I love to see great people come back. I also joined the ambassadors to give the school a Black face," Charlie explained. Charlie, a senior, majored in chemical engineering, and while not involved in the WSU Black Community, was involved in NSBE, Caldwell, and the general WSU communities. Membership practices in the Caldwell community are characterized by involvement in engineering-specific organizations such as the Caldwell Student Ambassadors (CSA) or engineering fraternities/ societies (see Figure 7.1). By these standards, fewer than half of the participants were active members in the Caldwell community.

Caldwell, as an institution, is enmeshed within students' lives. At the minimum, all of the Black undergraduate engineering students have experiences within Caldwell by way of their engineering courses. The school of engineering also provides funding for NSBE events and meetings as well as subsidizing travel to NSBE conferences. In this way, Caldwell helps foster the NSBE community, albeit indirectly. Caldwell also created the Multicultural Engineering Office (MEO), which acts as an institutional space intended to serve Black engineers and other groups labeled as "diverse" (see Figure 7.1). Through the MEO, students have access to a physical space within the school of engineering where they can convene, study, use computers, print, or decompress. In order to describe Caldwell in greater detail, I offer two points about life for Black students in Caldwell. First, different majors within engineering have different cultures. Second, perceptions of the engineering school's racial climate, while varied, were generally positive.

DIFFERENT MAJORS, DIFFERENT EXPERIENCES

Regardless of race, Caldwell students have a rigorous workload and strict course requirements to major in engineering. When I asked students what all Caldwell students have in common, four students, in some fashion, mentioned "a lack of sleep." While much important research examines the unique experiences of STEM majors (e.g., Choi et al. 2020; Esters and Toldson 2013; McGee and Bentley 2017) or, more specifically, engineering majors (e.g., Burt et al. 2018; McGee and Martin 2011; Morgan et al. 2020), even the classification of engineering can be too broad-based.

Caldwell is home to more than thirty majors across ten different engineering disciplines. Black students are spread across majors. Aside from sometimes vastly different course requirements, different majors in engineering have different cultures. Biomedical engineers, or BMEs, often take classes similar to students intending to go to medical school. Given the high attrition from the major, BMEs were jokingly called "Business majors eventually." Johnson and Alexis, the two industrial and systems

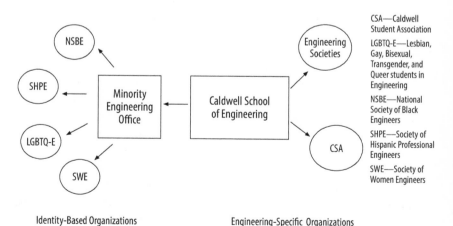

Figure 7.1. The Caldwell Social World.

engineering majors alluded to the stigma held by other engineers that industrial and systems engineers were not *real* engineers because they do not have the skill set to create a product. Computer science/engineering is the most popular in Caldwell. Dealing with computer programming, coding languages, and innovation in the tech sphere, Caldwell was a leading university in producing employees for Silicon Valley. In sum, distinct majors lead to diverse campus experiences.

NSBE Faculty Night provides another example of the differing experiences of students of different engineering majors. NSBE e-board officers coordinated an event for NSBE members to meet Caldwell faculty. Nineteen faculty, most from computer science and civil engineering, came to the event. One student in aerospace engineering, for example, sighed, "I met all these professors, but I'm literally not going to have any of them." While the event was a success and useful in that Black engineers met engineering faculty outside of the circumstances of class, the event could not necessarily meet the needs of students of all majors. To be sure, this is not a knock on NSBE—the event was well founded, humanized professors, and facilitated relationship building with an ice-breaker. The event becomes even more remarkable when taking into account the fact that NSBE Faculty Night was organized by full-time engineering students busy with school work. Rather, I make this point to demonstrate that meeting the general needs of engineers might not meet the specific needs of an engineer with a certain major.

THE CALDWELL RACIAL CLIMATE

Engineering is sometimes characterized as calculating and formula-driven without room to engage with politics, identity, or issues of equity. This is a stereotype. However, institutional structures indeed shape students' societal awareness beyond their disciplines. With such a rigorous course load, engineers have to focus on the requirements of their major and have fewer opportunities to immerse themselves in the social sciences.

Professor Carson, a computer science professor who also worked on Caldwell diversity initiatives, addressed a tension between engineering and issues of politics and identity. He explained that "with issues of diversity, and campus climate and justice . . . there's a lot I wish I could say. In engineering, so much of your classes are [already scheduled] so they won't get discussed." The majority of the participants, however, described the racial climate in positive or neutral terms. Laurie, for example, said that if more Black students were in Caldwell, "I would definitely feel like I belong more." Yet, she knew Caldwell was making an effort to "diversify" suggesting that "they can only do so much." Despite being one of two Black people in her major, Laurie likes Caldwell: "It's been a good experience. I have nothing bad to say." Others, such as Demi, felt like his race did not shape his experience at Caldwell at all, and had nothing but positive words to say.

While students did not always have the words to describe Caldwell, they provided various critiques of the climate in the engineering school. Students' words about Caldwell were often coupled with qualifications that told a more complex story about the campus climate. Black engineering majors, for example, engage with the objective reality of few Black engineering students in different ways. For some, the limited number is not an issue. "If you don't care, and you maybe have Black friends on the side, you don't see them everyday type of thing, then you're fine in engineering," Alexis, for example, noted. She continued, however, noting the marginal numbers of Black students, saying, "If you have to be around Black people, or you want Black people in your class. Nah, it's not for you." For other students, the limited number compels them to co-create social worlds with other Black students, perhaps in the NSBE or Black WSU communities. As I show throughout the chapter, Black students cannot be expected to experience the climate in the same manner.

The Tension between Diversity and Invisibility

Students appreciated and acknowledged the work Caldwell does for diversity. Short of recruiting more Black students, students did not know what else Caldwell could do to make the environment more welcoming for Black engineers. Only three students perceived the Caldwell climate in an explicitly negative manner. Students *saying* that the climate was neutral or positive, however, does not paint an accurate picture of how students *experienced* the engineering racial climate. In this section, I highlight how the unique challenges or experiences of some Black engineers are occluded within Caldwell's diversity efforts.

Caldwell does more than talk about diversity, they invest capital in diversity, creating a space like the MEO and creating unique initiatives, programs, and supports for students from diverse backgrounds. Keith, the assistant director of the MEO, even described the current moment, saying,

"It's like the golden era of diversity . . . when I first started, diversity was more or less a checkbox." Caldwell also invested in recruiting and hiring a director of equity and inclusion. By many regards, one might think of Caldwell as a leader in diversity efforts. Most students pointed to the MEO as an example of Caldwell's dedication to diversity and making the school welcoming for Black students. After observing the MEO for hours, as well as speaking with Black engineers about their perceptions of the MEO, however, I noticed a tension surrounding diversity and invisibility.

Despite their recitations of the ways Caldwell supports underrepresented populations, an air of nostalgia wafted through the words of Black staff in Caldwell. Place matters. Black students, in recent years, were using the MEO space less and less. After my interview with Keith, I asked him about the writing on the whiteboards in his office with quotes and students' signatures. He laughed wistfully, "Oh that was the kind of the golden age of MEO." "What do you mean?" I asked. "More people popping in, you know? More Black folk." A week later, when interviewing Carmen, the director of the MEO, I was surprised to see the same thing in her office. Signatures of students and quotes written by students more than three years prior were left untouched on her whiteboard.

"Why do you keep that there?" I asked Carmen, pointing to the words from Black engineers that had not been erased for years. Looking at the board smiling, she said, "It really was afternoons where just students, kind of checking in, felt comfortable enough to write on the whiteboard." Continuing, she said, "I felt like it was a stronger community and over time it's just sort of, I don't know . . . that piece is missing." Whiteboards, like colleges, are transient spaces. While the structure remains, the characters, words inscribed, and lessons, are no longer visible. At the most, one can barely make out a faint tint from overuse. Despite the nature of the canvas, Keith and Carmen held on to a warmer memory of years past—attempting to make something permanent on a plane built for erasure.

What gets lost in the push for diversity? Carmen and Keith in the MEO, as well as Tae in the Black Cultural Center, all seemed to fondly recall a time when a more cohesive and visible Black community existed at WSU. Keith, for example, noted a distinct "golden age" for diversity in Caldwell and a unique "golden age" for Black people in the MEO—they were not the same. The Black engineers certainly exhibited and held onto the idea of linked fate. Yet, as I explain later, perhaps Black administrators were feeling what I noticed in observation—for some Black engineering students, racial identity did not play a central role in their campus lives.

Regardless of students views on race, however, they all experienced objectively small numbers. Further, while Black people were often visible individually, their presence as a community was not always recognized.

EXPERIENCING HYPERVISIBILITY

While Caldwell made institutional commitments to diversity, Black students were burdened with hypervisibility by virtue of their small numbers. The director of equity and inclusion provided an example of just how visible Black engineers were at Caldwell. Organizations such as MEO, she told me, should nudge Black engineers to "show up." She explained, "The problem is we are not stepping up at the same rate. We are not showing up." Dr. Pittman is a Black woman and speaks in a collective "we." She pointed to other students showing up for invited Caldwell lectures, "The White kids in Caldwell? They don't care who is the speaker, they show up . . . they're there for every lecture." While her observation was more hyperbole (I attended four such lectures myself), her statement speaks to the hypervisibility and invisibility of Black students. Their presence, or absence, is easily noticed. Their responses to hypervisibility, however, are varied.

"Every teacher usually remembers my name . . . if anything you get more personal attention," Charlie mentioned about his visibility. "Professors always notice you. Like they'll know my name. . . . I feel like I can't get caught slacking," Robert told me. He also shared an instance of his professor, in a large lecture hall, commenting on his absence in a prior class. From that experience Robert knew, by virtue of his visibility, he was not afforded the same luxuries of his peers. Other students could take days off and go unnoticed. Robert, and other Black students, could not.

The majority of the Black engineers I interviewed responded to hypervisibility similarly—working twice as hard as their nonblack peers. Being the only one, or one of few, in a classroom came with added pressure or responsibility to perform academically. Encouragingly, many of the students rose to the occasion and appreciated the opportunity to represent. Black engineers sometimes attributed their motivation for success in engineering to something greater than themselves—they persisted in engineering for the culture, for Black people.

Black students cannot simply be individuals because they are simultaneously cast as representatives of the entire Black community. This is the fact of Blackness—Robert, for example, is responsible for himself, his race, and his ancestors (Fanon 2003). Frantz Fanon (2003) describes the fact of Blackness as the constricting, overwhelming experience of being Black under the white gaze. Under this gaze, Black people are not individuals, but walking stereotypes, with "a thousand details, anecdotes, and stories" grafted upon them" (Fanon 2003, 63). The hypervisibility participants experienced as a result of being one of the few, if not the only, Black people in classes was punctuated by a sense of linked fate (Dawson 1994). In primarily nonblack spaces, linked fate plays a pronounced role, even for a lone Black student in a Caldwell classroom. A high test score or correctly answered question in a lecture can potentially shape how others view Black students in general. On the other side of the coin, however, so does a failing grade or not showing up in class. Whether positive or negative, participants often viewed the Black community's fate, and more specifically Black students at Caldwell, as tied together.

With the immense burden and responsibility of representing and progressing in engineering "for the culture" came both pride and pressure. Lisa even said, "I would get a kinda pride out of [being the only Black woman], like 'Look at me. Look at me doing it! Representing my people.'" William did not find the pressure of being one of the only Black students debilitating—rather, he found inspiration in the pressure:

> It's a motivation thing. Like I feel like if I'm the only person I'm going to put forward a good impression. Also I just feel like, it's more I just want to expand like I'm not just a Black person, I'm my own person. So it doesn't matter where I am, I'm still going to do the best I can.

This motivation led William to study outside of his courses anywhere between six and eight hours a day. Kenya felt pressure saying, "You're always trying to prove yourself. . . . I guess it's a responsibility—a huge duty. Other than that I feel like it makes me a stronger individual, and it makes me work that much harder." Thomas spoke more to the burden of representing the race in Caldwell classes, saying:

> I feel like I have to be, not just one step ahead, but better than the next person because I feel like I constantly have to prove . . . like it sucks. I don't wanna have to prove myself, but I kinda have to. . . . Black people, we have to prove ourselves—every single day.

Thomas, like others who understood their burden of working doubly hard as a given, demonstrates a sense of racial realism. Racial realism, as the Critical Race Scholar Derrick Bell argues, begins with the "hard-to-accept-fact" that "Black people will never gain full equality in this country" (1992, 373). One sees the racial realism on a microlevel in Thomas's words. He had no desire to prove himself daily in Caldwell, but did not have a choice. Antiblackness would not simply evaporate from the school or the minds of his nonblack peers—he knew that—so he had no choice but to contort himself, working harder than his peers.

Thomas continued, referring to his hypervisibility in classes, saying, "You get stares, I swear to God. It's really sad. I swear to God, I've been to classes, and you just . . . side eye, you just see this look of like, not even amazement but like, 'when and how?'" Microaggressions are not always verbal (Sue 2010). Similar to the experiences of other Black people in primarily nonblack spaces (Anderson 2015; Posey-Maddox 2017), stares can be psychologically damaging. In addition to the normal pressures of showing up for class, keeping up with lectures, and answering questions posed by the professor, Black students have to do so under a spotlight, with a feeling of constant scrutiny. In such conditions, participants' achievement might be understood as a form of resistance (Carter 2008; Okello 2020)—succeeding in spite of racist structures and interpersonal interactions.

Thomas, Kenya, Lisa, and other students who use negative stereotypes or their hypervisibility as motivation is an example of stereotype management (McGee and Martin 2011). Students are not always crushed by stereotype threat (Steele 1997)—a phenomenon describing the anxiety surrounding awareness of an academic stereotype that leads to a negative impact on achievement. Rather, on the one hand, as McGee and Martin (2011) argue, students can use their awareness of stereotypes and the permanence of racism as a necessary response to achieve. On the other hand, the process of using stereotypes as motivation or using hard work as a coping mechanism in response to racist structures can also lead to symptoms related to chronic stress (James 1994; Quaye et al. 2020; Smith et al. 2011). Shouldering a burden of any sort, from lifting weights to being in a perennial spotlight in class, leads to stress. Stress can spur growth; but stress can also bend and break.

As I mentioned, however, some students, such as Demi, Funke, Nubia, Kareem, and Martin did not feel the same pressure to work twice as hard. While they were all hard workers with high GPAs, they did not attribute their success to a racialized motivation or a feeling of hypervisibility. I discuss the differences in how students understood being the "only one" in greater depth in chapter 8.

EXPERIENCING INSTITUTIONAL INVISIBILITY

Despite the hypervisibility Black students experienced, staff hinted at the Black student population's being lost in the concept of diversity—a phenomenon I term diversity dilution.[1] Concerning Black students in Caldwell, Carmen said:

> I do feel like for Black students they're kind of an afterthought until someone brings it up, like maybe the Dean has been somewhere and he comes back and says, "Okay, for Black students, what's the percentage?" And it is a small percentage.

The 2016–17 engineering handbook's demographic highlights of the incoming first-year class is telling: "450 students; 39% Women; 20% African American, Native American, or Latino; 18% International." Rather than disaggregating data by race for women, Caldwell simply lists a raceless percentage. Given the underrepresentation of women in engineering (National Academies of Sciences, 2020), highlighting the near 40 percent proportion of women signals to prospective students that Caldwell is a more inclusive environment for women. Without disaggregating by race, however, the wrongful assumption underlying this data point is that women, united by their gender, have the same experience (e.g., Chambers and Poock 2011; Crenshaw 1989; Winkle-Wagner 2009). In its institutional messaging, Caldwell adopted a single-axis framework in understanding identity (Zinn et al. 1986). In single-axis framing, only one identity, such as gender or race, is highlighted—a student is a woman, or a student is Black. Adopting single-axis framing is not only imprecise, but the framing occludes experiences of people with multiply marginalized identities, such as Black women.

Further, Black students in this data display, are lumped into a category with Latinxs and Native Americans. Of this 20 percent, Latinx comprised the majority and Black people made up less than 3 percent. The numbers, however, were not listed on the Caldwell website. Black people, after Native Americans and Pacific Islanders, were the least represented in the undergraduate Caldwell population.[2] The statistics advertised on the Caldwell website group Black people, Latinxs, and Native Americans together, likely because of the paltry representation of Native Americans and Black people. This is an example of diversity dilution. Black representation becomes lost within a broader category of who might be considered diverse, or in this case the underrepresented racial minorities category.

Through the process of diversity dilution Black students' needs are mainstreamed through Caldwell's diversity efforts and oftentimes get lost. Ayana's effort to create an NSBE-specific event informing members about the Fundamentals of Engineering (FE) exam serves an example of diversity dilution. In an e-board meeting, Ayana asked, "How many of y'all know what the FE exam is?" None of the students raised their hands. "That's what I thought," she said and explained that some engineers need to take the Fundamentals of Engineering, or FE, exam in order to be licensed. She only knew the exam existed, she said, because her father is an engineer and asked her when she planned to take the exam herself. Ayana and the e-board came up with the idea to have someone from Caldwell come to a NSBE general body meeting to explain the FE exam to members.

Caldwell Student Affairs liked the idea so much they publicized the event to the entire Caldwell undergraduate community. To the frustration of the NSBE e-board, instead of having someone come to the NSBE general body meeting on a Monday, Caldwell held the FE exam talk on a Tuesday evening. Of the audience of more than twenty students, only three were Black. "And this isn't the first time Caldwell has done something like this," Ayana complained to me later. This information session was originally conceptualized by and created for Black engineers. In the process of collaborating with Caldwell, however, the session became less about NSBE and more about Caldwell undergraduates in general.

While I did not inquire further, the schedule change from the Monday night NSBE meeting, to a 5 p.m. Tuesday evening, I think, made it clear that the event was no longer specifically for Black engineers, but for everyone. Events for "everyone" can be alienating—namely for the already marginalized Black engineers. For NSBE students, questions would have been directed to the speaker in the comfort of an all-Black audience. In reality, however, the talk mirrored a classroom setting, rendering the few Black students in attendance marginal and hypervisible.

Black Caldwell students, like Black people more broadly in higher education and society in general (Allen 2018; Brooms 2016; Noble 2013; Posey-Maddox 2017; Winkle-Wagner 2009), struggle with the tension between hypervisibility and invisibility in the Caldwell social world. Participants experienced what Dorinda Carter Andrews (2012) termed racial spotlighting and racial ignoring. Racial spotlighting, or how Black students are rendered hypervisible when they would rather not be, occurred as a result of being one of the few Black people in a class. Racial ignoring, or how Black students are made to feel invisible by nonblack others when Black students would rather be seen and acknowledged, occurred interpersonally in groups, categorically in data representation, and structurally in how Caldwell served its "diverse" students.

THE MULTICULTURAL ENGINEERING OFFICE AND DIVERSITY DILUTION

The Multicultural Engineering Office (MEO) provides an example of the tension between diversity and diluting. In a conversation with the Caldwell Director of Equity and Inclusion, she commented on the MEO saying,

> [I]n the room, you got Black students, somebody who could be disabled, somebody who might be lesbian, gay or transgender. Again, all of the populations should be paid attention to too. But, I do think that how we combined them under diversity, has left out the populations they were intended for.

The original purpose for the MEO was to support underrepresented racial minorities. Similar to other programs (Newman 2016), offices such as the MEO can play a pivotal role in the retention and persistence of Black engineering students at HWIs. Over time, as research illustrated the unique challenges of various groups in engineering, Caldwell responded by adding them under the umbrella of support provided by the MEO. In Caldwell, diversity is something students *have*—underrepresented students in engineering are seen as diverse. Military veterans, women, Latinx students, Black people, Asians/Asian Americans, and other groups are considered "diverse." Diversity, at WSU and beyond, is often seen as something that is achieved rather than as a dynamic process. The MEO staff and director of equity and inclusion were keenly aware of the complexities of diversity—less clear, however, was whether Caldwell or WSU in general were in agreement with this view.

"What questions do you have about Black students in Caldwell?" I asked the director of equity and inclusion, Dr. Pittman. "One of the things that I've noticed is that you will never ever find a Black student walking around Caldwell. I've seen you more than I've seen Black undergraduates," Dr. Pittman reflected. Speaking about how her office is located in the same building where many engineering classes take place she continued, "I don't see them. Where are they?" Continuing her train of thought, considering where Black engineers might be, she said:

> Latinos and Asians seem to be holding it down at MEO. . . . Are [Black engineers] in the Black Cultural Center? If that is where they are, that's fine. Because what we've done in making everything so broad, is that, in our own spaces, they're not comfortable.

Black students do not frequent the MEO. This struck me as odd, given that most participants, in my beginning interviews, pointed to the MEO as an example of how Caldwell supports Black students. Most students, while they appreciated having the space, did not congregate or study there. They mainly just used the MEO to print. In latter interviews and casual conversations, I dug deeper into understanding the space.

While staff likened the MEO to a "home," the reality played out differently for Black engineers. If anything, the MEO was a home base for Latinx engineers. While some Black engineers struggled to come up with a reason why they did not use the MEO, others cited the number of students who frequented the space and a difficulty to concentrate. Bianca, for example, said, "In the actual MEO room, people are always talking so you can't really get work done." In explaining her guess as to why Black engineers made little use of the MEO, Ayana offered:

> My guess would be, one, there are more Hispanic students than there are Black students, so then you get back into the, White people study together, Hispanic people study together . . .

In the MEO, one can often hear students speaking Spanish to each other. Sneezes solicit choruses of scattered "bless you's" and "salud's." The MEO houses six computers—clunky black desktops used for little more than printing assignments. Outside of the Latinx engineers, a diverse array of students come to the MEO, but only for resources, not necessarily to mingle. The MEO, like other spaces where students of different races interact, can be a site of racial tension. In the social world of the MEO, Latinxs might be considered the dominant group. In the small common room that can comfortably fit twenty students, Latinx students often make up the majority.

In a space dedicated to diversity such as the MEO, Black engineers, rarely present, can be an afterthought. Black Caldwell students as a categorical group get lost in the continually expanding umbrella of diversity. This categorical occlusion of Black students is related to what the Black Studies scholar, Jared Sexton, identified as "people-of-color-blindness." Sexton describes the phenomenon as, "a form of colorblindness inherent to the concept of 'people of color' to the precise extent that it misunderstands the specificity of antiblackness and presumes or insists upon the monolithic character of victimization under White supremacy" (2010, 73). I suggest that, more than people-of-color-blindness, the MEO faces the challenge of diversity dilution. As Dr. Pittman mentioned, the MEO was tasked with serving students of color, LGBTQ students regardless of race, differently abled students regardless of race, and other minoritized populations in engineering. All of these groups, while deserving of targeted support, are grouped under the broad banner of diversity, stretching the resources of the MEO to many different groups. With so many groups to attend to, a concentrated effort to support Black students becomes more difficult. When an institution or organization exhibits diversity dilution, the unique needs and positions of Black students are occluded under the category of diversity.

The Tension between Membership in NSBE and Other Engineering Organizations

Similar to other social worlds, it is possible to be a Caldwell student but not part of the Caldwell community. Membership in the Caldwell community is signified through involvement in Caldwell/engineering-specific organizations. In this section, I first describe how NSBE, a Caldwell-sponsored organization, exists in relation to other identity-based engineering organizations. In the latter half of the section, I illustrate the benefits of joining engineering-specific organizations as well as challenges Black students face in such groups.

IDENTITY-BASED ENGINEERING ORGANIZATIONS

The relationships between student organizations are often neutral, depending on the temporal moment and organizational memory. For example, during the NSBE e-board retreat, members learn about how outgoing e-board members feel about other organizations. Relations between the Society of Hispanic Professional Engineers (SHPE) and NSBE, for example, used to be stronger. Some NSBE members, including Robert and Olivia, even regularly attended SHPE meetings as first-years. With the exception of one woman in my sample who was raised in Nigeria, none of the Black women in the study were involved with the Society for Women Engineers (SWE).

NSBE AND SWE

Each identity-based group is loosely organized around a singular facet of identity outside of engineering. NSBE is centered on the racial identity of Blackness. SHPE is centered on ethno-racial Latinx identity. SWE is centered on gender identity, and women in particular. A danger of organizing around a single identity, however, is the tendency to prioritize the privileged members of a group (Crenshaw 1989), alienating multiply marginalized members. In spaces organized around Black racial identity, for example, students who are privileged in terms of gender and class—middle and upper-class cisgender Black men—could potentially dominate the group. No space, NSBE included, is exempt from the forces of identity-based oppression. While not the focus of my study, recall, for example, how Alexis suggested that NSBE members operated as if everyone in the group was middle class or higher.

SWE was another matter. While created to support women in engineering, SWE catered to White women, rendering most Black women in Caldwell invisible. SWE served as a textbook example of the limitations of a single-axis identity framework—while created for all women, SWE, in actuality, created a culture that centered White womanhood in particular (Hull et al. 1982). Absent an intersectional approach to programming in SWE, students described an organization that seemed to adopt a false "universal sisterhood" that rendered White women the prototypical members (hooks 1981; Mirza 2014).

Olivia put it bluntly, "We don't fuck with SWE. The reason we don't fuck with SWE is that they're like a White sorority. But it's mostly within the e-board, though, because we've had such bad experiences with them." She explained that she felt like a minority within a minority in SWE because of her identity as a Black woman, chuckling, "So what you go through is not what I go through, and I don't fuck with you." She

added, "But lemme think. The problem is, if the leader doesn't like them
then it'll eventually spread. . . . It just happened naturally though. . . . It's
something about their aura." Jessica, who attended meetings for SWE and
other Caldwell organizations, also referred to a negative aura of sorts saying, "I think a lot of the academic based groups [in Caldwell] are kind of
show off-y." Comparing NSBE with other Caldwell organizations, Jessica
said, "Everyone seems to be trying to one up each other and [in NSBE]
everyone is super collaborative. We have a GroupMe and everyone is like,
'Here's an awesome opportunity, go for it.'" She could not say the same
for the SWE community:

> I talk to SWE people and they would only tell me about
> opportunities after they applied or after the deadline and I'd
> be like, "Wow you suck." SWE is kinda like that. A lot of
> women groups are like, "Yes feminism! Girl power!" But then
> like, "I'm gonna be a girl boss, so I'm not going to tell you
> how I'm getting there."

Olivia, Jessica, and other Black women either had no desire to attend SWE
or only attended one or two meetings before deciding that SWE was not
for them, often commenting on the Whiteness of the organization. Other
Black women shared similar sentiments as Laurie, who said, "I feel like, in
Caldwell, my race matters more." Alexis, implicitly referring to the salience
of her racial identity in Caldwell, said, "There's more chicks in [Caldwell],
but there's still no Black people." Alexis implicitly associated women in
Caldwell with nonblack racial identity. Gender, race, class, and other
identities intersect to simultaneously structure students' experiences. Yet,
as stated by Margaret Anderson and Patricia Hill Collins (2004), specific
identities can feel more salient than others in certain circumstances: "At
any moment, race, class, or gender may feel more salient or meaningful
in a given person's life, but they are overlapping and cumulative in their
effect on people's experience" (7). Given their limited free time and the
salience of their Blackness in Caldwell, most felt that their identity as
Black women would be more appreciated and time well-spent in NSBE.

NSBE and SHPE

Olivia's experience with Latinx engineers is useful for understanding the
terrain of relationships across race and between organizations. During our

initial interview, a dawn of realization overcame her as she explained her interpretation of the racial climate, "But now that I think about it, most of the [racist] stuff that happens comes from Hispanic students." Olivia, however, emphasized that SHPE was not the problem, but rather individuals within the organization saying, "You can't blame that on SHPE—you can only blame that on the people." She recalled a time when someone from SHPE made fun of NSBE for having low membership. In another instance her lab-mate, a member of SHPE who would later be president, said, "'I thought you were a bitch before, but you're not that bad.'" In response, Olivia said:

> And I'm like, why would you say that to me. . . . What the fuck you think I'ma respond to with that? But I'm in a lab so I can't go off on her. 'Cause now I'm the crazy Black girl and now I'm the bitch . . . the thing is, I'm sitting there thinking . . . we didn't have a conversation really before this class, so what would've led you to believe that? Is it because I wasn't talking to you? Is it because I wasn't smiling all the time? Or is it because I'm a Black girl with a face and okay, because I'm not smiling I'm a bitch?

A Latina—a fellow student of color and woman—delivered one of the most memorable verbal assaults Olivia experienced at WSU. To say Olivia is experiencing racism is true but imprecise. The same goes for sexism, antiblackness, and White supremacy. What Olivia described was gendered antiblack racism—misogynoir (Bailey and Trudy 2018). The controlling image (Collins 2000) of the "angry Black woman" stereotype (e.g., Walley-Jean 2009) works in two harmful ways here. First, Olivia's Latina classmate assumed Olivia was, in fact, an angry Black woman. The controlling image of an angry Black woman stereotype created an expectation of Olivia based purely upon her racial and gender identity. Yet, in order to avoid acting out that very stereotype, Olivia quelled her rightful anger and disdain. In this interaction, one can see how the racist and sexist controlling image shaped the Latina's actions and Olivia's response.

Before recounting one final moment of racial friction, Olivia said, "Oh man, now that I think about it, I really don't like them," referring to Latinx engineers. Up until the year prior to my fieldwork, her junior year, she was a member of the SHPE GroupMe messaging app. She prefaced her story saying, "You know, when you're in urban communities, people pick up other slang words, right?" "Someone said, 'nigga'?" I predicted. She nodded and told me that someone in the GroupMe said "nigga" a few times in the chat, so she wrote something like, "Did you really have to use that word?" She felt compelled to say something. "One of them responded—not the one who said it, but someone else said, like, 'I don't see why we can't say the word.' And then some other people joined in like, 'You guys, let's just all get along.'" Nobody said anything else in the GroupMe for several hours, so she left the GroupMe. Recalling the end of the digital debacle, chuckling and shaking her head, she said:

> My friend, who's the vice president, said the whole GroupMe exploded after I left. Because it's like, you made someone leave the GroupMe because you made them feel uncomfortable. So from a president or vice president standpoint, that's not okay. So they disbanded the GroupMe.

This GroupMe was a counterspace for Latinx engineers. While counterspaces are understood as a safe haven for students of color at HWIs (Keels 2020), counterspaces are not inherently welcome to all racially marginalized students. In a short message exchange, this counterspace for Latinx students turned into an alienating and antiblack space. While Black and Latinx students are both victims of White supremacy, Latinx students can also enact antiblackness toward their Black counterparts, suggesting that the elision between Black and Latinx students can occlude how nonblack Latinx students also enact antiblackness.

Olivia's experiences with Latinx engineers are telling. Because of her proximity to this group and their comfort level with her, she encountered more racial slights or assaults. She sums up the relational nature of microaggressions, reflecting, "When I think about it, it's happened more in SHPE because they were the people I spent the most time with that weren't Black." Curious as to why she did not encounter as many racial microaggressions with other races, specifically White students, she explained that in her racially diverse high school, she was the victim of countless racial slights and insults from White students. "I don't hang out with White people. I stopped doing that in high school," she said. As I explain in greater detail in chapter 10, racial microaggressions and slights depend upon students' proximity to other races. For Olivia, Latinx students were the main racial aggressors not because Latinx students are uniquely antiblack, but because of her closeness to Latinx engineers.

ENGINEERING SOCIETIES

Active members in the Caldwell community participate in Caldwell Student Ambassadors (CSA), like Nina and Charlie, and/or join engineering societies. While the majority of Black engineers were involved in NSBE, only three were involved in CSA and eight participants reported regular involvement in engineering societies. Busy with a rigorous course load as well as NSBE meetings, it may seem natural that a small fraction of Black students would also be involved in engineering societies. Rather, more than a result of personal choice, the lack of Black engineers in engineering societies might be attributed to the alienating behavior of engineering societies, lack of representation, and time constraints. The lack of Black engineers in such societies is concerning, given that membership in engineering societies can afford increased career capital that NSBE does not provide.

In a conversation with a computer science professor, I asked, "How important are engineering society type groups?" He responded, "More and more I feel like, along with internships, that's another way to learn outside of just the classes, which I think . . . sets you apart in terms of finding jobs." The professor continued, explaining that engineering societies, "really give [students] a launching point to learn more on their own and create, design, and have something in their portfolio that they can show they've done." I asked the dean of the engineering school, "What's the benefit of joining these engineering societies?" "Big," he said,

> You learn how to work together . . . they are not for credit. No one is getting a grade . . . it's all driven internally by the students. They organize themselves, you know the way you create a team and how you compete as a team. That's really what it is. It's almost like being part of a football team and you want to compete with another football team. Except that in this case it's like, how do you build the best rocket and have it go to the highest altitude?

Dr. Pittman, the Director of Equity and Inclusion, commented on the exposure members of the engineering societies had with trustees of Caldwell. Of those engineering society members, "not a one" was Black. Dr. Pittman emphasized that getting good grades and getting engineering degrees is no longer enough.

I asked students who participated in engineering societies to explain the difference between engineering societies and NSBE. Funke, for example, joined the aerospace engineering society, and worked with the team to launch a rocket. As an aerospace engineer, the society experience was invaluable and she attributed her involvement to helping her get an internship at NASA—an accomplishment even more impressive after taking into account that this was just after her first year at WSU. Engineering societies can sometimes provide relevant experience that makes students attractive candidates for competitive internships.

Bianca and Dajuan both explained that engineering societies helped give them a more relevant skill set for their environmental engineering majors. "In NSBE . . . of course you work on your resume and your pitches, but like in these groups, they get you hands-on activities like building boats, sailing, and you're working with concrete," Dajuan told me. Similarly, Bianca, an environmental engineering major, said, "NSBE is cool but they aren't very like, environmentally focused." Through her engineering society, however, she said she can "actually apply what I've learned in class to an actual water treatment process. So it's kinda fun to actually put it together and actually make [the water filter] do stuff."

For a variety of reasons, Black engineers opted not to join engineering societies. For some, time was the deciding factor, and students felt like they could not commit to another organization outside of NSBE. For others, engineering societies were not appealing because none of their friends were in the organizations. Anthony, for example, explained, "It was kind of hard to get involved and get interested in it, 'cause I didn't know anyone that was in it." Because Black students were not prevalent in such groups to begin with and because Black engineers lacked a critical mass, integration into the teams was even more difficult. Ayana, however, reiterated that for any engineering student, joining another organization can be taxing because, "Caldwell, overall is overwhelming."

In some engineering majors, 100 percent of the Black students participate in engineering societies. Given the small numbers of Black engineers, however, this can mean one or two students. For example, the two Black civil engineers in the same graduating class were both involved with a related engineering society. The same can be said of the two environmental engineers.

Within other engineering majors, however, a lack of Black representation on engineering societies seems cyclical. Without many Black engineers in Caldwell, few can possibly join engineering societies. Incoming Black students often form bonds with other Black engineers and have difficulty building lasting relationships with nonblack people in their major. Thus, the likelihood that they have a friend or someone they know in a society is low. Consider Charlie—although he is active in Caldwell in that he served as a Caldwell Student Ambassador (CSA), he has no desire to be part of the chemical engineering society: "I'm probably not as much a part of that org just 'cause I don't have many friends in it. And any club that I don't have that many friends in I'm just not going."

Professor Carson, who taught computer science and engineering, recognized the importance of both identity-based and engineering-focused organizations: "I think both are critically important. Both play roles. The NSBE role and the research or extracurricular engineering societies." Rather thoughtfully, he considered a specific tension Black students might face in reference to their organizational involvement outside of class:

> [I]f you are a Black male coming into this context, you will likely be one or only two in your class and so, I think then, they draw together in NSBE or other groups, but I think then, I feel like they lose some of, they may lose some of the connection with their own major or discipline.

One mode of connecting to discipline or majors is through engineering societies. Black students' lack of involvement in such organizations, however, might be unsurprising if interactions between students at engineering society meetings are anything like interactions Black engineers often have with students in their classes.

Caldwell Organizational Involvement: In Summary

This chapter analyzes Black students' experiences in Caldwell organizations and offices. Diversity and its tensions arose as a central theme. In studying engineering students, one must be careful to generalize experiences across engineering majors that may have vastly different cultures. Within engineering as a discipline and Caldwell as a school, students have diverse experiences depending on their major. Black Caldwell students also experience, understand, and navigate Caldwell in various ways. While students have varying perceptions of the racial climate in Caldwell, all students experience the reality of being part of a marginal Black population. By certain standards, Caldwell is racially diverse, especially compared to other engineering schools. Yet, Caldwell is not Black. Through diversity initiatives, Black students' unique needs and Black student representation are occluded, exemplifying what I termed diversity dilution.

Student groups such as NSBE, SWE, or SHPE can serve as sites of study to better understand engineering students' engagement across racial lines. In order to learn about specific student groups, scholars tend to construct student organizations as discrete objects (e.g., Guiffrida 2003; Museus 2008). Indeed, student organizations can be understood as social worlds of their own. But groups do not exist in isolation; they exist in relation to each other, creating a web of groups at the same university. Daisy Reyes (2018), for example, demonstrated how Latinx student organizations at the same campus vied for resources and how group cultures built identities in relation to other groups. Similarly, NSBE at WSU took its shape in relation to other organizations and was shaped by Caldwell as a social world. By examining the relationship between organizations one can see how groups potentially distanced themselves from NSBE or from Black students more broadly.

Concepts of student involvement and engagement provide entry points to understanding campus life (Astin 1984; Kuh 1995b). Further, student engagement opportunities are important to examine because they can result in positive educational outcomes (Pascarella and Terenzini 2005; Quaye et al. 2019). To think of student groups only in terms of transaction, or how involvement can be translated into positive educational outcomes, to be sure, is overly simplistic. Students might join a group to make friends, gain social status in a campus social world, party, develop a skill, get to know a crush, network, or to see people that look like them. It is worth noting, however, that some groups are more related to students' career interests than others. Involvement in an engineering society, for example, can result in capital accumulation for students in the engineering career field in ways that involvement in NSBE or the Black Student Union cannot.

In their research on how college affects students, Pascarella and Terenzini (2005) suggest, "The impact of college is largely determined by individual effort and involvement in the academic, interpersonal, and extracurricular offerings on a campus" (602). Yet, race, and Blackness in particular, mediates students' involvement, what organizations they join, how much time they spend, and their level of engagement. Like any student, participants joined organizations and invested their time and energy in endeavors of interest, but also where they felt welcomed and validated. As was the case of some engineering organizations and societies, nonblack students' antagonism toward Blackness foreclosed opportunities for engagement. Antiblackness in Caldwell created a boundary felt by Black engineering students that limited substantive involvement in certain engineering societies.

Students of color, broadly, do not have the same engagement opportunities as their White counterparts at HWIs (Quaye et al. 2019). As Black Caldwell students show, however, student of color engagement does not equate to Black student engagement. As I highlight throughout this book, being Black is different from being a nonblack student of color. The antiblackness of nonblack students of color created a barrier to Black student engagement opportunities. Antiblackness manifested interpersonally with antagonism toward Black students. On an institutional level, antiblackness manifested in diversity dilution in the MEO as well as the small Black student population in engineering. In the next chapter, I highlight challenges Black students face in more informal settings while working with other Caldwell students.

8

Informal Relationships

The (Im)Possibility of Peer Collaboration

My race kinda pushed people away from helping me in a sense.

—Chantelle

The electronic brochure for incoming Caldwell students reads:

We foster a collaborative, non-competitive space. You won't compete or have to worry about the grading curve. Group projects will be present throughout your curriculum—it never takes just one engineer to solve a problem.

For some students, this claim rings true. Faculty and staff also supported this notion. One computer science advisor nodded, while the other advisor described the WSU computer science program:

It's very collaborative. You don't code in a bubble . . . usually you code with other people. You do your own work but it's part of a larger process. So oftentimes your code has to match with someone else's and so you work in teams.

Professor Carson described the culture of engineering, saying, "There is a real team mentality to engineering. So, I think, folks that I interact with want to solve problems that will help people. . . . It feels like there's more team camaraderie."

An industrial and systems engineering professor implied that the Caldwell environment lends itself to collaboration and asking for help, saying, "[Students] are supposed to, if they have trouble, to look for help. . . . But in real life, some students have trouble and they don't speak out. They keep failing and failing and failing." During the same interview, the professor also mentioned, in his classes of about twenty-five to thirty students, he has never had more than two Black students in the same class, noting, "Usually Chinese group among Chinese . . . White group among White. And Black as well. So that is common I guess in all activities. That is not new." While the professor admonished the hypothetical student for failing to ask for help, he unwittingly provided a rationale of why collaborating with other students, as a Black engineer, can prove difficult. In engineering classes, groups sometimes segregate by race. For Black students, racially segregated grouping can mean isolation and exclusion. Of the fifty-eight Black students in Caldwell during my study, thirty-five (60%) were the only Black students in their major for their graduating class. No more than three Black students shared the same major during the same year. Certainly, classes—especially in computer science—overlap, yet the numbers are noticeably small.

Collaboration is central to engineering coursework as well as in STEM and innovation more broadly (Chang et al. 2014; Gasiewski et al. 2012; Marra et al. 2016). Peer collaboration is often viewed as an engaging, thoughtful pedagogical practice in STEM. Group work, however, needs to be reconsidered. As I show in this chapter, the civility and collegiality of peers is sorely taken for granted. Interestingly, what we know about collaboration in STEM says little about the very relationships that make groups what they are. Study groups are implicitly constructed as static units, or substances, rather than dynamic webs of relationships (Emirbayer 1997). When groups are understood as substances, the students and the study group are constructed as static entities existing independent of each other. Of course, groups do not exist outside of the students that make them. However, this fact is taken for granted by faculty, staff, and scholars studying STEM alike. Joining a study group or collaborating with peers is described as a mechanical transaction similar to showing one's ID to gain access to a university library. Yet, the reality is far more complicated. When one understands group work as a relational process, one gains insight that is closer to the social reality, appreciating the dynamics of collaboration, how collaboration is usefully facilitated, and the boundaries stymieing productive group work. For example, how does one understand peer collaboration when your peers want nothing to do with you? As I show in this chapter, Black Caldwell students faced barriers to effective collaboration due to the racism and sexism perpetuated by their peers. In other words, antiblackness created a social boundary.

Race is relational and dynamic (Omi and Winant 1986). While the societal status and relations between races change over time, an antagonism toward and distancing from Blackness has remained consistent across racial lines (Douglas et al. 2016). Historically, individuals from other races have increased their proximity to Whiteness by purposefully distancing themselves from Blackness and Black people (Ignatiev 2012; Ray et al. 2017). The same antagonism toward Black people occurs at WSU and in higher education in general (Dancy et al. 2018). Participants recounted, and I witnessed, instances where both White and nonblack students of color in Caldwell participate in antiblackness. While a growing body of literature exists (Abrica et al. 2020; Ray et al. 2017), sociologists of education rarely examine how nonblack people of color reinforce and engage in antiblack racism. Afropessimist thought (Sexton 2010), however, provides a useful lens to analyze and understand antiblackness. Afropessimism suggests that antiblackness, while related to white supremacy, is a unique form of oppression that only Black people experience. Through this logic, personhood and citizenship rights are measured by a distancing from Blackness (Ray et al. 2017). In other words, the closer a group is to identifying or associating with Black people, the fewer rights they will have recognized by the state.

Similar to how nonblack people of color historically distanced themselves from Black people for access to citizenship rights, I noticed a distancing from Black Caldwell students. Rights from the state in the context of Caldwell might be considered rights to social status, access to study groups, or the even the right to be seen as a Caldwell student. To be sure, some students, depending on their major, have more access to Caldwell social status. But for too many participants, Caldwell social status is out of reach, it seems, simply because of their Blackness. Nonblack students actively distanced themselves from Black students. While it's outside the scope of this paper, I wondered if nonblack Caldwell students subconsciously thought that their social status would be marred by a connection to Black students.

In this chapter, I discuss two tensions concerning more of the informal relationships within the Caldwell social world: (1) the tension between group work and being the only Black person, and (2) the tension between expecting and experiencing racism. Similar to the previous chapter, I show how antiblackness creates a boundary for Black students in Caldwell. Opportunities for productive collaborative work or access to study materials for courses were foreclosed simply because of participants' Blackness. To spotlight the ways nonblack peers are complicit in perpetuating antiblackness at Caldwell, I conclude this chapter with a vignette of a NSBE Study Day during final exam period.

The Tension between Group Work and Being the Only One

Foundational research concerning Black students' attrition in STEM fields cites Black students' tendency to study by themselves as a factor in their low achievement (Seymour and Hewitt 1997; Treisman 1992). This ethnography, however, tells a different story—challenging the notion that Black students need better study habits. Group work, I found, while potentially beneficial, can be a site ripe for antiblackness and alienation.

Many students, regardless of race or major, can likely recall nightmarish tales of group projects. However, the challenges faced by some Black engineers during group projects at Caldwell are uniquely racialized and gendered. Their difficulties in group work manifest in two main ways: (1) access to groups, and (2) access to collegial behavior and respect from peers.

"Has race mattered at all during your time here in college?" I asked Alexis. "I think in terms of being selected for groups," she replied candidly, "I've always been the last one, because people assume that you're lazy, or you're here because of affirmative action. . . . That's happened a couple of times." Her peers never said anything, but she always noticed that she was the last person to find a group. Chantelle felt similarly and offered an example of nonblack peers alienating her:

> My race kinda pushed people away from helping me in a sense. I feel like that was a reason. Because like people would come up the same time as me and I would see them be befriended by their race, you know what I mean? And I would try to join in and then they would do this thing where they would speak

in their own language so I don't know. So like I just, became very standoffish.

Chantelle explicitly identified her race as a boundary to peer collaboration. Her inability to find many collaborators was not a fault of her own, but a result of antiblack attitudes from her peers. Outside of her friends from NSBE, she felt like she was only able to make friends at Caldwell "by a stroke of luck."

Kenya, a computer engineering major, feels uneasy whenever professors say, "Okay, let's pick partners." To herself, she thinks, "Okay, who's gonna pick me?" She wondered how much of her unease was a creation of her own making, explaining to me, "It's like, you kind of already start making your mind feel like something is gonna happen. I can say I felt that way, but I don't know if it was really that way, you know?" While rarely said explicitly, Black engineers, especially Black women, are sometimes made to feel unwelcome by nonblack peers.

Jessica told me she was frustrated with trying to work with people in her classes outside of her friend Payton, a fellow NSBE member, recounting, "I would ask for help . . . it is primarily guys, but they would kinda act like I was dumber. So that made me not want to work with them. So I was never really included." I asked her if she thought gender played a role in her exclusion. She responded, saying:

> I think it's just the intersectionality for sure, because there were other girls in there that were not Black. . . . I don't know if it's because the guys had a crush on her, I don't know if they thought they were smarter, but the other girls, I feel, were more connected.

While nonblack women seemed to have access to collegial peer collaboration, Jessica did not, exemplifying a gendered antiblack racism.

The most egregious stories of racialized insults and disrespect from groupmates came from the women I interviewed. Ayana, for example, recounted a semester-long group project that was "hell." The other three people in her group were White, two men, and one woman—Karen. They refused to answer Ayana's messages in their GroupMe, met without her, scheduled meetings last-minute, and complained to the professor about her. Ayana mentioned that Karen seemed torn between being kind to Ayana and showing her loyalty to the guys. Karen, after all, was the only person to even respond to Ayana's messages. While Karen, at times, acknowledged Ayana's existence, Karen was very much complicit in alienating Ayana and making her experience "hell." No sense of "sisterhood" connected Karen to Ayana. Ayana and Jessica were not excluded in their groups because of their identities as women—they were excluded because of their identities as *Black* women.

In another example, Hanna had already done much of her group's project herself, when the rest of her team, three White men, scheduled a last-minute meeting that she could not make. "We're meeting in 15 minutes," a group mate texted her, but Hanna reminded him that she had work. Someone else in the group responded to Hanna in the GroupMe saying, "Excuses are like assholes, everyone has them." Hanna was not friends with these men, so that message could only be interpreted as mean-spirited. The next morning, Hanna recounted, "I get an e-mail from my professor saying that my group wants me to leave. And I was like, um let me get back to you on that 'cause we're about to . . . I'm about to throw down." Hanna responded with "receipts." "I really wrote six paragraphs explaining how I did all the work in the group," Hanna continued with her story, "I did the only diagram that existed for the team. I did the entire power point in Google docs to keep track of all the changes that I made." Her group mates ended up getting docked points, but the professor did not, to her knowledge, say anything to them about their behavior. Her group mates, White men, actively attempted to make her effort invisible. Were it not for Hanna engaging in the added labor of documenting the work she did for the group, challenging her group mates, and advocating for herself, she might have received a lower grade or have been tasked with starting a completely new project, with her old group claiming her intellectual effort as their own. Despite her hypervisibility, she was made to feel invisible, and similar to Posey-Maddox's (2017) findings concerning Black parents' experiences in a White suburban school, Hanna's contributions, however central, were completely disregarded.

Black women at Caldwell faced a complex set of challenges due to their race and gender. Their experiences rendered them, paradoxically, both invisible and hypervisible. Grace, for example, shared a couple of experiences that were rude and imbued with racism. In a packed Computer Science lecture, the entire room was full with the exception of a seat next to Grace on the aisle. "This Indian boy decides to, 'Hey I'm going to sit on the stairs,'" Grace narrated, "The professor is just like, 'You can't sit there, it's a fire hazard . . . there's a seat available up there,' pointing to me." Shaking her head, laughing, she said, "He literally left . . . walked out. And he had to walk by me to walk out of class." Of course we cannot say for sure why the student left class, yet I can say for sure how that incident made Grace feel and that she believed it motivated by antiblackness. Consider the possibility that for this nonblack student of color, the potential embarrassment of leaving class while all eyes were on him paled in comparison to the embarrassment of being seated next to the only Black woman in the class.

Continuing her list of racist experiences, she paused in a moment of reflection, saying, "It's never from White people. It's mainly Asian people and Indians. Not to generalize . . ." Grace's eyes misted and voice cracked while recounting the next story. She described her experience in office hours for a computer science course. She had the same question as an Asian American woman who was in front of her to get help from the TA. Grace asked her if she could go over what the TA told her, reiterating, "I have the same problem." Her classmate looked at her and said, "What does it matter? At the end of the day, you're going to get a job and I'm not." Grace was "shook" upon hearing her response. What made matters worse for Grace, however, was the indifference of her peers: "The kicker was that, I looked around to see if anyone else heard. . . . They all did. And nobody said shit. They all were looking up on their computers and I'm just like, 'Y'all gonna let her accost me like that?'" Grace's experience highlights the specious nature of grouping students of color together in an analysis on account of a shared oppression. Other students of color did not come to Grace's aid at that moment. Another person of color was the offender. Grace was the only Black person in that space. If any coalition existed, it was positioned against her, explicitly through an insult and implicitly by her classmates' silence. Working across racial differences posed a problem for many Black engineers, not because of a lack of effort on the Black students' end, but rather because of an unwillingness of the nonblack students to work with them. This finding is particularly troubling considering study groups are, in many cases, central to success in engineering.

Microaggressions, racial slights, overt racism, and other negative racialized encounters are dependent upon proximity. Many Black engineers, for example, reported that Asian students, American and International, were the main offenders of racist slights or actions. How are we to make sense of antiblack sentiments or microaggressions from other "people-of-color"? In this majority-minority context, nonblack students seem to be displaying a distancing from or dislike toward their Black counterparts. Nonblack students displayed antagonism toward Black students, socially and even physically distancing themselves from Black students. One might question to what extent Caldwell's culture constructed an image of an ideal Caldwell student in opposition to Black racial identity.

THE IMPORTANCE OF GROUPS

Students can potentially achieve in engineering without study groups/ partners, but having a group makes the workload more manageable. A computer science professor, for example, impressed upon me the importance of groups saying, "You can't really get through successfully without a mini-cohort of people in your major." Chukwu's experience with study groups demonstrates their academic benefits. I first met Chukwu as a first year in mechanical engineering. He was raised in Nigeria, speaks with a baritone voice, and has a natural burly build. He is an introvert and ran for Membership Chair of NSBE to force himself to speak to more people. Chukwu mainly worked by himself for a little over half of his first year.

I asked what difference working with people made for his studies and he replied, "That mechanical engineering class, for instance, I was doing twelve, thirteen hours. Got cut down to four hours." Being able to share ideas and discuss concepts together made homework and learning in general easier. Jumping to a conclusion, I asked if joining a study group was more difficult because of his race. He corrected me, "I don't think it's harder because I'm Black. I think it's just because I'm just that kind of person." Aware of his introverted nature, I asked him how he made friends, to which he replied, "A lot of people are just friendly, introduce themselves . . . I wasn't really the person to go up to . . . when they'd come up to me, I'd just see the opportunity." While not the primary focus of this project, I was curious about the role of his ethnicity and gender in his perceived approachability. This possibility comes to fore when juxtaposing his experience with Ayana's.

Ayana, a senior and the same major as Chukwu, had a very different experience in working with people in her major. "It's hard. Engineering isn't really designed to do by yourself," Ayana explained, "For example, there's some projects where it's like, 'Oh, we could do it with one or two people.' Most of the time, I do it by myself. Because, one, it's easier to do it by myself than to find somebody." Demonstrating her thought process in a sarcastic voice, she said:

"Okay, let me talk to Becky over here who doesn't actually want to talk to me,"[1] and, kind of pretend like I care to do this project [with her] when the professor said I didn't have to do it with another person. So I just do it by myself.

For Ayana, working by herself was a more attractive option than working with a nonblack classmate. Outside of projects, she also worked on problem sets for homework by herself. "So, you get two weeks to do twenty problems, right?" Ayana began. "Other groups will take that twenty problems, split it amongst themselves. Collect it," she told me, "I will do all twenty by myself. Which is what you're supposed to do. But, that's hard to do when you have five other classes to worry about." Her sentiments are influenced by racial realism (Bell 1994). After being snubbed many times in group work, she did not consider the unrealistic yet idealistic possibility that her nonblack peers would suddenly change their feelings toward her. Through her sense of racial realism, Ayana was free to view the reality of the situation and understood she was presented with two unfair options: work with someone who does not want to work with her or complete a group project by herself. Either way, she was at a disadvantage in comparison to her nonblack peers who had access to study groups.

In addition to academic support and camaraderie, friends in the same major served as emotional support. For example, Payton was upset that Jessica considered changing her major from computer science and actively worked to convince her to stay in the major. The two often studied together, worked together, and even cried together about the difficulty of assignments. Another student, William, for example, considered switching from computer engineering to just computer science for a lighter workload. He decided to finish out the more rigorous program partly because of his friend, Robert, whom he first met in NSBE and who was also in computer engineering: "I think because my friend Robert, he's like, [in computer engineering] too, and we're the only two Black people in that class. So I thought I might as well just finish it with him." Because many Black engineers lack access to the central source of support found in study groups, same-race friendships were especially important. With smaller numbers, their sense of linked fate is heightened. Without Jessica, Payton would likely have no one to study or perhaps even talk with in her major. William did not switch majors because he did not want to leave Robert by himself. Their otherwise individualistic decisions to stay in a major were linked to their relationships with the other Black person in their class. Echoing prior research, these students' motivations to stay in their majors shows the importance of same-race friendships for Black students at HWIs (Brooms and Davis 2017; Grier-Reed and Wilson 2016; Harper 2013; Keels 2020; Ong et al. 2018; Thelamour 2019). With their friends, they could form a Black counterspace within an otherwise nonblack class; a safe place and study group of two.

FORMING STUDY GROUPS AND WORKING ALONE

A few of the engineers described how their experiences of feeling alienated were not emblematic of all Black engineers' experiences. Robert, for example, said, "The experience is lonely—just very lonely . . . it also depends on who you are kinda . . . if you grew up a lot with a lot of nonblack people, you can integrate fine because you're used to that anyway." Providing me with even greater clarification, Robert said, "You're probably already interested in those same things as those people . . . kinda like Thomas." "Bitch," Thomas yelled at Robert, without turning around from his game of FIFA with Anthony. We all shared a laugh, "Thomas kinda gives me that vibe," Robert continued, still laughing. "Of what? Of what?" Thomas asked with faux indignation. "That you hung out with a lot of Whites and Asians before here," Robert responded. "Yeah, I kinda had to," Thomas admitted with a laugh. Thomas attended an elite private, preparatory school and was, indeed, the only Black person in his high school class. Bringing it back to our conversation, Robert said:

> Which isn't a bad thing. 'Cause he can easily talk to them and befriend 'em all, but I don't know. . . . I've only been interested in strictly hip hop kinda stuff. My culture that I'm used to isn't necessarily popular with people in my major so I have to do more to try to befriend people.

While Robert makes this point, Thomas, as I mentioned earlier, also felt also felt hypervisible in the Caldwell classroom, feeling as though he had to work twice as hard as his nonblack peers. Despite Thomas's background, he likewise, albeit differently, experienced antiblack othering through racial spotlighting in the classroom.

As Robert explained, one's background prior to WSU played a role in how seamlessly one fits into the WSU engineering culture. Interestingly, I noticed after analysis that all of the engineers I interviewed who were born in Africa had little trouble making friends across races, forming study groups, and seemed more accepted by other students. Majors, however, have unique cultures, and chemical engineering was known to have more of a collaborative culture. Joseph, who was born in Ethiopia, also made friends rather easily in his computer science class:

> It's a CS class in a series . . . kind of a weed out class, one of the more difficult. It has the steepest learning curve. So you make friends in war . . . like when you're stressed out and stuff. So I have some close friends from that. And in CS a lot of classes you take with them too.

While I cannot provide further explanation beyond this trend by their own accounts, a possibility could be that students' immigrant status within a heavily immigrant populated department such as Caldwell allowed them greater access into the engineering community.

Other students, similar to Thomas, were very much used to attending predominantly White and Asian environments and were either adjusted to working by themselves or could gel with students of different races. Nubia and Ayana, for example, both attended predominantly White and Asian high schools in New York City. Both were well adjusted to working by themselves. Other students, such as Thomas, Gary, Martin, Charlie, and Noelle, attended high schools with similar demographics but had more friends of other races. Gary, for example, looked at WSU and stated, "For me, personally, it's pretty consistent with what I've grown up with." For students like Gary, who came from higher income backgrounds and attended predominantly White high schools, their habitus, or backgrounds, aligned well with WSU and Caldwell. One might suggest that Caldwell catered to this specific "type" of student. However, as I highlight through-out the next chapters, a specific background does not render one exempt from antiblack racism.

As mentioned earlier, different majors have different cultures—some more accepting and cooperative than others. Laurie, in civil engineering, had a racially diverse study group. In an NSBE study session, Laurie and two of her classmates, an Asian and a White woman, joined us to work. Bianca, although majoring in environmental engineering, also was taking the same class. They had an assignment about concrete production. While concrete is a fascinating topic by itself, I was further intrigued by Laurie's reaction to something Johnson said: "Man, these teachers don't give a fuck about us." Laurie stopped her work and said, "Speak for yourself," and looked at her group members, "Don't you all think we have great professors this semester?" and they nodded in affirmative. "Not even trying to be irritating, but I love my professors right now," she added. Further, the camaraderie between the students also might have been something unique about the major and that class. In sum, not all Black engineers faced challenges joining study groups or working on group projects.

The majority of the students I interviewed, however, mentioned that they tended to study by themselves. Others, who had difficulty making friends, still made do. Kenya, for example, about the difficulty of joining study groups, said, "I'm not complaining. You get through it. Like I said, it's an advantage, but it's not necessary." Anthony also noted the nature of studying with friends and getting distracted as a reason he chose to work by himself. Beyond concentration, however, he also alluded to the dearth of Black students within Caldwell as another possible reason for Black engineers working by themselves:

> There's not many of us in most of our majors anyways. There's not always a lot of people to ask for help, so we've kind of learned to study well by ourselves. We have our study nights, too, so . . . but even then, you won't see a lot of NSBE people at those either. So maybe it's something just having to do with studying well by yourself. 'Cause you kind of have to know how to do that well, as well as studying with other people.

Anthony alluded to the objective reality of Black Caldwell students having few people of the same race in their engineering classes and the resulting culture adopted by many Black engineers—an inclination to study in isolation. The formula for study habits, as I demonstrated, is not the same for all students. It also depends on where the student is from, what type of high school they attended, as well as their major. Study habits also depend on exercising agency in different ways—from Robert going out of his way to put his classmates at ease to Ayana doing group projects by herself to save herself the psychological strain of working with people who disrespected her.

CHEATING AND COLLABORATION IN CALDWELL

Study groups also afforded something else—an avenue to engage in other, perhaps more unorthodox and discrete academic practices. In other words, study groups were resources for cheating or extensive collaboration. College students of all races likely engage in academic practices that would frighten professors or violate academic honor codes. Further, the line between cheating and collaboration can be hazy, especially within engineering. Access to cheating, or ethically compromising collaboration, emerged as a reoccurring theme.

I originally did not have any questions in my interview protocol about academic dishonesty, but I heard from a Black Caldwell graduate student that groups of Asian students would cheat on tests. I broached the topic hesitantly with Ayana, saying, "Someone told me that, and I don't know if this is a grad school type thing or whatever, but that a lot folks cheat or whatever. Is there—" "There's rampant cheating in Caldwell. That's how you pass your classes," Ayana said, cutting me off. "Really?" I asked. "I swear to God."

I asked if Black students cheated. She clarified:

Yeah, but it's hard to cheat when you do [the exams] by yourself. For example, how can I cheat in a class if I'm sitting by myself in the exam? Or, if I didn't get five years' worth of the professor's exams? We already have a natural disadvantage because of the fact that we don't have that type of support system.

Referring to two Black students who greeted us earlier in our interview she continued, "They just came out of [a foundational engineering class]. I took that class two years ago. They have my stuff, and they have Nina's stuff." To be clear, the point here is not that Black students want to cheat—students, regardless of race, collaborate in orthodox ways. Rather, the point is that nonblack students, specifically racial groups with larger representation, have easier access to unorthodox collaboration and study resources. In other words, nonblack students often have an unfair advantage and are literally cheating, working together, while Black students typically have to play by the rules and work by themselves. As students pointed out, they do not receive a gold star or award for playing by the rules. Professors and job recruiters do not see how a student earned a grade, they just see an A and an excellent student, or a C and a student having a difficult time.

Maahka, who was joining the engineering fraternity for her major, knew she would have access to the fraternity's test bank once she became a full member. In the meantime, she struggled finding old exams to study. In one instance, she asked a few classmates if they had older exams, and was surprised to see that the person who finally emailed her an old exam received it from someone she considered a friend: "I looked at the e-mail. It's literally like a [nonblack] friend that I see three times or five times a week who sent the e-mail to another person. So you really have to beg sometimes." I asked why her friend did not initially send her the exam and Maahka struggled to come up with an explanation, saying, "They don't give it to you like unless you . . . I guess they . . . I don't know, maybe they just cross you out?" Maahka did not offer a reason for why they crossed her out, but it is worth noting that she was the only Black person in her major in her class.

Using old tests is a rampant practice. While not necessarily a form of cheating, some students have access to more exams, and older exams, for the same course. Access to more study materials and potentially similar exam questions can give an unfair advantage to students. Continuing her explanation, Ayana said, "They're cheating when you go to the exam room, and I've done it sometimes. By any means necessary. I'm like, 'I'm really gonna fail this exam today. Maybe I should put a little extra something in my notes.' Whatever." She reiterated, "There is rampant cheating, which is why the White people sit with the White people. And the Asians sit where the Asians sit. And the Indian students sit with the Indian students." Recall the words of the professor at the beginning of the chapter who noted that students tend to group with their race: "Usually Chinese group among Chinese . . . White group among White . . ." The reason Ayana posed for the racial grouping, however, was related to hoarding study resources and the potential to collaborate on tests without fear of a classmate reporting them.

Chantelle, a computer science major from the Caribbean, provided an example of the hazy line between collaboration and cheating, the difficulty of working across racial lines, and the limitation of grouping women's experiences in STEM together. Computer science has been likened to a clubhouse dominated by men where women are the outsiders (Margolis and Fisher 2002). Yet, as Chantelle shows, White women and nonblack women of color likewise distance themselves from Black women in the computing space. Intersectionality is needed to specify the unique experience of not just women of color, but Black women in particular (Charleston et al. 2014; Gaston, Gayles, and Smith 2018). In what follows, I describe her tumultuous experiences with nonblack women of color in her class.

Chantelle learned that trust is hard to come by in her major. Outside of the four other NSBE members, all men, who also majored in a CS-related concentration and were in similar classes, she had two other people, White and Asian, with whom she studies and trusts. She previously worked with two additional people, both Asian women, but had to "cut them off." One girl, Mary, thought her boyfriend liked Chantelle. "She just asked me if I liked her boyfriend back. And I'm like, 'Dude, no.' So I'm like, really? Girl code 101," Chantelle laughed, shaking her head. Rather than question her boyfriend, Mary had questioned Chantelle, implicitly finding fault in Chantelle's presence rather than Mary's relationship with her boyfriend. Mary's thought process was likely shaped by the racist and sexist controlling image of Black women as hypersexual beings (Harris-Perry 2011). In Mary's mind, Chantelle's proximity to her boyfriend was a lingering threat to her romantic relationship. The other infraction was related to academics.

Chantelle explained that she would often help Allie with work. When Chantelle needed help with an assignment, however, Allie was reluctant to offer help. "So instead of her helping me out herself, she sent me a copy of someone else's work," she said. "She's Asian, so she gets help from her Asian friends." Allie was able to figure out her computer programming assignment, but rather than send Chantelle a copy of her program, she sent a copy of one of her Asian friends' work, saying, " 'I'm not sure if this is even right. So yeah, see if you can figure it out from there.' " Their friendship, if it ever truly existed, was over. "That's all I needed to know," Chantelle said. I asked how Allie even had access to her friend's program, or code. After talking to a few computer science professors and advisors, I knew that cheating in computer science could be detected with software. Chantelle told me what she knew about some Asian groups' study techniques:

> You can't use exactly someone else's code. But at least, most of the time, what they do, what I found out is what they do in the Asian community, they work in groups, and some codes are wrong, some are right. So they figure it out. They figure out the right way and they try to alter it a bit.

Reliving the event as she recounted it for me, she continued, "If I look out for you, I expect you to look out for me. If I need your help, don't turn around and make up a lie like other CS students, you know what I mean?"

I pushed, asking if Black CS students studied in the same way. She shook her head, saying, "We more so talk about them, the concepts. And yeah, we look at each other's code. So it's like, 'Okay, for this block, this is what I did.' [or] 'I think you need to add this.'" Their method of studying together was "more like learning . . . and trying to help each other out," she argued. While she demonstrated how the Black CS students worked together in a different, perhaps more ethical, way, she also acknowledged the intrinsic collaborative nature of CS and programming:

> You need an extra set of eyes when you're working on code. 'Cause sometimes the mistake is in front of you but you can't see it, you've been staring at it for so long. And someone else comes by and it's like, "Oh, it's because you missed some semicolon."

Grace majors in math and computer science, and also witnessed rampant cheating. Her classmates, she feels, already seem like they have a better handle on the course material and are reluctant to help her: "Half of the class is like friends and they're sitting together. You'll try to ask them if they can explain something and they don't really . . . it's frustrating." She pointed to a recent occurrence, giving me an example of cheating saying, "The other day we had a quiz and I didn't know shit on it. I didn't know a damn thing. I was gonna take the L."[2] To add insult to injury she saw six people cheating, "Sharing papers. Speaking their language. Asian guys." Staring into the distance, her voice quivered, "At first I'm confused . . . just frustrated. I felt like really dumb in this class. I don't know this information as well as I could, and all of these other people clearly know it 'cause they're doing better on these quizzes." She continued, with disgust and incredulity in her voice, "So I'm sitting here feeling bad about myself and you cheat."

Her computer science exams were even worse. Held in lecture halls, auditoriums that can seat two hundred people, computer science exams were rife with dishonest academic conduct. Grace described how people cheat, saying, "They just have their sheets on the floor and whisper to each other. I can't even do that. I have no one to do that with." Even if Grace wanted to partake in the same practices, she could not. As a junior, she only recently made her first friend, in her graduating computer science class, "a nice Filipina girl." More than academic dishonesty, other students' cheating practices have tangible impacts on those who do not cheat. As Grace pointed out, "You're messing my grade up, you're fuckin with my curve."

Alexis, an industrial and systems engineer, never cheated on an exam. However, she shared a story about someone cheating off of her work:

One time, I felt cheated because there was this Indian guy sitting next to me. He was trying to copy off my test. I literally got up and moved across the room, just because I feel like the professor was gonna say I was the one cheating off of his test instead.

This tells us both about how she thinks professors view her as a Black woman in addition to the standards she holds for herself, likely because of the hypervisible nature of her identity in engineering classes. Even when practicing academic integrity, her position as the only Black woman in class, she believed, rendered her vulnerable to suspicion of academic dishonesty.

Tension between Expecting and Experiencing Racism

A tension also exists between the extent to which one experiences racism and to which one expects racism. At times, Nubia and other students such as Alexis might notice microaggressions, or a differential experience based on their racial identity, but credit little significance to such actions. Other students, Nubia included, simply do not notice a difference in experience. Funke, for example, concerning how race has impacted her Caldwell experience, said, "I haven't seen [race] impact me directly, but like maybe it's happening under the scenes and I can't see it. . . . I haven't seen any racial aggression yet." Nubia was often oblivious to seemingly racialized assaults or slights. She has pride in her racial identity as well as her scientist identity. A biomedical engineering major, she joked with me once, saying she was probably the first person in her lab to have dreadlocks. While working on her applications to neuroscience PhD programs, she asked for my advice about writing a diversity statement. I assumed she wanted help brainstorming ways of writing the statement. However, I was wrong in my assumption. After I had explained my thought process of how I wrote a diversity statement, she said:

My problem is different. I actually don't want to write it. I don't want them to accept me just because I'm Black. Like, I don't want to be wondering why they accepted me, like, is it because I'm a good scientist or because I'm Black?

She told me she did not want to have that thought lingering in the back of her head if she were accepted.

Her intense focus on science and being a scientist has shaped how, if at all, she perceives or interprets racial slights. She attended a predominantly Asian, STEM-oriented high school. I asked her if it was difficult being one of the few Black women, and she replied:

> No. I've talked to other Black students who went to that school who found it difficult sometimes. But the reason that it didn't bother me was because I was too focused on other things to really notice any of the other problems that they had.

She was focused on "being a scientist," she explained later. I asked if she experienced WSU in a similar manner, and she explained that, although she was still very focused, she is more aware of her race:

> I was sitting with a few other people in NSBE talking about the problems that they had while they were here and I realized that I had actually experienced some of those things, except I hadn't really attached the same significance to it that they did. . . . Like, no one ever initiating conversation. That had never been something that I considered a problem until I realized that that's not applied to the whole group as well.

Nubia generally views the racial climate as positive in Caldwell. Her perspective is shaped by her laser-like focus on being a scientist. Her summative point, however, speaks to the different ways Black engineers experience the campus racial climate: "People can interpret the same actions totally differently. Things that others might see as rejection, I might write them off, but it's still actually an issue."

Similarly, while some Black engineers took offense for people not expecting them to major in engineering, others did not. Gary, for example, found it entertaining: "When people ask your major, they're not expecting someone like me to say mechanical engineering. But that's part of the fun, I get to see the 'Oh.'" Other students, in similar situations, however, expressed their hurt or anger of someone seeming surprised by their major.

Students who had friends of the same race and rarely interacted across racial lines in Caldwell also had positive views of the racial climate. In a way, their NSBE and/or Black community membership could shelter them from some negative racialized encounters. Payton, for example, said that race had not negatively impacted her time in Caldwell:

I feel like maybe if I collaborated with more people I would experience more, just 'cause like you know, through personal interaction you can see true colors. But I don't think so. Like not from my professors, from my peers, or anything. Yeah, but that's probably because I don't talk to them enough.

Surrounding oneself with Black students and engaging with the Black and/or NSBE communities, however, could not completely shelter students from racial slights or assaults. Kenya, for example, reiterated the importance of NSBE, saying she expected to be the only one in the class, "You know you have NSBE to stand on, but in your classes NSBE isn't there with you."

Students' opinions on the campus racial climate, I believe, were also shaped by a racial realist ideology, or the belief that racism is endemic to society and will never disappear. While students did not refer to the Critical Race concept of racial realism in name, they seemed to hold a belief that racism was permanent. With this assumption of racism, they were able to view Caldwell as positive, or doing the best it could. By mediating their expectations of the university, the department, and society in general, they were relieved of some of the psychological stress of wondering why their experiences were different in Caldwell.

Recall how Thomas said, almost as a truism, that as a Black person he has to work harder than people of other races. While unfair, he accepted a racial realist logic—because society is racist and unfair, he will have to work harder than other races to achieve. Ayana, relatedly, could not identify the types of racial microaggressions she dealt with, saying, "Maybe it's 'cause I'm used to it . . . I also expect a level of microaggression in the classroom." Ayana did not doubt the prevalence of microaggressions or racism; rather—either subconsciously or consciously—she did not seem to recognize racist slights as noteworthy. Microaggressions became mundane.

Kenya also adopted a clear racial realist perspective of her experience in Caldwell. When I asked her how, if at all, she dealt with racial microaggressions, she replied, "That's in the world." Being the only one, and a "double minority" of being a Black woman, she explained can be very challenging: "Like it takes a lot of . . . how do I put it? It takes a lot of foundation within yourself, and a lot of confidence, understanding, and belief in that what you're doing is actually possible to accomplish." Kenya's take on dealing with a negative campus racial climate, microaggressions, and only-ness, has an air of racial realism, accepting racism as a fact:

I feel like I've come to realize that even though it definitely exists, whether it's microaggressions or stereotyping, they exist. . . . And they're not right, of course. We know that. We can see that. But like I said, that's the world. As we work towards fixing it and reshaping these stereotypes, we just have to. . . . Me, in general, just . . . trying to be successful and trying to shake up those stereotypes, etc. . . . I feel like they exist in Caldwell, in the world, everywhere, but you just know it, you move forward, and you push through them and on the way work on changing it.

For students of the severe minority in classes, a racial realist perspective can serve as a coping mechanism and a way of life. Learning to shrug off racial slights or assaults is a matter of course when one has hours of studying to do to prep for classes. Perhaps this perspective allows them to view the racial climate in the engineering school as mainly positive or neutral. I wondered how beneficial it would be for Black engineers in my sample to be able to name, identify, and understand racial microaggressions that they encounter on a daily basis. The majority of the engineers I spoke with, if they recognized microaggressions in the classroom in Caldwell, adopted a similar approach as Kenya.

Study Days

The campus is slow during the week before exams. Libraries, study lounges, and classrooms are full of people studying. Without classes, campus feels empty. The usual rush that happens around ten to the hour, when classes let out, is gone. Students wear study attire such as basketball shorts, flip-flops, and sweatshirts. Making the most of the weather at the cusp of summer and their relaxed schedules, some students were on the campus quad bumping volleyballs to each other, tossing footballs, or lying in hammocks between trees. I walked past the frolicking students to the NSBE study session in a humanities building, Room 214.

The room holds thirty-eight desks, most of them unoccupied. Seven, mostly full, pizza boxes are resting on tables in one corner. "NSBE FINAL STUDY SESSION," was written in chalk in large letters, nearly covering the entire blackboard. In smaller letters, between the "final" and "study," read, "Time: 10am-The day we die. We don't stop." Under the somber ending time, were the ghostly chalk remnants of an "11PM." "Thomas, did you do that?" Robert asked. Thomas, wearing a White hat with the NSBE symbol and WSU basketball shorts, looked up from his computer only to make eye contact with Robert and nod with a closed lip smile, before focusing again on his work.

Grace, Robert, Payton, Thomas, and Thomas's girlfriend, an Asian American woman, were in the room. Robert made sure to let everyone know that he saw Grace holding a guy's hand the past weekend. Grace's eyes squinted behind her black framed glasses, annoyed, before she hunched over her laptop again, studying for her statistics exam. She wore a hoodie on her head, and blanket on her legs, fully prepared to study in the near-uncomfortably cold air conditioned room. Payton complained about the cold but would not go home. "I'm here now, and if I go home, I'm sleeping."

NSBE members came in and out—some to say hi, some to study, and most to grab a slice of pizza. Most of the time, folks were studying, mainly by themselves, but a few times students asked for help. "Hey, Thomas. What's extrapolation? It's for business statistics," Payton said. Thomas, Robert, and Grace converged by Payton's desk to help.

Anthony walked in during the afternoon wearing a navy NSBE shirt and track pants. Thomas broke his concentration to start talking trash about Anthony, "Boy, why you look like your hair never had waves though." We all laughed. Waves, after all, required a lot of work and can only be achieved by near constant brushing. I joked that waves were a sensitive topic for me because I never had waves.

Bianca walked in, "How are you all studying if you're yelling?" "How you gonna come in with all that?" Grace retorted. Bianca eyed the pizza. Robert caught her too, "Daaaamn," he said, stretching the word for added affect, "Hungry, hungry, hippo." "Whatever," Bianca replied. Laurie soon walked in wearing a small white T-shirt with writing on it in permanent marker. Payton laughed, "Is that like a T-shirt from elementary school or something?" Laurie explained that she had CSA, Caldwell Student Ambassador, training and the outgoing CSA members wrote notes on their shirts. Payton asked how many Black people were in CSA. "One and a half. Me and Nina. Nina's the half." Everyone laughed. I said, "Oh, no Black men?" Payton and Laurie agreed that Dajuan could have gotten the position but that he would not apply because it would be "too many Caucasians for him."

Picking up a slice of pizza, Laurie said that the rest of the CSA members were going to get dinner together, but she needed to study.

Grace commented, "Nina still went, huh?" Laurie nodded in an affirmative. "She's a finesser. She's buddy buddy with all of her professors . . . they aren't going to ruin her life," Robert said, as if pardoning Nina for not studying like the rest of them in the room.

The day was a mix of studying and talking. Intermittently someone would spark conversation and provide an organic study break for everyone. During a later conversation, Payton mentioned that she was taking twenty-one credits next semester. I heard gasps. She said she hates Caldwell and is just "trying to power through." "Don't kill yourself trying to power through," Robert cautioned with a chuckle at the end to lighten his somber statement. Living true to his self-appointed title of "Dumbledore of NSBE,"[3] he provided his wisdom, adding, "Also, think about your GPA. You can have a GPA of two-point-five or take an extra semester and have a three-something."

Somehow we got into a conversation about the Netflix series, *Dear White People*. I only saw one episode and said that I did not find it realistic. I was referring to a scene where a White guy was angry he could not say "nigga" in a rap song playing at a party. "I just can't imagine that happening," I said. Payton and Grace disagreed, explaining their experiences of White students saying the n-word in songs around them. "It's a real thing," Grace said.

I took the opportunity to ask everyone in the room how they felt about using the n-word. Grace only recently starting using the word in college. "I think, just being around people who said it so frequently when I got to college, it desensitized it. I use it as a colorful decoration to my language now." Payton said, "I use it all the time because it's my word. And my mom says it a lot." Erving felt like we, as in Black people, cannot be upset about other people using the n-word if we say it so often. Bianca felt similarly, "I feel like either everyone uses it, or no one uses it." Robert emphasized the relational aspect of the word saying, "It's about context sometimes though . . . like would you want someone else calling your mom, mom?" Anthony agreed, "Like you have to have a connection to it."

That evening, a group of us were still in the classroom, including Grace, Payton, Anthony, Thomas, Robert, Bianca, Laurie, and Maahka. Erving had left to study with his girlfriend in a neighboring classroom. Laurie was in and out of the room. "Why you keep leaving us? We not good enough for you?" Robert asked. "No I just need to study," Laurie said in a rushed tone. "So we not studying?" Payton asked. Robert emphasized

Payton's point, motioning with both hands in an exaggerated motion to his work. "I mean, they're studying for the same class I am so . . . I might come back," Laurie replied. She did end up coming back later because, as she explained, "I was just helping people and answering questions. But like, I need to actually study." In her predominantly White and Asian study group, she felt like she was the one who was being held back.

As time progressed, the studying got more relaxed. Robert hooked up a PlayStation 4 to play FIFA. Anthony played music on his portable, Bluetooth speaker box. Jasmine was on the phone with her father for at least an hour. She used her headphones to keep her hands free. She alternated between watching Thomas, Robert, or Anthony play FIFA and studying and talking to her dad. "Put it in your book, Antar. Jasmine loves her father very much," she said in third person. Even though she was not actively talking to him, her dad on the other line gave her comfort while she worked on her project.

While playing FIFA against Thomas, and losing, Anthony, putting extra bass in his voice, rapped along part of a J. Cole song, "Deja Vu," that seemed antithetical to his mild-mannered personality and suburban background. It was too much for Jasmine who cracked up, "You said that with your soul!" "This your song, huh?" Payton added. Anthony smiled explaining his fandom of J. Cole.

For dinner, we all shared chicken wings. Jasmine only ate the fries and carrots. "Are you a real live vegetarian?" Payton asked. "Like a whole vegetarian?" Laurie asked, laughing at the new way of using "whole" as slang. Jasmine told them she was a pescatarian. At one point, we were all standing, eating wings. Referring to the scene of Black folk eating chicken, Payton commented, "We're like the stereotype." I noticed Anthony throwing a wing away with too much meat left on the bone. Robert also caught this violation, "Nigga, you better finish that! All that meat left!" "It's in the trash now," Anthony shrugged. "Shit, reach back in," Robert responded. We all shared a laugh.

A little after 10 p.m. a South Asian man walked in the room looking at Robert and Thomas playing FIFA, saying, "Yo, no lie, I'd put money on a game right now, if you're down." "This sounds like a hustle," Robert said. A White guy wearing a red hat and shorts accompanied the South Asian guy and said, "Yeah, he's honestly not good. He's all talk." Thomas, speaking with the same certainty he would have used to talk about the weather, said, "Definitely a hustle." The new guys asked if they could join us studying, and we obliged.

"You putting this in your book?" Jasmine whispered to me, "Gentrification." Two White women came in to join the newcomers about twenty minutes later. They sat on the opposite side of the room. Without asking, the White man erased "NSBE" on the blackboard to write out a number tree.

"This is why Thomas stays up all night," Laurie said, as Thomas danced. "Robert, may I borrow you?" Jasmine asked. Robert said, "Sure," while doing almost a choreographed dance with Thomas to the music playing. Anthony, Thomas, and Robert went over to help Jasmine. Thomas and Robert continued dancing as they tried to figure it out.

"It's hot as fuck," Robert said. "Cuz you was killing 'em with the moves. Chris Breezy with the dance moves." Jasmine laughed. Robert finally settled down to help, saying, "Man, I need some deodorant," then grabbed the chalk, looking at Jasmine's computer screen and saying, "Yeah this is kinda easy."

Robert, Thomas, and Jasmine crowded the blackboard putting up complex equations that looked like hieroglyphics to me, but looked like probability equations to them. They all spoke in math speak, to the point where Jasmine could better comprehend the concept, scrawling numbers and variables on the board all the while. Between his words of advice and thoughts on the project, Thomas continued to dance to the rap music.

Around 11:30 p.m., life seemed to imitate art as the coincidental nature of the day reached its zenith. Robert and Thomas walked over to talk to the group that asked to come into the room, all White and one South Asian. The two men showed Thomas and Robert something on the computer screen laughing. I started to walk over to see the commotion. Robert laughed questioningly, "You're going to take out the n-word right?" and looked at Thomas out the corner of his eye. "Yeah, definitely," the South Asian guy said. "Oh, of course bro," the White guy added. To Thomas, Robert said, "Alright, let's rap it but take out 'nigga.'" The newcomers put on an instrumental of a popular song and Thomas and Robert rapped the lyrics, "All day, them HITTAS gon splay. All day, them HITTAS gone splay."

Thomas did not get the memo the first time and said "niggas" instead of the "hittas" that Robert was substituting. Robert said "hittas" loudly and glared at Thomas. The rest of the rap were allusions to a Computer Science (CS) class. I was shocked to see that the word document with the seven lines on it actually held the word *nigga* on two of them. Robert ended up freestyling a few more lyrics of his own before leaving. I asked him what it was about and Robert said, "They're taking CS 104, so they're probably freshman."

Robert's freestyling was not limited to the lines he rapped over the instrumental. He handled the interaction with the nonblack students with grace—mirroring an emcee, improvising, moving with and directing the crowd, all while following a strict, unforgiving beat. Such microaggressions, understandably, often leave those on the receiving end in shock, unable to utter a response (Solórzano et al. 2000). Many, myself included, probably would have tripped up in his position, unable to find the beat, that is, the right words and a constructive response. Robert's freestyled response of managing the situation, correcting his nonblack peers, and even using humor at the end demanded creativity and poise. His response, however creative, could only have been the result of practice in racist encounters. While I admired his quick response to the situation, I was enraged and saddened by thinking of a world that socialized him to be well-practiced in responding to racism.

Walking out of the room, I still could not believe the two men had the nerve to show their written lyrics with the the n-word on it to Black men. I said, "Maybe they just copied the lyrics and didn't change that yet?" Robert side-eyed me saying, "Eh, everything else had references to CS, so . . . I mean that's why I asked if they were going to change it. You gotta say something about that stuff. If you don't, they're going to think it's cool." We changed the subject and they parted ways. Payton, Laurie, and Jasmine went to a midnight brunch in one of the cafeterias. I was still shocked at the occurrence, and so was Robert, who said, "We were JUST talking about this." I was amazed by his composure. He checked them, laughed, lightened the mood, and kept it moving. I also made sure to text Grace the next day, saying the scene in *Dear White People* basically just happened only a few hours after our discussion.

As Grace said, it happens. It happened before my eyes. The students, as far as I know, were not very troubled and moved on to discussing what swag they got from job interviews. No complaints were filed with student affairs. No blogs were written. No anonymous submissions to bias reporting. We simply shared a collective experience with a quick debrief. I mention our collective reactions neither to make light of the situation nor to suggest that this infraction was simply brushed off by myself or NSBE members. To the contrary, I use our reactions, or lack thereof, to show the violent mundanity of antiblackness.

NSBE went through the proper channels to schedule a room during exam period, a time when study space is scarce. After welcoming the nonblack students into their space, NSBE was repaid with an unasked erasure of their signage on the chalkboard and the shock of learning that the visitors were making a song peppered with the n-word. One might call the actions of the nonblack students microaggressions. One might incorrectly suggest that NSBE, and myself, were simply being too sensitive. These interactions wear away on Black people's spirits (Love 2016; Pierce et al. 1977; Smith et al. 2011; Quaye et al. 2020).

After the entrance of nonblack students, what started as an affirming, joyous Black place turned into a site of Black suffering (Dumas 2014). Michael Dumas (2014) uses Pierre Bourdieu's concept of "la petite misère" to articulate everyday Black suffering, denoting "a broader range of structural and cultural assaults that make everyday living difficult for populations living under certain conditions" (6). Suffering is not only the extraordinary, vulgar crimes and insults of antiblackness, Dumas points out, but also the microaggressions and difficult to describe everyday suffering Black people experience. In other words, suffering is not just being called the n-word, suffering is also seeing nonblack students, after welcoming them into your space, write and joke about using the n-word in a song.

Yet this room, this study session, should not be singularly understood as a site of suffering. Room 214 in the humanities building was also a site of resistance led by Robert. Room 214 was a site of grace and kindness extended by NSBE members to their nonblack peers. It was a site of collective struggle and productivity. For a few hours, Room 214 was a Black place—a site of joy. The racial conflict is necessary to highlight and understand, but consider what is missed when Black suffering, alone, takes center stage. One can easily miss the life, agency, and expansiveness of the social reality experienced by Black Caldwell students.

The Caldwell Social World: In Summary

Black engineers often face unique, racialized obstacles in traversing the field of Caldwell. Some Black engineers report dealing with microaggressions, while others do not. Some Black engineers have study partners and working groups for their classes. Others do not. The varying perceptions and experiences are shaped by multiple factors, including personal background, the culture of a major, as well as attitudes toward racist slights or other byproducts of racism.

How students experience Caldwell is also informed by their proximity to and relationships with other students. Recall how some students fostered a sense of engagement within the NSBE and/or Black communities but not necessarily with the Caldwell community. Proximity also relates to microaggressions and the racial climate. Olivia, who was in closer proximity with Latinx students, reported that most of the racial slights and assaults she encountered came from Latinx students. Grace, who was in close proximity with Asians, experienced the most microaggressions from Asians, and so on. This section also highlights the unique way the campus climate in an engineering school is felt. Students' experiences are very much shaped by their majors and the culture of their major. Given the unique nature of engineering students' experiences in college, scholars might consider new ways of analyzing campus racial climate with engineers in mind.

THE BOUNDARY OF ANTIBLACKNESS

Nonblack students' antiblackness served as a boundary to participants' access to peer collaboration and a greater connection to Caldwell. Antiblackness in the classroom, for many students, was not a possibility—it was a fact. Such racial realism, or the belief that racism is permanent, was not a defeatist logic; rather, racial realism was a knowledge of the worlds they inhabited and traversed. Consider the words of Kenya concerning her approach to dealing with racism: "You just know it, you move forward, and you push through them and on the way work on changing it." Her words are strikingly similar to advice that the character Baby Suggs, in Toni Morrison's (1987) *Beloved*, gave Denver concerning navigating a world full of antiblack terrorism:[4]

> *"But you said there was no defense."*

> *"There ain't."*

> *"Then what do I do?"*

> *"Know it, and go on out the yard. Go on."* (244)

For students with a racial realist logic, such as Kenya, they know it—the possibility of racial slights, their hypervisibility, the legacy of racism—and they move through campus and foster a sense of engagement despite such conditions.

The resilience of participants despite such conditions, however, should not distract one from the very real oppression they faced. Caldwell, and group work in particular, can become a site of Black suffering (Dumas 2014). As a researcher, and as a Black man who attended a HWI himself, I could not shake the images of these students as they recounted instances of antiblackness. I recall the misty eyes and tears escaping eyelids, the shrugs, the hollow laughter, the shaking heads, the calloused indifference, the worn-down apathy, and the varied looks between confusion, sadness, and rage. Consider Ayana, who stated that she expects "a level of micro-aggression in the classroom." Or Kenya and Alexis who noted the sick feeling of knowing that they would be picked last for group work. Imagine how it feels to be presumed incompetent in study groups or in the classroom for no reason other than your identity. While not the totality of their experiences, participants often experienced Caldwell spaces as sites of Black suffering.

How students navigate Caldwell is shaped by their racial realism, reactions to antiblackness, and gendered racism. This chapter builds upon Ebony McGee and Danny Martin's (2011) work on stereotype management, or how Black engineering students purposefully respond to racial bias and stereotype threat. Working alone, for example, might be considered an example of stereotype management. Yet, participants faced more than stereotypes. Students worked alone and even achieved in response to out-right antiblackness—to nonblack classmates shunning them, picking them last, verbally assaulting them, taking credit for their work, and showing outward disrespect.

Many Black students mentioned studying alone, but Black women seemed to have the least access to peer collaboration. They shared the most examples of nonblack students alienating them in classes and in groups. Black women expressed that they felt like they were picked last for group work, felt as if nonblack peers treated them as if they were not intelligent, and provided examples of standoffish, hostile behavior from nonblack peers. Maahka felt like her peers "crossed her out." Nubia displayed a supreme focus on becoming a scientist. Ayana and Jasmine did group work individually so as to not deal with antiblack peers. Hanna advocated for herself when her group insulted her and attempted to take credit for her work. Black women, depending on their major in Caldwell, experienced a unique gendered antiblack racism.

Black women, however, were not passive victims—they were agentic, using a variety of strategies to cope with and resist gendered racism in Caldwell. Lewis and colleagues (2013), in their study of Black women's experiences coping with microaggressions in higher education, found that Black women use various "strategies as a form of self-protective coping to shield themselves from the cumulative negative effect of these subtle microaggression experiences" (68). As the authors point out, supposed inaction is not passive coping or avoidance. Participants who opted to work by themselves, who used their voice to set the record straight with professors and peers, who leaned on their Black peers instead of the nonblack majority, or who let their silence speak in response to racism were deliberate in their responses. Such strategies prioritize one's peace while simultaneously resisting and/or exiting toxic antiblack sexist group environments.

The will and fortitude of Black students, especially Black women, to persist in the face of such antiblackness is remarkable. To lionize the incredible effort, creativity, fortitude, and brilliance of Black Caldwell students without also decrying inequitable conditions in Caldwell, however, would be wrongheaded, only showing part of the story. The game is rigged. Nonblack Caldwell students have more resources, alienate Black students from study groups, and even cheat during exams and assignments. The odds stacked against Black students are considerable and manifestations of antiblackness. A school or class that accepts such inequities can only be understood as antiblack.

9

Nina's Story

Nina is a leader and is confident. Her statements sometimes end with a, "right?" almost precluding disagreement with her point. Nina's proficiency as an engineer, her creativity, leadership, and dedication resulted in a full-time job offer from a big tech company at the end of her summer as a rising senior. Some of her success, she believes, is from her ability to code-switch, or change her behaviors, presentation, and/or speech in a specific context (De Fina 2007). Micere Keels's (2020) work on campus counterspaces similarly shows how students code-switch depending on the cultural context both on and off campus. Code-switching requires contorting oneself, muting certain aspects of identity and altering others, such as speech, so as to be more accepted in the given context. Nina was able to show, beyond engineering knowledge, that she could adjust socially to the company's culture.

"So, I think I've mastered the code-switching shit," Nina laughed, recounting an experience she had in Japan while interning for the tech company during the summer. She was referring to her ability to associate comfortably with her Black peers as well as nonblack executives. "Especially because I'm biracial. Code-switching comes natural to me," she continued, before updating me on her experience with her colleagues. Similar to her mastery of code-switching, Nina moves between worlds with ease. Nina is an example of a student who is engaged with both the NSBE and Caldwell communities. Her peers playfully describe her as "so Caldwell," because of her heavy involvement in the engineering school. Nina's story, however, shows how involvement does not always grant one acceptance from nonblack peers.

Nina was born in Virginia. Her mom is Black and her dad is White. The first to graduate from college on her side, Nina's mom graduated from college when Nina was little. Her dad, however, did not graduate but joined the military. She describes her upbringing as upper-middle class. Despite her background, Nina said, "It's not like I grew up in an environment where college was heavily emphasized or anything like that." Her trajectory, interests, and socioeconomic status changed when her family moved to a military base in California. Describing the city where she grew up, she said, "It was just like millionaires. . . . I really felt uncomfortable in school, but that's where I saw this whole college thing . . . and was exposed to other areas and as a female student being exposed to the Society of Women Engineers."

Faith and good works come to mind when thinking of Nina. Her parents ran the Sunday school at the church they attended. Her mom attributes Nina's success as an engineer to "having God's favor." Similarly, when telling folks about her prior internship opportunities and full-time offer at a big tech company, she mentions that she is "blessed" or "really fortunate." Yet, her good fortune and faith is met with an impressive work ethic.

Nina's parents are "go-getters." When other churchgoers said "no" to the pastor, her parents would say "yes." She remembered an occasion when their pastor, about her parents, said, " 'Everyone else used to say this can't be done and y'all just do it. They hem and holla, but y'all just do it.' " She adopted a similar work ethic and holds high standards for herself and her peers. When others fail to meet her expectations, she doubles down, doing more work herself, leading by example. During the e-board retreat with the outgoing and incoming e-boards, Nina, the incoming president, walked around the conference room during a break, throwing away other members' trash from breakfast. She did this without asking for help or making much ado about it. She is among the first to come to NSBE events and among the last to leave, doing thankless work without looking for recognition.

The Engineering School and Black Engineering Community

Caldwell held the engineering job fair during February. Twenty minutes before noon, Nina, Grace, and Johnson sat at a desk under a tent helping direct Caldwell students to the tables of different companies and answering logistical questions. Nina, who already had a summer internship lined up, only came to the career fair to volunteer with NSBE. She was dressed casually with a denim jacket. Johnson, who did not have summer plans yet, was dressed for the fair, wearing a suit with a V-neck sweater under his jacket. An NSBE pin was lodged in the lapel of his suit. He had just finished meeting representatives from two companies at their tables.

I asked why they decided to volunteer to help staff the Caldwell career fair. "We just love Caldwell that much," Johnson responded in a sarcastic manner. "Hey, some of us actually *do* love Caldwell," Nina said with a smile. "Okay, Caldwell Ambassador!" Johnson said in concession. "We get paid for participating," Grace said, answering my question. Members of Caldwell student organizations volunteered during the fair in exchange for added funding for their organizations. In other words, the more NSBE members that signed in and helped staff the fair, the more money Caldwell would deposit into NSBE's account.

"So how are you, Antar?" Nina asked me. During my response, an Asian woman asked Nina, who was wearing her black Caldwell Student Ambassador shirt, how long the companies would be out for the fair. Another student, a first-year Asian man wearing flip-flop sandals hopped off of his skateboard and asked, "This is just for engineers? Did we get an e-mail about this?" Nina engaged with two more people asking similar questions while I was present.

Logically, NSBE and Caldwell are intertwined. NSBE is a WSU-sanctioned organization within Caldwell and is connected to Caldwell institutionally through the MEO. For Nina, the two communities often overlapped. During an NSBE fundraiser, for example, I was the only person helping Nina for at least half an hour. Peeved with the lack of support from other members, she said, "I appreciate you coming out, but you shouldn't have to do this." She printed a sign for the churro sale fundraiser off of her computer, ran to the engineering school, and came back with the poster and tape. Nina did not need to sign out the tape because the woman in the Caldwell office trusted her. Nina's friend, upon hearing the story, said, "That's what happens when you sell your soul to Caldwell, I guess." They laughed.

While selling churros, she mentioned that she needed to prepare for her lab in a couple of hours. The only part she was worried about was the presentation, so she needed time to prepare. In between selling churros, texting her friends to come support NSBE and buy churros, and dancing to the music blasting from a laptop speaker, she somehow prepared for her lab. Nina, despite her many responsibilities finds time to balance them all, and even have fun in the process.

In understanding Nina's love for NSBE, it helps to understand her grandmother who grew up in rural North Carolina during the Jim Crow era. If you ask her grandmother, Nina said, segregation was fine. Black folk did not bother White folk and vice versa. Despite her grandmother's feelings Nina explained:

> She didn't have the same education and access and so, for me, that's why I'm so passionate about NSBE. When I went to [the national NSBE] conference there were just so many Black professionals who were there to give back for that cause . . . they hadn't removed themselves. Like when we're lobbying in Congress, to have these initiatives to have a certain amount of Black STEM graduates, that for me, like, is wow. That's why I do this.

Nina told me that she understands why "bougie black people" would leave the communities they were from as opposed to going back to "help it out." NSBE members, however, did not remove themselves, and operated with service to the Black community in mind. Likewise, Nina chose to maintain involvement in the Black engineering community on campus.

Nina's experience and active membership in both NSBE and Caldwell in some ways shapes how she moves in both communities. She implores other NSBE members to become more active in Caldwell, and uses her membership in Caldwell to represent NSBE in hopes of recruiting more Black engineers.

Outside of being a mechanical engineer, a Caldwell Student Ambassador, Caldwell Academic Peer Leader, e-board member and eventual president of NSBE, Nina adopted the mission of increasing the visibility of Black engineers. In the beginning of the Spring semester in the NSBE GroupMe, Nina and Charlie posted about hosting prospective students and volunteering for other events for prospective Caldwell students:

> NINA: Charlie and I can't be the only Black faces of Caldwell lol. So y'alls help is super encouraged.

> CHARLIE: This is the process of us getting more black people here. We need your help.

NINA: And on that note apply for Caldwell First-Year Coach and [Caldwell Student Ambassador] too! I'm literally the only Black face and I'm light bright as it is.

During the Spring semester, Charlie and Nina were the only Black Caldwell Student Ambassadors (CSAs). With nudging from Nina, Laurie joined CSA the following semester. Membership in CSA is selective and the application process is competitive; only twenty-six undergraduate Caldwell students are CSAs. Donning the recognizable Black polo inscribed with a white "CSA" above the area where breast pockets are located comes with responsibility. CSAs work with Caldwell Admissions staff to plan events, act as liaisons for prospective students, and help design Caldwell publications. Given their position representing the Caldwell School of Engineering's undergraduate population, CSAs meet industry representatives and school leaders.

Nina pressed students to consider applying to become ambassadors on multiple occasions prior to when the CSA applications opened. Leaving a general body meeting early, Nina, wearing her Black CSA polo, asked to make a quick announcement. Her foot propped the door open for an easy exit. She promoted CSA, answering a couple of questions about the position including GPA requirements and recommendations. "Why do you do so much?" someone jokingly asked. "She's so Caldwell," Grace commented in response. Nina shrugged the veiled compliment off, scanning the group to see if anyone else had questions. Before leaving she emphasized that CSA needs more Black people and that NSBE members should apply, saying in mild frustration, "I'm not representative of the whole fuckin' Black experience." Many of the NSBE meeting-goers laughed after her statement, including the two middle-aged Black engineering professionals who came to the meeting to promote a scholarship. Less than twenty minutes later Nina messaged the NSBE GroupMe saying, "When you realize you dropped the f-bomb in front of industry," accompanied with an embarrassed emoji.

Nina initially got involved in Caldwell because she found herself, nearing the end of her first year, unhappy, napping too often, and unproductive. She thrives off of "being busy." Charlie, one year her senior and a member of NSBE and CSA, told her she would be good as a Caldwell Ambassador. In her application to be an ambassador she stated, "I did not know any engineers." Her closest friends were in the Black community: "I only did Black things and it just really was not great academically, because there are not a lot of Black engineers—especially in my major." Nina is the only Black person in mechanical engineering in her graduating class. Through her role in CSA she represents Caldwell, meeting with incoming students and going to galas with donors. Through CSA, Nina explained, "I know the deans, I know everyone in admissions, that type of thing." CSA is also a paid position, funded by Caldwell, which is added incentive for students to join.

More than providing a community, CSA provides Nina an opportunity to meet people who are different from herself. "My friend would always tell me I don't have enough White friends . . . it was a good way to break out and meet other people," she told me. I told her that I did not have many White friends in college myself. "Maybe you should diversify yourself," she said in a playfully scolding manner. "But why?" I retorted. Caldwell students of other races, outside of the NSBE community, she explained to me, were engaging in interesting, cool activities that a lot of NSBE members were not.

Nina pointed to a friend of hers in Caldwell that was participating in the Engineering Social Entrepreneurship Challenge—a competition sponsored by a Caldwell alum that provides WSU students the opportunity to use engineering and technology innovations to develop sustainable solutions for society. Her friend used 3D printing to create sanitation cups for women in developing countries. "Not to dog the Black community, but none of the people in NSBE take advantage of those challenges, just because they are not so Caldwell," Nina continued, saying, "They're not looking for those opportunities at Caldwell."

Nina is outgoing, so joining Caldwell organizations "just fits." Because Nina is involved in Caldwell organizations, she finds herself different from other Black engineers who are "all trying to go about their business and get their degrees." She also attributed the lack of Black students in other Caldwell organizations to representation. "They just don't see anyone doing it," Nina postulated. "The other Black CSA who graduated, other than Charlie, he did not come to NSBE at all, was in a White frat, so he was not fucking with the Black community." Using the same language as Johnson, Nina describes herself as a bridge, but a bridge between the Caldwell and NSBE communities: "There is no one to like bridge that gap and I felt like I could be that person."

Despite Nina's comfort within Caldwell and her outgoing nature, she still faced a challenge in the classroom. Typically, Nina studies by herself. Only recently, in her junior year, has she started studying with other people in her major. "I'm still looking to find those groups. I'm very jealous of people who have really tight groups. You just do better," Nina told me. She lamented her lack of friends in her major, saying, "When it comes to group project time, I don't have anyone I can be like, 'Hey do you want to be in a group?' I send out a mass e-mail to everyone and then wait for replies back." She seemed to place the blame on herself, commenting, "If I'm not pushing, it's not going to happen," or "I haven't been doing a good job of, 'Let me get your number,' and let me push myself in here."

Nina's actions and other accounts suggest that her lack of a study group is not a fault of her own. People segregate into different groups based on race and Greek Letter affiliation, Nina noticed, saying:

> The Hispanic people, shit, they are tight. They study their asses off together. . . . I feel like the Asians and the Indians, they are pretty close, I think. They think they're smarter and don't want to be bothered. . . . I'll see someone in the library studying the same thing and I'll be like, "Can I get in?"

She laughed talking about her effort to push her way into groups, continuing her thought process, "Anyone who is Greek and fratty or in a sorority, they all study together." Despite her feelings of fitting in Caldwell organizations, she faced a boundary to engineering career capital in the form of study groups likely because of her identity as a Black woman.

"I feel like anytime I've been part of a study group, no one has asked me, I've always texted a few people," she admitted. Her involvement in CSA, however, has proved useful in meeting more people. She told me that she was worked into a group in a class because another CSA member, in a way, vouched for Nina. Going into her senior year, she has two people in her major with whom she can consistently study. She gave an example of the benefits of having a strong group culture by pointing to the chemical engineers: "The seniors download all the material and then send it to them, the homework answers. They'll split it up, they do very well . . . they rely on each other heavy." I asked why NSBE students could not do the same. "Because we are all different majors," she replied. Without a critical mass of students, Black students are often the only ones in their classes.

Nina, despite doing everything "right"—putting herself out there by asking to join groups and deeply involving herself in the Caldwell community—did not have steady study partners until her junior year. While I thought otherwise, Nina did not attribute her lack of a group to antiblackness. That simply is not how she moves. She is a pragmatist, focusing on how she can operate, how she can change, or how she can work harder to meet her goals. Thinking about other people's biases, pragmatically speaking, was not the best use of her time. Nina's experience silences those who might suggest that Black students simply need to work harder to integrate themselves into engineering schools to tap into these resources. Nina did just that. Yet, however "Caldwell" she was, it is worth reiterating that even as a junior with friends throughout Caldwell, nonblack peers were resistant to studying with her.

Nina is confident, intelligent, and strong. Her positive, assume-the-best attitude about her Caldwell experience and challenges joining a study group probably help make her experience manageable. Yet, as Lindsey West and colleagues (2016) demonstrate in their study of the Strong Black Woman stereotype, strength, while positive, sometimes comes at a price of emotional and mental well-being for Black women in college. Nina shrugged off the fact that for three years she struggled to find study partners—but would other Black women be able maintain their composure and smile through or perhaps even ignore it all like Nina? As Nina mentioned and showed in a number of ways, she loved Caldwell, making the best of her experience. I wondered, however, to what extent Caldwell, especially Caldwell students, loved her back.

"So is Caldwell a good place for Black students?" I once asked Nina. "I would say I think so," she replied. The negative aspect of being Black in Caldwell, however, was that, "you're not seeing Black professors, you're not seeing maybe as many Black students as you want, so you have to seek that out." At an HWI such as WSU, NSBE serves as an avenue to create such a community. Nina accepts the fact that she may be, and often is, the only Black person in her classes but reiterated, "You can get that outside. And we have a strong NSBE community right now." Caldwell is a good place for Black students, she thinks, because of the opportunities Caldwell students are afforded. Nina attributed securing her internship with a big tech company to being a WSU student, WSU's reputation, and also WSU's strong professional network.

The Black Community

Nina does not attend BSU meetings and does not have much time to attend other Black organizations' events. Despite her busy schedule, Nina is grounded within the Black community by way of her close group of friends. Her core circle of friends, affectionately called, "The Yard," are predominantly Black and active in the Black community. Black student groups also held parties at The Yard's house. Nina's friend group actually hosted Brown Sugar, the NSBE party I highlighted in chapter 5. She smiled when thinking of them, saying, "We post about each other on Instagram. We're so proud of each other. And everyone in the friend group, everyone, has an internship this summer, so it's kinda dope." In addition to living together and partying together, Nina's friends motivate each other academically. "I'm proud of that," she said.

Nina from Ayana, and Ayana from Olivia, inherited indifference bordering on irritation with the Black Student Union (BSU). Ayana and Olivia would regularly mention how BSU had snubbed NSBE or they would critique BSU's programming. In Nina's first e-board retreat, the NSBE leaders dedicated near half an hour to their relationship with BSU. Some participants recalled how BSU leadership scheduled events at the same time as some NSBE events. Nina asked, "Well who was at these meetings where they came up with these events? Who's in the room?" No one answered.

Nina argued that despite BSU's programming and past relationship, NSBE should be present, if only to represent the Black engineers at BSU. "We're invested too," she mentioned. For Nina, representation, or having someone "in the room," matters, and is tied to individual and community success. She pushed NSBE members to join more Caldwell organizations to have more Black engineering representation. She was inspired by the power of representation of Black engineering professionals at a national NSBE conference. Nina even made a point, followed by laughter, by saying, "I mean come on, Antar shouldn't be the only NSBE member going to BSU meetings, right?" Although Nina herself could not always make time to attend meetings or sometimes held personal feelings of indifference toward the BSU, she made sure NSBE was represented. During her tenure, for example, Nina required at least two NSBE members to attend BSU general body meetings. Similar to Ayana, Nina worked to increase the visibility and representation of Black engineers within all of the communities at WSU.

THE MAINSTREAM WSU COMMUNITY

10

Negotiating Racism

Is Mainstream Campus Life for White Students?

Many Black people approach the White space ambivalently, and ostensibly for instrumental reasons. When possible, they may avoid it altogether or leave it as soon as possible.

—E. Anderson, "The White Space"

Black engineering students take pride in their WSU identity. Along with other students, participants go to sporting events and cheer along with their peers. They wear WSU gear, have pride in their school colors, chant WSU's fight song, and buy into the *illusio*, or traditions and symbols (Bourdieu 1984), of the WSU social world. To an extent, all participants are involved with the WSU community given their status as WSU students. The connection to WSU, however, is complex. Most participants' sense of engagement to campus came from involvement and membership primarily in other social worlds. In other words, they were attached to WSU *by way of* the Black, Black Engineering, and/or Caldwell social worlds.

Outside of the rituals of tailgating and sporting events, fewer students fostered their engagement through what might be considered the mainstream, or dominant, WSU community. I defined participation in the mainstream WSU community simply as having membership in a student group on campus that was not explicitly centered on race. This, of course, is not to say that student groups without an explicitly racial focus, such as an a cappella group or the WSU band, are not racialized. These groups' names or goals, however, indeed give the guise of being race-neutral. White and Asian American students, who numbered the majority of WSU's student body, primarily made up this mainstream WSU community. Either through participation in historically White Greek life or alternative organizational involvement, four Black undergraduates in the study sample demonstrated strong attachment to the mainstream WSU community. In my analysis of Black campus life in relation to mainstream campus life, I began struggling with an underlying question—is mainstream campus life at predominantly or historically White institutions simply a nicer way to say White campus life?

I considered titling this book, "Campus Life." Yes, this book centers on Black campus life—why consider a title that is vague at best and mischaracterizing at worst? Perhaps by entitling this work broadly, "Campus Life," I, along with the narratives of my participants, could point out the wrongheaded impulse in higher education to name race only when the topic applies to people of color. Critical Race scholars demonstrate how the traditions and symbolism at HWIs were designed by White people for White people, and that the campus experience is racialized through and through (e.g., Allen et al. 1991; Dache and White 2016; Harper and Hurtado 2007; Patton 2016). It follows, then, that a traditional or mainstream campus experience is, to an extent, a White campus experience. Despite the knowledge that the campus experience is racialized, too often scholars avoid thorough discussions of race or avoid in-depth study of students of color in their research on campus life. In other words, I am suggesting that many titles concerning campus life or how college works might be more aptly titled "White Campus Life" or "How College Works for White Students." By neglecting to name the centrality of Whiteness in studies intended to be about campus life more generally, scholars reify Whiteness as the norm.

I hesitate to call the social world of the mainstream WSU community the "White campus community," however, because of the strong participation of Asian American students as well. Admittedly, I say the least about this campus social world, mainly because most participants had little to say about it themselves. For the purposes of this text, I refer to this social world simply as the mainstream WSU community, with the knowledge that this social world is dominated by White and Asian American students.

In order to better illustrate students' experiences in the mainstream WSU community, I first highlight Noelle's experience. She joined NSBE during her senior year but first found a place in the larger WSU community. Most of her close friends are Asian American and lived in the honors residence hall with her during her first year. When I asked if she ever experienced racism on campus she mentioned that during her freshman year, one of her friends, an Asian American woman, drunkenly admitted, " 'Oh, I know this is really bad but when you're not around, Noelle, I say the n-word.' " Noelle told her, "That's not okay." In another instance, Noelle sent a message to a different Asian student who posted as her Facebook status, "Me and my day one nigga," telling her why her use of the word was offensive.

While Noelle neither had many Black friends in her predominantly White high school nor at the beginning of her tenure at WSU, she enjoyed being around Black people. She was lukewarm about being a member of Jack and Jill, an elite, nationwide organization of Black families, but really started to enjoy being around other Black people at her first internship. Noelle thought, " 'Oh, Black people are really lit.' Then that's also why I joined NSBE too. I was like, 'Oh, I need to make Black friends.' "

Outside of NSBE, Noelle was a highly involved member of a popular women's service group on campus. While she made friends in this group she was one of the few Black women. She described the group, as "all White feminists." Noelle was particularly put off by their reaction to Trump's inauguration:

All of them were crying after Trump was elected. I was like, "I don't know why you guys are crying. It's only because this is the first time your rights have ever been taken away and been put in jeopardy." I was fine. I was like, "This is my normal life. This is just what happens." [They had] Just such a strong reaction. I was like, "And, honestly, you guys are at least upper middle class White girls."

Noelle began to understand her service organization like other Black women understood the Society of Women Engineers (SWE) chapter at WSU—a White space catering to White women under the guise of universal sisterhood.

Noelle is an illustrative example of how one might experience the WSU community. While she is comfortable in different spaces in the WSU community, she sometimes negotiates negative racialized interactions with other students. Her story, like others, is complex, and she is anchored in various communities—the NSBE community and the WSU community. As I show throughout the chapter, Noelle and other students face two main boundaries to participation in various facets of mainstream WSU life. First, Caldwell students have time restraints because of strict course loads as engineering students. Second, Black Caldwell students, in different ways, negotiate the boundary of antiblack racism they might experience in the mainstream WSU social world. In what follows, I describe two tensions Black engineers faced in the WSU community: (1) the tension between WSU life and Caldwell responsibilities, and (2) the tensions of doing diversity and negotiating racism.

Tension between WSU Life and Caldwell Responsibilities

Homecoming is a big deal at WSU. Alumni come from across the nation for the festivities. Three Black fraternities have annual tailgates, each with their own DJ, jungle juice, and food selections. Hundreds of Black WSU students, alumni, and Black students from area schools come to join in the festivities. The tailgates are on a field at the center of campus.

During WSU's homecoming festivities, Thomas was working. Without giving the festivities a second glance, Thomas, in a stoic manner—uncharacteristic of his typical jovial and joking demeanor—unlocked his bike and rode home to do more studying. Johnson stayed in the library to finish up his work while one of the biggest WSU student events transpired outside. Certainly, other engineers partook in the tailgating. The point here is, for engineers, their engineering student demands infringe upon some of the experiences that are common among WSU students. Alexis, reflecting on her WSU experience, lamented her lack of time and freedom to enjoy WSU as a member of her sorority, saying, "I love [WSU]. I just feel . . . I wish I had more time," before recounting the heavy course load she was saddled with her last two semesters. Timothy, albeit hesitantly, also noted the difference between the Caldwell experience and the general WSU experience, "No offense, but non-pre-med [or] engineering majors sometimes could have a totally different set of priorities. Not trying to generalize but . . ."

The prospective student brochure began the section on Caldwell student life with an encouraging statement: "Of course you will work hard, but that doesn't mean you can't have a real college experience at the same time. We want you to have a life!" The words from a 1957 *The West Side* issue, however, ring more true for WSU engineers' experiences: "The mastery of any particular aspect of engineering can and at times must become a 24 hour-a-day job." Given the unique structures of the engineer's course requirements, a tension existed between the engineering student experience and the experience of students with other, non-engineering majors.

Similar to the tensions in the Black community social world, the boundary of time, again played a role in students' capacity to engage in mainstream WSU life. The amount of time and energy a student can expend toward any endeavor in higher education is finite (Astin 1984). The extent to which a student can be engaged in university experiences outside of the classroom, or campus life, is shaped by students' majors. Student engagement, and campus life more broadly, may look fundamentally different for engineering students and, potentially, other STEM majors, with labs and greater course requirements to degree. For engineering students, their immense time spent studying dictated their time outside of class.

I asked Black undergraduate engineers at WSU a variant of the question, "What is unique about the engineering student experience at WSU?" The answers, although varied, most often referred to the immense amount of work Caldwell students were tasked with, as well as their limited amount of free time. "I think Caldwell students work a lot harder than the average student. [We] spend a lot of time studying, spend a lot of time doing work, and honestly a lot of classes," Charlie began. His sentiments toward being a Caldwell student as well as students in other majors were echoed by other Caldwell students in informal conversations and meetings:

> [Being in Caldwell means] Feeling that you're kinda smarter than everyone, but also feeling like you work harder than everyone. When anyone else says, "Oh my gosh, I have so much work," It's kinda like, "Fuck you," kinda thing. It's like, "No you don't."

With more work however, comes less time.

"They probably don't have a lot of sleep," William said, with a laugh, in response to my question about what Caldwell students have in common. The lack of sleep, while comical, often was cited as another commonality of engineers. Laurie, for example, described the difference between Caldwell students and students of other majors, saying,

I just think it's harder. I hear my friends, like my roommate, she annoys me so much because she gets to sleep. And she's like in bed at ten o'clock but I'm like getting home at eleven-thirty, and I still have all this stuff to do. I'm like, "Must be nice."

Saul, a first-year student who also ran track said, "I get such little sleep now, it's crazy. I went to bed at five this morning. It's bad, bro. I'm trying to get everything to work, but . . . some things are giving." Athletics and engineering did not often mix because of time constraints. Laurie played soccer seriously in high school and was even recruited by a school in her home state. While she was not recruited by WSU and had no interest in playing, she knew the engineering workload would be too much to do both, saying, "I couldn't do engineering if I played soccer here."

Testing is different for engineers. Students start taking exams only a few weeks into the semester. Johnson, jokingly said, "We shouldn't even say midterms for engineers. We'll have like three exams before a final." Thomas, who idolized the work ethic of tech moguls like Elon Musk and Mark Zuckerberg, said:

> I did a little experiment and woke up every day at eight a.m.
> It was nice. Even though I went to bed at four a.m. I would
> wake up at eight a.m., and it would be nice because I have
> the whole day.

WSU engineers are sometimes forced to be stingy with time, given their course demands. When I asked Noelle how she stayed organized, she showed me her iPhone calendar, I saw a full calendar of different colored blocks for the week, signifying her classes, groups, study time, interview prep time, and time she allotted for jogging. Looking at a sliver of a rectangle, I noticed that she only scheduled thirty minutes for our talk. She laughed and shrugged saying she needed to work. One Black engineer, who graduated a year prior to my fieldwork, was named the Caldwell Valedictorian. NSBE students spoke of him with mythic qualities. His work ethic, and time spent studying, was known by many students. Nina, for example said, "He would roll into [the twenty-four-hour library] at two a.m. and stay until six. He was learning, but he really liked what he was doing. Really invested in having a quality education, I guess." Being an engineering student at WSU was unique, and by certain measures (e.g., strict requirements for engineering degrees) more rigorous. Martin, for example, could not imagine any major experiencing the same feelings he felt as an engineering student: "Unless you're an engineer, you will never fully understand the engineer struggle because it's hard. But at times, you're just like, 'I can't do this. I want to be done with everything and I just want to quit.'"

Active involvement on campus—outside of coursework—benefits students academically and socially (e.g., Astin 1984). What are we to make of the time constraints and reality of having limited opportunities for campus involvement? These students' accounts compel scholars to examine how campus life might look different based on one's discipline and resulting outcomes.

Tensions of Doing Diversity and Negotiating Racism

Students engage in a constant process of negotiating racism through various decisions such as deciding whom to associate with, where to party, where and whom to avoid, and what groups to join. By negotiating racism, I mean, to what extent and how students deal with or manage racist encounters from nonblack peers. The theme of negotiating racism came to the fore in many participants' discussions of the mainstream WSU community, which could be understood as a White Space. The sociologist and ethnographer Elijah Anderson (2015) describes "The White Space" as predominantly White neighborhoods or spaces that Black people must often traverse. The Whiteness of higher education has been noted by critical geographers and higher education scholars alike (e.g., Cabrera et al. 2016; Gusa 2010; Inwood and Martin 2008). From the naming of campus buildings (Brasher et al. 2017) to the dominant campus culture (Allen et al. 1991), HWIs are, at least in part, White Spaces. White Spaces on WSU's campus similarly manifest in different forms.

"Are there any Black or White spaces at WSU?" I asked students this question over the summer of my fieldwork, and the answer was fairly consistent—the Black Culture Center (BCC) or Black Student Union events were understood as Black spaces and Fraternity Row, or "Frat Row" was seen as White space. "Frat Row is definitely a White location," Robert laughed in response to my question. "I guess Frat Row is literally just a White space. But as far as campus of course the BCC is a Black space," Laurie echoed.

FRATERNITY ROW

Frat Row plays an influential role in the mainstream WSU community, or, as Grace said, "That's part of the culture here. Everyone here at some point goes to Frat Row when you're a freshman 'cause that's all you really know." Frat Row is comprised of ten sororities and seventeen fraternities lining both sides of a street almost a quarter-mile away from the main WSU campus. Some of the houses look more like mansions. The Greek letters of the organizations frame the entrances of the houses.

At night Frat Row takes a different look. The number of Black and Latinx people who work as security on Frat Row eclipses the number of Black people and Latinx students who are members of the actual fraternities and sororities on Frat Row. The smell of beer mingles in the air with blasting music. Sometimes the Greek Letter Organizations play house and electronic music. Often, they play popular rap music. The music selection typically was more diverse than the partygoers themselves.

The birth of WSU's so-called campus climate era was spurred by an incident on Frat Row in 2015. Someone from one of the fraternity houses threw a beer can at a volleyball player and called her a racial epithet. Protests, forums, and student demands followed. Some members of the student government saw campus climate as an event, or time period, as opposed to an omnipresent subjective quality of campus. WSU's Frat Row and historically White Greek Letter organizations in general are common sites of racism and exclusion across the nation. For example, White Greek Letter organizations are the common hosts of racist parties, "where guests are invited to show up dressed representing racial stereotypes or to mock any racial or ethnic group" (Garcia et al. 2011, 6). Research continues to show how historically White Greek Letter organizations contribute to the maintenance of White Spaces on campus (e.g., Park and Kim 2013).

Frat Row, while a focal point in dominant WSU community and social life, remains a White Space. Membership in the dominant WSU community, by way of Frat Row, made membership in the Black community difficult. Recall, for example, how one student qualified membership in the Black community as, among other requirements, a disdain or indifference toward Frat Row. Many Black students avoided, had little interest in, or felt excluded from Frat Row. Consider the implications here—historically White fraternity and sorority social events—often understood in scholarship as a mainstay of campus life—were actually tangential, unimportant, or avoided completely. By decentering White students and meeting Black students where they are, scholars and administrators will be better positioned to understand much of Black student life.

Erving, an aerospace engineer and member of a Black Greek Letter Organization, described his initial experience with the historically White fraternities on The Row:

> First I looked at the White Greek life. The social connections . . . and maybe [the fraternity can] help you with a job later on. And then I went to Frat Row. I mean, I didn't like the White frats at all. I didn't get no love out there. I didn't want no love. . . . We didn't fit in.

More than a White Space, Erving and others alluded to Frat Row's being an economically privileged space. He continued, describing the people on Frat Row saying, "They kinda think they're better than you. They come from money, most of them . . . they don't want to get to know you." Clarifying his feelings, I asked, "But you're not necessarily like, 'Oh be my friend'?" "Yeah, I don't care," Erving responded:

> But you know, I definitely experienced that freshman year. And I feel like the first two, three weeks you try to hang out with them. You hang out and drink. And I just felt like I didn't fit in. I would feel uncomfortable sometimes. Like I just couldn't see them as my friend, like, "Dang, why am I here?"

Or consider Grace's sentiments of Frat Row. She had little interest in trying to venture outside of the Black and NSBE communities because of her interactions with people on Frat Row. In describing Frat Row, Grace said:

> It was just like a callous disregard for other people, constantly. You could feel the entitlement of a predominantly White community, like it was oozing from them. It was just like "you don't belong" type of mindset. Not letting Black girls in your party . . . they don't do it as much anymore.

I asked Dajuan if he dealt with any negative racialized interactions at WSU and he replied, "I'm pretty sure there's some racist stuff going on in the fraternities . . . I don't go to Frat Row at all . . . I know they sometimes are like, Black people can't get in." Dajuan corrected himself, saying, "It's not like that, but it's like people that aren't in the frat don't go," which, given the dearth of Black people in fraternities or sororities on Frat Row, provides the optics of Black folk not getting into their parties. Continuing our conversation, I asked Dajuan, "So where do you go [to party]?" "Just like, I guess you could say the Black parties," he responded.

Frat Row, while a site of revelry and partying for many WSU students, is not a destination for most Black WSU students. While some people cited exclusion, more often, participants had little desire to join the social activities on Frat Row. The question, for Black WSU students was not, "Why can't we party on Frat Row?" Rather, the question was, "Are there any Black parties this weekend?" Some students complained about the rock and roll or electronic music that some "White parties" played. One student, albeit not an engineer, said she stopped going to Frat Row because she knew she would have to suffer hearing drunk White partygoers slurring the n-word along with rap songs that were playing.

Understanding how many Black engineers understand Frat Row to be an unfriendly, closed-minded space where Black people are not welcome, one might be surprised to learn that two participants were involved with Frat Row. Martin, whom I feature in the next chapter, and Kareem are members of fraternities on Frat Row. While attending a predominantly White high school is not an indicator of being involved in Frat Row or the dominant WSU community, both Kareem and Martin attended predominantly White high schools.

Kareem, a computer science and business major, described NSBE as "a very open and inviting community," but said he's been "in and out" of the group. He explained, "I think people are there for different reasons. Personally, I'm there to network. Like obviously I want to make friends with people but I have a lot of friends outside of NSBE, so I use it to mainly network." For Kareem, mainstream WSU provided a sense of engagement. Studying students like Kareem is important, as Blackness is not a monolith. Further, by exploring the diverse mechanisms Black students use to foster a sense of engagement, we might learn how to better support them.

DIVERSE FRIENDSHIPS AND DIVERGING VIEWPOINTS

Much scholarly work engages with diversity and examines how diversity is "done" on campuses (e.g., Ahmed and Swan 2006). Yet many institutions and students themselves think of diversity as an achievement or characteristic of a population, rather than a process. A few students hold-ing this viewpoint were very clear about their appreciation of the racial diversity in representational terms at WSU. Saul, for example, provided a brochure-worthy response concerning his friend group:

> So most of my friends come from my floor so it's a huge col-lection. There's no real predominant [race]. . . . And outside of those friends I definitely have a lot of diverse friends . . . I'm happy about it. It makes things interesting. Diversity is the spice of life so I just want to have a different taste of everything.

Willis, who attended a majority White high school, likewise spoke glow-ingly about the diversity of WSU, saying, "I've learned so much about other cultures. Like just being in my halls and listening or talking to my friends, hearing the things that they do. . . . So I like culture a lot." Diverse friendships, however, can lead to diverging viewpoints. Stu-dents with more racially diverse friends generally expressed more patience in how they reacted to potential racial slights or microaggressions. Lisa, for example, said,

> I really give people the benefit of the doubt. I don't want to immediately jump to an, "Oh they're racist," or "They did this because of my race." And so with that kind of mindset I've been less inclined to see things [as racist].

Similarly, Joseph gives others the benefit of the doubt. He gave an example of people on campus avoiding eye contact with him, saying, "It's like, are they being rude or is it because I'm Black? I do wonder that. But more times than not I take it as they're being rude." Gary, in describing his positive perception of the campus racial climate said, "It's been pretty liberal. Even if someone says something that was a little distasteful, it doesn't generally come from a place of anger or hatred."

Dayo likewise makes a case for patience in reference to diversity and misunderstandings around sensitive issues. "I tell people, 'Everyone comes from all over the world to go to college.' I think college is a great mediator. That's why, if we didn't have this knowledge beforehand, you gonna learn over time in college," Dayo began. "People come in as fresh-men and you know, I don't blame them 'cause wherever they came from maybe that was okay," Dayo continued, "They should learn quickly that's not okay anymore. But I feel like they deserve some time to adjust, slash, become aware."

In Funke's study group with fellow aerospace engineers, she told me her Latina friend said, as if embarrassed, that "they might not be fully in support of the Black Lives [Matter] movement." Funke responded to her classmate, saying, "Well, you're allowed to say that. You have an opinion. Like, tell me why you think it's not necessarily a good thing. And I'll tell you why like it's there in the first place." Tough conversations about identity, she thinks, are important, but made easier when she knows the person:

> [The conversations] could be hard sometimes but I think because there's friendship there already, there's respect. So it's just like we know that we'll talk about our different stance. And I know I may not be able to convince you in this conversation but we're still talking about it.

Relationships shaped how students understood racial microaggressions as well as how they engaged with people with conflicting viewpoints about identity. "I think it depends on my relationship with that person," Gary explained, "If I'm really close to that person, and then they drop something [racist], then it's like, 'Ah, I think I thought a little higher of you.'" He told me however, that he would still take the time to correct them on their slight because, "other people might not be as nice." In most cases, he gives his friends the benefit of the doubt:

> I kind of know people aren't really used to dealing with a lot of diversity. My friend from Minnesota—me and my other friend are his first Black friends. Then you have questions, like, "Do Black people tan?" Yeah. It's not that he's racist, he just doesn't know.

Charlie, a chemical engineer, who attended a predominantly White private school prior to attending WSU, feels similarly about highlighting the nuance of relationships when experiencing the campus climate and racial microaggressions. He feels fortunate because he feels comfortable in both worlds, Black and White, because of his background. His ease around White students however, has garnered negative attention from some of his Black peers, he explained:

And it's like, "Oh Charlie? He hangs with the White kids," or, "Oh Charlie, he has all the White friends, blah blah blah," and I'm like that's who I grew up with. I hang out with everyone. It's not like, "You're White, I want to be your friend." It's like, "You're cool and you have some kinda likeness to me, we're gonna be friends."

Emphasizing the importance of relationships Charlie, said:

I know I probably do things that upset people, so I wanna give people the benefit of the doubt. There are some people I cut off because I'm not close with either way, but with friends that I know or whatever, I'll sit down and talk to them.

He gave an example of a discussion with a White friend of his in the "top frat" on Frat Row. Pointing to the incident on Frat Row where a member of a fraternity hurled a racial slur at a volleyball player, he recalled how his friend said, "'I don't get this. It's fuckin' up Frat Row . . . racism doesn't exist that much anyway.'" Replaying the conversation for me, Charlie told me he challenged his friend:

He asked me, like, "Have you ever felt that something racist happened to you?" and I was like, "Straight up, yes, I have." And I told him and he was like, "Oh. Okay never mind." And it was a sincere, "I'm sorry, I didn't know." And he was like, "I understand even more that I'm ignorant to a lot."

Beyond diversity and equity officers, student demographics, or programming highlighting various students' cultures, the students, themselves, make diversity *happen*. A racially diverse student body and meaningful cross-racial interactions can lead to positive outcomes for college students across various metrics (e.g., Bowman and Park 2015; Chang 1999; Gurin, Dey, Hurtado, and Gurin 2002). Diversity, however, is not simply achieved, as these students' accounts show. Rather, diversity is an ongoing, sometimes painstaking process. Diversity across racial lines comes at the price of labor from marginalized groups, specifically Black students. In the process of becoming more culturally and racially aware, for example, a nonblack student might learn that reciting the n-word in a song is never a good idea, why a movement like #BlackLivesMatter exists, or how to work with and respect people of different races. These lessons however, often come at the cost of a Black student's energy and emotional well-being. Such work might necessarily fall on the backs of Black students. My point here is to make plain the work being done by students to make diversity happen. Participants did not describe the work and patience they exercised in bringing nonblack peers up to speed on matters of Blackness and racism as a burden. Yet, one might consider their patience and dialogues with nonblack students a type of invisible labor or racialized equity labor.

An Expectation of Racism

Black engineers' expectations concerning the racial awareness of people with whom they did not have relationships are comparatively lower. For people Gary does not have a relationship with, he said, "You keep your expectations a little low." Some students seem to expect a level of racism. Charlie, for example, said, "I'm very oblivious to it, like either I don't pick up on it or I just," and snapped, continuing, "like no matter where you go its gonna happen." Another student, Bianca, sighed before laughing, saying, "It's sad that we have to kinda adjust what we expect like, that we know racism isn't going anywhere. But it's really not." This expectation of racism is part of racial realism (Bell 1992). Racial realism, as these students show, shapes how students "adjust" themselves to peers and their expectations of nonblack others. At the base of racial realism, as Bianca and Charlie show, is the clear-eyed approach to reality—racism is permanent.

Black engineers often compared the way they experienced the campus racial climate or racial slights to Black students with other majors. Bianca, in describing how she interpreted the climate, brought up her friend, a humanities major: "Yeah, I'm definitely one of those people who . . . 'cause my friend Leonie is super like . . . not like makes everything about race but makes everything about race." Using Leonie as her reference point, she said:

> You can say one thing and she'll go on this huge rant and tirade and I'm just like, "It's not even that serious, just chill. Can you chill?" And she's just one of those people, and I'm just one of those people that's like, I don't know, I guess maybe I'm accepting of it, or I'm just used to it, but I just don't make a big deal of that stuff.

As mentioned in the earlier section, engineering as a discipline does not always lend itself to discussions or reflections concerning race and identity. "We talk about numbers," Ayana laughed, "When you go on to [The School of Humanities] everybody's on edge, 'cause they been talking about race for the last four hours and ain't nobody like each other. Over here, it's not really a conversation like that." Payton also mentioned that she never, to her knowledge, experienced any racism. Thinking about the rigor of her computer science major, she laughed, "Like I don't understand how you could be racist in an environment where everyone is just super stressed out. Like I don't know, like how do you have time to be racist?"

Payton's words, although masked in humor, convey an intriguing point. Some participants, and likely other engineers, indeed suggest that race is less of a factor in engineering than other disciplines and careers. Yet, consider a Bourdieusian analysis using his concept of *field*. A Bourdieusian analysis might suggest that the *field* of engineering is working just how it should, ensuring that racial characteristics of the "typical" engineer remain static, reproducing limited numbers of minoritized engineering majors. An absence of discussions of race or the intersection between structural racism and other forms of domination and engineering is thereby business as usual, becoming an implicitly understood practice in the discipline. Within the *field* of engineering, employing a race-neutral logic "confers on the privileged the supreme privilege of not seeing themselves as privileged" (Bourdieu and Passeron 1990, 210). The privileged, in the engineering field, are White cisgender men. Coupled with CRT, one also assumes that race is always at play in every *field*—even within a major dedicated to seemingly raceless equations, programming languages, numbers, and permutations. On a structural level, for example, one might rightly argue that the small number of Black engineers at WSU is a manifestation of the legacy of antiblack racism (Bullock 2017; Moses and Cobb 2002).

NOT IN A PLACE TO EXPERIENCE RACISM

"So have you ever dealt with anything you felt like was racist on campus?" I asked Erving. "I would say I haven't really been faced with that because I try to keep away from it," he responded, "Especially Frat Row, you stay away from Frat Row . . . that's it for the most part. I'm mostly studying, I don't have time." Black engineers who were more attached to the Black or NSBE communities often were not in a place to experience negative racialized interactions. As engineers, their time was often accounted for, studying or in classes. As active members of the Black or NSBE communities, they were mainly in racially homogenous settings with other Black students.

Cole, in another case, described his friend group as "mainly Black folk." He continued, "I think I sort of developed a certain prejudice towards other races coming here." Curious as to why he felt he developed a prejudice, Cole explained that his feelings came from his experience in his first-year residence hall which was also home to a sizeable amount of people who were interested in life on Frat Row. Cole's roommate was friendly and introduced him to people in the residence hall. For some reason, however, Cole felt like none of the people wanted to be his friend:

> If I was walking down the hall it wasn't like, "Oh what's up Cole?" it was, "Oh, that's Keith's roommate. Hey Cole." But that's just 'cause like I wasn't part of that community. I was seen a little different. I think that turned me off that community at WSU. Which is kinda wrong in hindsight.

I pushed back, saying, "Ehhh, but I mean, they weren't being real friendly to you, though." Cole nodded, "Yeah, true shit, but I do believe it's not based off of dislike, it's just xenophobia. . . . I came in, I didn't look like them, didn't act like them . . . so it wasn't like them being out to get me." While Cole articulated this boundary as xenophobia, the act of nonblack students distancing themselves from Cole and other Black students might still be understood as antiblackness.

The majority of the students who were engaged with the WSU community attended predominantly White high schools. Attendance in a predominantly White high school setting however, did not guarantee a sense of comfort in the WSU community. Students such as Ayana, Nina, Thomas, Laurie, Nubia, among others, for example, attended majority White and Asian high schools, yet they were not attached to the WSU community. Laurie could not articulate just why she mainly hangs out with Black people at WSU, saying, "I was always around [White people] because I played club sports . . . my soccer teams were predominantly White. I just didn't connect with them I guess."

Grace described her friend group at WSU as the opposite of what her group was in high school, all-Black now, and all-White in high school. She felt like her friend formation happened naturally at WSU, saying, "It's just that I really related to Black people that I met here and there's a large variety . . . and the White people and other races I met were just like, not really nice." Grace found a home in the Black and NSBE community. Her involvement in these communities was not a simple reaction to the hostility of Frat Row or wider WSU community. Grace clarified her feelings, saying, "It's not like, 'Fuck them.' I'd just rather not deal with that. . . . I'm cool where I am."

Anthony, a senior at the time, reflecting on his time at WSU and any instances of racism or prejudicial interactions, said, "Overall, I don't notice it as much. Maybe that's just because I'm mostly around Black people. But other Black people, they notice it more than I do, just 'cause their experiences with other groups." Anthony himself did not notice negative racial attitudes from others because he was predominantly around other Black students and shielded by the Black and NSBE communities. He also acknowledged differences in how Black students interpreted the campus climate, attributing their varying interpretations to their friend groups.

The WSU Involvement Fair

I shake the professor's hand, thanking him for letting me interview him. His office is on the second floor of the six-story electrical engineering building. The building has a no-frills décor with walls that are bare with the exception of plaques, flyers, and room numbers. Walking out the office toward the elevator, I see a brown, South Asian man with a goatee sitting in an office with the door wide open. We make eye contact and I smile. He returns my smile with a hint of curiosity in his eyebrows. "You're an engineer?" he asked. I give him a rundown of my project and he laughs, "Oh, okay. I was asking because I've seen you in the gym downtown." He's an electrical engineering PhD student.

Would the student have asked me that question if I was of another race or was he just being friendly? What good would it do me to know his true thoughts? The next day would be the involvement fair for new WSU students. I make a mental note to ask NSBE members what they thought of the situation.

The summer weather intensifies just around the time school starts in September. The weather during the involvement fair was scorching. Fortunately, NSBE had a table in the shade. At the beginning of the fall semester, WSU holds an involvement fair outside, lining the walkways around the center of campus. It makes for a difficult time walking by.

Hundreds of students, mainly first-years, crowd the main paths, walking slowly to observe the displays of the different organizations.

NSBE had their own table and display. Next to their poster sat their many regional and national NSBE awards—a plaque, a fancy award made of glass, and two other trophies. I thought of what the past president told me, "I like to win. That's what we do. We win." Members of the new e-board were stationed at the table, Laurie, Bianca, Grace, and Payton, each wearing their grey NSBE T-shirts. It was a team effort, chatting with any students who stopped by the table. "What's your major?" one NSBE member would inevitably ask. "Computer Science." "Aerospace engineering." "Biomedical." "Civil." Whatever the engineering major, the NSBE members rejoiced, often with an obligatory, "Aaaayyyee!" One of the e-board members, usually Bianca, then had the new students sign up for the mailing list and handed them a flyer, made of "that good paper," as Payton observed with a laugh. The flyer advertised upcoming events, the location and time of the weekly general body NSBE meetings, the NSBE barbeque, and the NSBE bowling night.

Some students came who had majors that were not exactly engineering. One girl who was majoring in biology asked if she could join. Bianca explained that NSBE is an inclusive organization and that people of all different majors are welcome. During her explanation, Bianca glanced at me and furthered her case saying, "I mean, we have Antar, too. He doesn't even go here." Laughing, Grace introduced me as the unofficial "NSBE dad." Laurie doubled over, "NSBE dad. I like that."

Remembering my situation with the South Asian man, I gave Grace and Laurie the play-by-play of the situation to get their feedback. "Like, why wouldn't I be an engineer? I'm not, but, why not, you know?" Grace said it seemed like he just wanted a friend. "Maybe he wanted a workout partner? Yeah, I don't think that was racist," Laurie added. Bianca, being Bianca, suggested that I stop being sensitive, and asked the rhetorical question with faux seriousness, "I mean, are you an engineer, Antar?" We shared a laugh and I relented.

I asked Thomas about how his summer ended. "Yeah, we gotta talk, bro . . . hold up . . ." Thomas said, registering the chords of the popular rap song "Magnolia" on somebody's speakers. We paused our conversation to start Milly Rocking, a dance that involves waving your arms in spherical motions—a move that Johnson was known for in the Black WSU community. I checked to see if someone from NSBE brought speakers.

I found the source coming from about ten feet away from us, a dance team. They all happened to be Asian. It was a good strategy—playing popular hip hop songs.

The "Magnolia" beat is infectious, begging listeners to dance. Some of the lyrics felt uncomfortable in the predominantly White and Asian American setting. Members of the dance group took turns freestyle dancing to the hypnotic beat. They were good. Yet, I became more aware of the n-word in the unedited songs they played. I asked Payton how she felt about it. "Well I just figure they're singing the songs in their heads either way, and I'm not going to be mad about that. That's kind of a waste of my energy. I might as well enjoy the music. I'm not mad." Grace, Payton, and nearly all the rest of NSBE continued to dance to the music throughout the involvement fair.

The Mainstream Campus Community: In Summary

This chapter highlights the myriad of ways Black engineers understand, experience, and negotiate negative racialized interactions. I found that many students give others a "benefit of the doubt" when experiencing a potential racial microaggression. Others negotiate racist interactions by avoiding White spaces whenever possible. Few participants were actively engaged in the mainstream WSU community's social world. The majority, however, found belonging and engagement at WSU through the other social worlds I highlighted. In interpreting a negative racialized encounter, relationships matter—trust between friends can facilitate constructive conversations and speaking across difference. In addition to the relational aspect of experiencing microaggressions, students also adopted a racial realist attitude to racism and prejudicial behaviors, understanding racism as a fact of life.

Racial realism is a mindset that acknowledges the permanence of racism and Black people's subordinate societal status (Bell 1992). Throughout this book, and this chapter especially, I aimed to make the point that racial realism might be used to understand how some Black students themselves understand and navigate their worlds. Most often in Critical Race Theory (CRT) research, racial realism is mentioned as a stance the theorist adopts. Less often is racial realism seen as something students themselves adopt. Many participants, while unfamiliar with the term *racial realism,* were familiar with the general idea of racial realism. In fact, beyond familiarity, a philosophy of racial realism shaped how some students navigated campuses and viewed race relations.

Acknowledging racism's permanence can lead to different responses. For some, it could mean becoming more of an activist. For others, it could mean deciding to resist in quiet ways, succeeding in a game of educational and career outcomes with odds stacked against them. For most, however, acknowledging racism did what Derrick Bell (1992) believed it could do—relieved students of constant racial despair and suffering. Bell suggested that through racial realism, one learns to find fulfillment in the process of living as well as the struggle against racism. This is not at all to suggest that one is happy with racism, but that one refuses to allow racism to define or dictate the sum of one's life.

Racial realism, in a way, can be seen at the involvement fair where I and the NSBE members were recruiting for NSBE. The predominantly Asian American dance group played music blaring with the n-word rapped throughout without, it seemed, any consideration for the Black people at the NSBE table or the fact that their group was made of only nonblack people. At the least, this instance was inconsiderate, at the worst it was outwardly antiblack, and one might also rightfully consider it both things. Payton's response, however, was not one of racial naiveté. She was able to dance and enjoy the music, precisely because of her awareness that most nonblack people are likely uttering the n-word, at least in their heads. Racism, and antiblackness specifically, is a fact. In what might be understood as a site of suffering (Dumas 2014), the beat goes on. Oppressive structures persist—one can engage in activism against them, attempt to avoid them, and/or navigate life with the knowledge that it exists—all can be understood as resistance (Solórzano and Bernal 2001). Payton and others, despite the real oppressions they face, prioritize the dance, prioritizing the life they make either because or in spite of inequitable conditions. The dance of campus life is complex, occurring across social worlds and is shaped, but not completely determined, by structural oppressions.

11

Martin's Story

When Martin is around Black people, he notices it. Describing a short vacation on Martha's Vineyard with his family before his junior year, he said, "I was at Ink Well in Oak Bluff . . . there's so many more Black people there." Laurie once explained an interaction with Martin after I told her I was about to shadow him in a class, saying, "I don't know him that well." Covering her face, as if embarrassed for laughing, recounted:

> It was so funny, like Martin with us at the [National NSBE conference] and he was just like, "Guys, this is like the most Black people I've ever been around." And like I laughed, but you could tell he was serious.

Martin, while a Black WSU student, is not an avid participant in the Black WSU community. He is only minimally involved in NSBE and sporadically attends ethnic student organizations, such as the Black men's group on campus. Martin finds a sense of belonging in other communities, building relationships and engaging with people in the Caldwell and mainstream WSU communities.

Martin stands at 5'10" and has a slim, athletic frame. "I used to be skinnier, but I worked out like nonstop for a challenge in high school," he told me. His cheeks fold into dimples when he smiles. Martin's parents are both ethnically Creole from Louisiana—a mix of European, Native American, and African heritage. Very light-skinned, some have confused his race, but his tightly wound, curly hair might serve as a signal of his African American identity. His hair is usually cut low with a fade and lineup—bald around the ears and progressively thicker moving up the scalp.

Martin graduated from an elite private, predominantly White high school in New England. Outside of his family, most of his interactions with Black people were on the court. He originally wanted to do karate, but his dad put him in basketball programs: "I started playing basketball when I was four. I was the youngest kid there. I could barely dribble the ball." They used to tease him, making fun of the way he talked and his lack of basketball skills, saying, "Why are you here? You can't even make a lay-up." More than skills, he differed in background. Most of the kids in the basketball program were from working-class or low-income backgrounds and attended predominantly Black and Latinx public schools. "It was just a different culture. They bullied me," he laughed. Ultimately, he was glad his dad put him in basketball, joking, "I see Black kids who cannot play basketball now, it's just awkward. Everybody's like, 'You don't play basketball?' "

He also played basketball throughout high school, which is where he had the most contact with other Black students. "I was mainly around White kids in my classes, you know? And I was totally fine, like not hanging around Black people my whole life," Martin explained. Sometimes, in reference to his high school experience, he spoke of other Black students as if they were a group he was not a member of, and, in some ways, he was not: "Like the Black kids were hanging out together. We had alcoves for each grade, and they kind of took over one section of one alcove. And that was the Black cove. . . . Nobody else would hang out there." Continuing his impression of other Black students at his school Martin said:

> Most of them were athletes, not always the brightest. They were bright people, but they weren't hardworking. So they didn't perform as well in classes, didn't speak up in class. . . . They were like, "I'm just here to reap the benefits of our school." Our school had a very good name brand, but they went places. They got into good colleges. But they didn't necessarily get there the same way that all of us working hard every day.

While racially Black, Martin did not engage in the Black community's social world at his high school.

Martin played basketball with them but clarified, "I never hung out with those kids. I didn't like avoid them, I talked to them but . . . we were friends, but we didn't hang out." His upbringing, being bullied by other

Black kids in his basketball league when he was young as well as being in predominantly White spaces, shapes his lack of comfort in predominantly Black spaces. Martin divulged to me:

> When you asked the question about how I feel like being a Black kid on campus, it's tough. I feel like a White kid on campus. But like I said, I'm not scared of Black kids anymore, but kind of like they do their thing. I do my thing.

Through further conversations with him, I knew this was not about aspiring to be White or self-hatred. For example, when I asked how he felt to be Black in Caldwell on a later occasion, he said, "I feel like I'm just another person in Caldwell." Without having the language, it seemed like he wanted to be seen without being signified by his race and defaulted to Whiteness as the norm. Martin's view of his racial identity was born of his upbringing and class status—his *habitus*.

The Mainstream WSU Community

Martin and I grabbed lunch. Walking out of the dining hall, he shared his excitement about his fraternity's party on Friday night. "It's going to be great. We're bussing in girls from [a nearby university]. Cleared out the entire backyard and first floor." he mused. Despite his excitement, he was worried about Saturday morning. "My girlfriend and I are running a 5K. . . . She really wants to do it," he sighed. "But I bought some Pedialyte," he clarified with a grin. His girlfriend at the time, Mandy, a White woman, was in a sorority only a couple houses away from his.

"Martin!" a Black woman yelled, to get his attention. "Oh, hey," he responded, somewhat off guard, and waved. As we walked by, referring to the woman who greeted him, he said, "She's so pretty. Like she's a model." He clarified, as if feeling guilty, "I mean, I'm happy with Mandy, but I mean, she's still pretty." Martin took the Black woman to his fraternity's formal, a party where fraternity brothers bring dates and dress in formal attire, and later invited her out to another one of his fraternity's events, but she could not make it. As the semester progressed, their communication dwindled, and Martin got closer to Mandy. "Of course now that I'm happy with a girl she starts talking to me again," Martin said with mock frustration.

Martin is a middle child; the only boy. His older sister attended WSU as well and told him, "If you don't join a fraternity, you won't have a social life." As a first year, Martin thought, " 'Okay. I'm going to join a fraternity.' But then at the same time I was like, 'I'm an engineer, so I should think about this a little bit.'" The fraternity he "rushed," Lambda, has one of the highest average GPAs on Frat Row. While shopping the different fraternities, Martin noticed:

> There were more engineers in [Lambda] than I had seen in other houses, and talking to them, they were basically like, "[Pledging] is definitely not easy. Just Caldwell in general is hard but there are people in here who will help you out and like we've been through it."

The Lambda brothers were referring to the process of becoming a member of Lambda, or pledging, and being a Caldwell student at the same time. The intake process, he said, was of course difficult. But membership, a built-in family, parties, attention from women in sororities, bossing around new members, and status on campus made the toil of intake into the fraternity well worth it. Further, membership in a Greek Letter Organization gave him a broader social life:

> I think being in a fraternity has allowed me to have a stronger social life than most. When I say stronger, I mean most widespread. I've met so many different people through Greek life that I would have never met otherwise. I wouldn't say I have better friends than other people, but I've just been exposed to more types of people.

Frat Row is exclusive. Beyond being seen as exclusive to Black WSU students in general, mainly those involved in the Black and/or NSBE communities, Frat Row even excludes people in certain houses/fraternities or sororities also on Frat Row. Martin for example, does not have access to all of the parties on Frat Row even though he is a member one of the frat houses, explaining:

> I go to all of my own parties, obviously. It's difficult to go to other people's parties because you have to be plus-one as a guy. I'll go to a lot of Chi Sigma parties because a bunch of

my friends are in there, but other than Chi Sig, I don't go to any other parties.

While his identity as a member of Lambda was foundational to his college experience, he confided in me, saying, "It is different being an African American in Greek life." He continued;

> Most fraternities are not nearly as diverse. They might have one Black guy. I think a third of them, maybe a quarter of them . . . have one Black guy in a class of twenty to twenty-five. They might have one or two Asian guys for each class. My house is very very different.

Based on my interviews with other students who painted Frat Row in a broad stroke of Whiteness I was surprised by any differentiation. In Martin's house, for example, he felt welcome, saying, "There's a bunch of Black kids in my house and even there's a bunch of Asians. We're a very diverse house." Confirming what I heard from other Black students, however, he said, "But on Frat Row in general, and some girls, you do get a little, like . . . some people go [mocking a woman's voice] 'This is the Black house. This is the Asian house. And we don't really wanna go there.'" Surprised, I said, "Stop playing!" "Yeah. . . . Obviously we're not the Black house. It's like thirty percent of us. It sucks, but most people . . . a lot of people I've seen and met are very open." Only about one-third of the men in his fraternity were students of color, and yet that was enough to mark that fraternity as different, as the Black house, in the eyes of White women frequenting Frat Row. The view of Martin's fraternity being less desirable because of its Black and Asian American membership, however, should not come as a large surprise. White Greek Letter Organizations are the most racially isolating organizations on college campuses (Park and Kim 2013; Park 2014). Rather, calling Martin's fraternity the Black or Asian house is on brand with the history and culture of White Greek Letter Organizations.

Martin usually tries to brush off microaggressions: "I try to, as much as I can, just move on, because dwelling on it is just going to make me angry." Despite his upbringing and sense of ease around other races, he also holds somewhat of a racial realist outlook on negative, racist interactions, explaining, "Really, nothing I'm going to say in that moment is going to change the way they think so I just move on and try not to dwell on it too much." Considering Martin's words, the fact that he is in a majority White Greek Letter Organization, and his lack of involvement in Black social worlds at WSU, his assertion that racism, and some people's perceptions of race, are permanent might be surprising. Martin is not naive about racism. Martin, however, is a cisgender, heterosexual, light-skinned, Black man from a high-income background. By virtue of his identity and higher income upbringing, he had access to experiences and spaces in an elite high school that many other Black people did not. While certainly not exempt from racism, he experienced oppression differently because of his economic privilege.

I witnessed one racist interaction while grabbing lunch with Martin. We ordered lunch from the food court and walked toward the plastic cutlery and small, six-ounce water cups. Martin reached for a cup, terrifying an Asian woman in the same area. She jumped back, recoiling, to get out of the vicinity of Martin's reach. Noticing this, Martin said, as if he were growing impatient, "Here," he paused motioning to the cups, "Go ahead." Shaking his head, he looked at me saying, "Like, I'm not going to attack you. Why did she freak out?" "It's not that deep, right?" I replied. "Exactly," Martin said, before updating me on his Algebra for Engineers course.

I brought this interaction up with him a few weeks later and he could not recall the incident. One moment, clearly racialized from my perspective and something I would remember, was a fleeting moment, unworthy of long-term memory, to Martin. Whether the woman who jumped away from Martin was simply startled by another presence or if her fear was born of a racist stereotype of Black men, we, of course, cannot say. This exchange, however, does show how Martin engages with perceived negative racialized interactions.

Out of the undergraduate engineers I interviewed, Martin is of the minority who are at ease and active members in the dominant WSU community. His engagement and comfort in the dominant WSU community can be attributed to his K–12 background:

> The culture of this school is very similar to [the] culture of my high school. . . . They're very similar, especially when it comes to people of this wealth and this demographic. I grew up with kids who were all upper class. All had pools . . . mansions. Like the kids here, basically. As a Black man, it doesn't feel that different than it was in my high school and I was already pretty comfortable there.

He seemed accustomed to friction between races or microaggressions. "I've never been personally discriminated against, but I've seen people say things that are, like, 'Whoa, that's not okay.' But then I've also experienced that in my high school as well. It wasn't new to me," Martin said.

His membership in Lambda, an institutionally recognized fraternity with a house on Frat Row granted him access and membership to WSU in ways foreign to most Black engineers. While some Black engineers explicitly described Frat Row as a "White" or "unfriendly" space, Martin found a literal and figurative home in Frat Row. His comfort in this space can be attributed to whom he was surrounded by prior to college, attending elite predominantly White schools.

The Black Engineering Community

I first met Martin at a NSBE meeting. I bought $10 worth of churros for a fundraiser to subsidize their travel to the NSBE National Conference. I tapped Martin, who was standing in line to buy a churro, himself, on the shoulder asking him if he wanted one. "Seriously? Wow. Thanks so much, man," he said, pausing for a moment, "Wait, what's your name?"

Martin started coming to NSBE meetings during his sophomore year. He used to get NSBE e-mails his first year, but between being a first-year Caldwell student with rigorous coursework and joining his fraternity, he had no time for other commitments. Outside of landing two job offers from a top tech company as a sophomore at the NSBE convention, he was excited to get to know other Black engineers: "Convention was amazing cause I actually got to hang out with all the kids in NSBE and really get to know them. Learn their names and stuff like that which was a lot of fun."

While not an avid member of NSBE, Martin appreciates having the NSBE community, even going so far as to say, "It's probably the closest-knit community I've seen at WSU. Stronger than my fraternity, actually." Likely because of his upbringing around predominantly White students, Martin, who identifies as Black and has never shied away from his racial identity, sometimes refers to Black people as if he is an onlooker as opposed to part of a collective—as a "they" instead of a "we." Tentative about laying claim to Blackness, he said,

> This is what I've experienced from being around Black people. From being around Black people not that much, the little

experience I have, everybody just wants to help everybody.
Everybody realized that there are the struggles and everybody
just wants to make sure that everybody is getting through and
getting by as much as they can.

Continuing his musings of NSBE, he told me, "I just felt welcome from
day one that they really wanted me there." The welcoming nature of NSBE
took Martin aback in a good way, recounting how other NSBE members,
upon meeting him, would say, "Oh, you're an engineer? Come join this.
Come do this with us. Do this with us." Martin concluded his thoughts
on NSBE, saying, "I love it. I love every second of it."

The Engineering School Community

Martin's experience and comfort in Caldwell is shaped by his engineering
exposure prior to matriculation into college. "Me and one of my dad's
friends," Martin recalled, "who was a computer engineer, built a computer
and my mom still uses it today. That was a huge project. It took us about
eight, ten hours." Reflecting on the impact of the project, he continued,
"That whole experience, building a computer and then also researching
the parts. . . . I also wrote a paper about the history of computers. That
was really helpful . . . putting me on the path [to] liking computers."
This assignment—building a computer, researching the parts, learning
the history of computers—was an elementary school graduation project.
He was in the sixth grade.

The following summer, going into his seventh grade year, his interest
in computing evolved into an interest in engineering. His parents put him
into a summer engineering camp at a local university. In high school, he
continued to excel in math and science classes, which made him consider
engineering more seriously. After his junior year of high school, he participated in a selective summer engineering program for students from
underrepresented racial backgrounds.

Martin sees Caldwell as welcoming. Yet, for people who "feel alienated," he explained, "there's like MEO, there's NSBE, there's places you can
go and connect with other people who look like you and talk like you and
come from the same background as you." While Martin identified different
"types" of Caldwell students, he considers himself like the majority who
are "hard workers" and "competent."

The Caldwell Martin experienced was cooperative more than competitive. "There's always a curve," he explained, "It's just like, 'How many points can I get?' . . . And everybody's trying to help each other prepare as much as they can so that they can get as much partial credit as they can." He also had no problem making friends and study mates in his electrical engineering courses. Because so many of the students have the same classes, friendships organically formed for Martin. He has a "crew" of three men in electrical engineering—a Columbian student, a White student from New York, and a student from Bahrain.

One other Black student is in his electrical engineering class, but he has a different study group. A group of White students in electrical engineering study together, but, as Martin said, "They're more nerdy. Less like me. I'm less nerdy and more just like, 'I just want to do it and get done.'" Concerning being one of two Black people in his class, he said, "I've never grown up seeing a lot of Black people in my classes, so it's not weird. It's just weird that [the majority are] Asian instead of White now."

Martin has an ease about his engineering classes and campus life. For example, he spoke glowingly about one of his engineering professors, Dr. Mark, and has a friendship with him. Martin was taking his second course with him: "I go to his office hours practically every other week. If I'm not there to do work, we just sit there and talk. We've grabbed coffee a couple of times." This semester, Martin was tasked with designing and building a makeshift guitar from scratch in Professor Mark's engineering course. The first time I tried to accompany Martin to the class he called, frantically, saying he could not find his guitar, and that there would be no point in going to class. A pledge in his fraternity, in cleaning the house, mistook the beginnings of his wooden guitar as junk and threw it in the trash. Martin called the pledge class leader and had him get the guitar. "On the bright side, the pledge drove a Jaguar and drove me back to campus, so that was nice."

Martin usually commits an hour a day to do homework. He ramps his effort level up, sacrificing sleep and pulling all-nighters as exams near. He has a "work hard when I need to, play hard" philosophy. He ends up doing more all-nighters than he would like, because he knows himself: "If I sit down in front of my computer for two hours, I know I'm going to do twenty minutes of productive work. It's not worth it. I'd much rather be getting lit or hanging out with my friends."[1]

Outside of his coursework and fraternity, he is heavily involved in Engineers Without Borders, a student-led Caldwell organization that designs and implements an engineering-service project abroad. As the president of WSU's Engineer's Without Borders (EWB), he spent about two hours a day on EWB-related work. EWB, like Caldwell engineering societies, is goal oriented. Therefore, EWB work does not stop during midterms and finals and presents a large time commitment. During the Spring semester, EWB was designing a well for a small town in a Central American country—doing research on the area, creating budgets, and using AutoCAD design software (commonly used by mechanical and electrical engineers) to create schematics of the well and filtration system.

"Tuesday night I kinda just don't expect to get much sleep," Martin said, referring to his weekly 7 p.m. general body EWB meetings. Anywhere between fifteen and twenty members show up to meetings. While Martin is the only Black man, the group is rather diverse—comprised of Latinxs, a Black woman, Asian/Asian American, and Whites. White women make up the majority of EWB.

Martin and Wesley, a Latino and the vice-president, led meetings, spending the first five or so minutes updating members, crossing off items on their agenda on the whiteboard, and listing goals for the meeting before getting to work. Most of the interactions seemed collegial, more like workplace interactions as opposed to a laid-back atmosphere.

During meetings, after presenting the agenda and goals for the night, Martin floats from group to group, answering questions and playing a managerial role. Martin made it look easy. After asking his vice-president if he was going to work with the filtration group, Wesley responded, "Nah man, Katherine took control of that. It's hers now. I mean, you can't stop inertia." Martin and Wesley doubled over laughing. In sharing their extended laughter, they missed a girl raising her hand trying to get their attention. When Martin finally looked up, his eyes seemingly directed toward her, she asked a full question about outside contractors. Martin completely missed it and started talking to me and Wesley. The girl, her pale skin turning red, looked down, embarrassed. I nudged Martin to let him know that she had a question. "Oops," he said, with a laugh, and lightly jogged toward her.

In addition to providing a service—free of charge—to a community in need, a free trip to a foreign country with friends, and learning tangible engineering skills, participation in EWB set him apart from other engineers in the eyes of industry recruiters. EWB provided valuable engineering career capital. Many of the recruiters, he said, were impressed with his work with EWB. Martin gave me the rundown of why he thought EWB helped him get his two internship offers at the NSBE Convention:

EWB was basically my starting point for my entire NSBE convention. And I had like forty pages of technical documentation that I could show people, like, "Hey this is what I've produced and you can look through it. It's technical plans, it's reports, it's everything." So I show that to people that I can do that and I have real proof which is great for a selling point.

Once, leaving an EWB meeting, he walked me to the door and said, "Have a good night, Antar." There is something earnest about Martin. His eyes are analyzing and alert. There is a bareness to him. He acts and asks questions, not tentatively, but with a simple authority. His private school pedigree and upbringing show, I think, in these moments, from the way he jokes with friends and manages people in EWB providing feedback. I do not think people question Martin's belonging in the engineering space. Martin, himself, does not question whether he belongs, either.

Martin does not necessarily need NSBE, but he benefits from and loves the space. While his involvement is not high, he benefits from NSBE as a vehicle for internships and networking with industry professionals. Recall how Martin pointed to resources Caldwell offers for people who feel alienated. Martin is not one such student. For Martin, Caldwell works as it was intended to.

Like other students, Martin's experiences in various communities or social worlds inform each other, and are overlapping. His prominence in the Caldwell community, leading a project-oriented group, afforded him greater success at the NSBE convention. Further, his ease in the WSU community likely facilitated friendships more easily in the Caldwell community. In some ways, Martin serves as a foil to Johnson. Martin has almost no presence or involvement with the Black community, but is submerged in the dominant WSU community. The converse holds true for Johnson. Their backgrounds are also far from similar. Whereas Johnson is from a low-income background, attended a majority Black public school and had little engineering exposure, Martin comes from a high-income background attending an elite majority White preparatory school. While both Black engineers, the ways they experience the campus racial climate as well as how they foster a sense of engagement at WSU are vastly different.

12

Sociology and the Blues of Campus Life

[Willie] Dixon explained and defined the blues as "the facts of life"—not just the hard times, heartbreaks, and troubles but also the triumphs, joys, boasts, and celebrations, and many things in between.

—O'Neal, "Foreword," in *Willie Dixon: Preacher of the Blues*

I wrestled with the question of how to understand Black life and agency within the constraints of racism as a societal force. I found an answer in the blues. Beyond an art form, the blues can be understood as a philosophy. As the famed blues artist Willie Dixon explained, the blues is more than the trials and struggles we face, but also our joys and achievements. Ralph Ellison (1945) suggested that the allure of the blues to Black people in the pre–Civil Rights South was its power to "express both the agony of life and the possibility of conquering it through sheer toughness of spirit" (211). A similar ethos emerged from Black students at WSU.

More than a community or culture, Blackness is a structural condition mired in antagonism (see Sexton 2010). My literal experience of writing *Black Campus Life* served as a reminder of the blues and the structural condition of Blackness. I wrote a good portion of the text at a university library. Near completing the last chapter, I left the library to walk around the campus to clear my mind before my next writing session. While I had used this library for years, I had never ventured beyond my normal path from the parking lot to the library. After sauntering through campus for about ten minutes, I returned to the library to continue working. I sat at my computer for a few minutes before I walked to a restroom. I

209

was interrupted on my walk back to my computer by two campus police officers. "We received reports that you were looking lost walking around campus?" "Are you a student here?" "Can we see some identification?" After I showed them my university ID, the officers left. I felt sick. I left the library and could not bring myself to write there for months.

Prior to this incident, that library was my favorite place to write. I mention this experience to show the tension of writing about engagement, agency, and student life while also understanding the permanence of racism. While I largely appreciated the library's resources and space, my experience as a Black man being questioned by campus police within this space forever changed how I viewed both the university and the racial climate at this school. Similarly, the force of antiblack racism should not be underestimated or overlooked in *Black Campus Life*.

I think of the nonblack woman jumping back from seeing Martin. I think of the South Asian student opting to leave class as opposed to sitting next to Grace in a lecture. I think of the noticeable presence and absence of Black students. I think about the labor, patience, or willful ignorance of Black students to engage with others across difference. I think about nonblack students cheating and disqualifying Black students from groups. I think of Black students learning to work by themselves with extreme effort to achieve.

While students deal with antiblackness to different degrees and respond differently, racism, and antiblackness in particular, is understood by many students as a fact of life. Students adopted a racial realist perspective. In education literature, racial realism is often understood to be an acceptance of the permanence of racism in society and education (see Harper et al. 2009). A racial realist perspective, I found, resulted in different responses. Some avoided interactions with the potential of racial aggressions completely. Others had a low expectation for nonblack students in terms of their racial awareness, thereby relieving themselves of the shock of a racial offense.

A sense of resolve sometimes arises from the antiblack attitudes of others. I did not cast Black engineers as victims because they did not understand themselves as such. Ayana completed projects intended for groups by herself. Jasmine studied hours upon hours in order to score higher than students who would not invite her to a group. Robert stared down nonblack others who looked at him questioningly in the engineering space. Thomas spent WSU homecoming weekend in the basement of a library. For engineering students in majors with exclusionary racial climates, racial despair, it seems, is a luxury they cannot afford—problem sets need completing, tests need to be studied for, and life needs to be lived. The campus experience, for students understanding racism and microaggressions as a fact of life, has a blue tint.

Despite Black students' resolve, we have to address their structural position. Institutions and society will remain antiblack. Racism is not going anywhere. Yet, by learning more about Black students' lives we might learn different ways to better support them. In *Black Campus Life*, my goal was to take the reader on a tour of campus life and begin some of the exploratory work of learning what Black students are doing on the ground to fashion a campus more amenable to themselves. I used the idea of social worlds to learn more about Black student life and unhinge "campus racial climate" and "campus life" from their static conceptions often employed in scholarship. These social worlds, or communities, can be distinct or opposing, yet some communities overlap. The worlds students engage with the most and their corresponding level of comfort shape how students interpret and experience the campus racial climate.

Social Worlds, Boundaries, and Tensions

The purpose of this book was to gain a qualitative understanding of campus life and the racial climate by examining the experiences of Black students in engineering and computer science at a historically White institution. To make sense of something as vast and multifarious as Black student life, I used the ideas of social worlds, boundaries, and tensions. By likening social worlds to fields (Bourdieu and Passeron 1990), I suggested that different social worlds are overlapping, yet are comprised of networks of people with distinct traditions and practices of belonging. Like an agent in a field, people in social worlds can tell who does and does not belong based on how others navigate the space. Social boundaries, however, hinder active engagement and belonging in a given social world. As such, students experience tensions related to their identity and engagement in campus social worlds (Table 12.1).

In Table 12.1, I include the tensions I have highlighted for each social world. The tensions are not intended to be exhaustive. Yet, the tensions do provide insight into how racial identity shaped how students

Table 12.1. Campus Social Worlds and Their Tensions

Campus Social World	Tension(s)
The Black Community	Collective v. Individual interests
The Black Engineering Community	Engagement v. Responsibility
	Strategic Essentialism v. Antiessentialism
	Family v. Engineering focus
The Engineering School	Diversity v. Invisibility
	Membership in NSBE v. Other Engineering Organizations
	Group Work v. Being the Only Black person
	Expecting v. Experiencing Racism
The mainstream WSU Community	WSU Life v. Caldwell Responsibilities
	Doing Diversity v. Negotiating Racism.

experienced varying aspects of campus life. In what follows, I expound upon three concepts that are interwoven within the fabric of the boundaries and tensions in each social world: (1) linked fate, (2) labor, and (3) antiblackness.

LINKED FATE

Black WSU students' feelings of linked fate came to the fore in the more homogenously Black social worlds—the Black Community and Black Engineering Community—as well as in the broader Caldwell Community. Linked fate is the acknowledgment and belief that what happens to others in a group, in this case Black people, will likewise impact individual members of the group (Dawson 1994). In other words, Black people who exhibit a sense of linked fate understand that life outcomes and experiences of one Black person are inextricably linked to the entire Black community. The concept of linked fate, however, tends to center upon racial identification without addressing other identities such as gender, sexuality, and ethnicity (Simien 2005). Such is also a limitation of this book. While I address gender, ethnicity, and class throughout the work, I primarily attend to race. Had I examined the homogeneously Black campus social worlds exclusively, for example, I might have been much more attuned to the heterogeneity within Blackness. Despite the clear limitation of the concept, however, linked fate was useful in understanding the thinking undergirding the words and actions of many students I studied.

While originally used to explain similar political behavior and public opinion in the Black population (Dawson 1994), a sense of linked fate also shapes how students navigated campus life. At the core of linked fate is the belief that Black people have a responsibility for both themselves and the larger Black community. For example, why would students invest hours doing organizational work for NSBE for no additional compensation? They were not coerced into this work. Rather, they felt a responsibility to each other and to fostering the development of Black engineers on campus. Recall the NSBE motto which students would say in unison at the close of every meeting: "To increase the number of culturally responsible Black engineers who excel academically, succeed professionally and positively impact the community." Linked fate runs through this motto both as a charge to increase the number of Black engineers but also to be a culturally responsible engineer.

Linked fate is related to living with and countering stereotypes. With knowledge that negative controlling images exist and that their singular actions may be grafted onto other Black people for no other reason than their race, Black students often felt an added pressure to perform in Caldwell courses. While students achieved as a form of resistance, and of course for individual purposes of securing a high grade, students also achieved for the culture. Arriving tardy for class or receiving low grades, many participants believed, would be a mark not only against themselves, but against all Black students. In this way, a sense of linked fate served as a response to antiblack stereotypes. By better understanding the linked fate of Black collegians, higher education stakeholders might learn how to better support Black students.

Linked fate runs counter to the values of the increasingly individualistic norms and values of society. During an ascribed time of self-discovery and personal development, some students adopted a sense of linked fate and prioritized the collective Black community. Exhibiting linked fate despite the individualistic reasons not to, I believe, is remarkable and worth learning from. I, for example, marveled at the lengths students would go to support each other and NSBE. To be clear, however, linked fate arises from oppression (Dawson 1994). The shared responsibility Black students often exhibit for each other, for Black student organizations, and even for future Black WSU students serves as response to the antiblack oppression that Black people have historically faced and continue to face at WSU. Students went out of their way to build and maintain community with other Black engineers. Black students' labor to create communities and make campus more appealing for themselves, which derives from a sense of linked fate, however, might be, and likely often is, exploited by universities.

LABOR

Labor speaks to tensions within the Black community and Black engineering community social worlds. A responsibility to the collective Black community or the responsibilities of NSBE both involve an element of work. Involvement in student groups or Black communities on campus, however, is not often constructed as labor. Black students' participation in ethnic student organizations and leadership across organizational types, for example, has certainly been well documented (e.g., Harper and Quaye 2007; Museus 2008). This body of work highlights how participation in such groups leads to a sense of engagement, involvement, belonging, among other factors that lead to positive educational experiences and outcomes. The same rings true for participants' involvement in NSBE. Yet, in addition to viewing participation in NSBE as a form of engagement, I also viewed participation in NSBE as a form of labor. By understanding involvement in such organizations as labor, one can better view the central role of students themselves in creating a more welcoming campus community. Certainly, all groups, to an extent, require work to demonstrate membership in some fashion. What differentiates Black student involvement in ethnic student organizations such as NSBE, however, is that such groups positively shape the campus racial climate, provide opportunities for engagement, and furnish places of belonging for Black students.

A positive or welcoming campus climate is not a goalpost or endpoint to achieve. Creating a positive climate is a never-ending process requiring intentional labor from various stakeholders and resources. Black engineering students turned out to be focal stakeholders in building a positive racial climate for themselves. When considering the hours and labor dedicated to maintaining an NSBE community that was generally welcoming for all Black engineering students, one might rightfully understand involvement in such organizations as a form of racialized equity labor, or the "uncompensated efforts of people of color to address systematic racism and racial marginalization within organizations" (Lerma et al. 2020, 286). Linder and colleagues (2019) likewise conceptualized students' activist work as a form of labor. While Black student organizations may not always be engaged in explicit activism, the work to create and maintain communities for racially marginalized groups might likewise be understood as labor and directly related to perceptions of the campus climate and diversity.

Racially diverse settings where students work or interact across racial difference are prime settings for racist interactions. How Black students negotiate racist interactions is also labor. Consider, for example, how Natasha Warikoo's (2016) work, troubling the idea of diversity, demonstrates how White students at elite institutions often view diversity as a bargain. As long as White students benefit from a more cosmopolitan experience and are not threatened academically by racial minorities, Warikoo argues, diversity is welcomed. My work provides further nuance to Warikoo's (2016) work, showing that diversity comes at the price of Black students' labor. Participants, for example, often displayed patience and understanding in meeting their nonblack friends where they were located on the figurative racially conscious spectrum. If a nonblack friend committed a racial slight, Black friends were tasked with correcting the slight or offense. These corrections or engagements are also a form of racialized equity labor. A diversity "bargain," therefore, calls for additional labor of Black students to educate peers about race, racism, and racial slights. Scholars might further explore the ways in which emotional labor manifests in the processes of diversity (see Evans and Moore 2015).

ANTIBLACKNESS

In 1903, Du Bois prophetically argued that the "problem of the twentieth century is the problem of the color line." The problem of the color line, in 2020, remains unsolved and will likely remain a problem for centuries to come. As scholars focusing on antiblackness argue, however, the color line itself is black. Cross-racial interactions remain sites of tension, but in settings such as Caldwell at WSU, nonblack students seemed to be united in distancing from and displaying an antagonism toward Black people. In other words, the color line remained a boundary in Caldwell, yet the boundary was uniquely opposed to Black students.

The Caldwell school of engineering presented an especially interesting site to study race because of its "majority-minority" classification and its commitment to diversity. Caldwell simultaneously invested in diversity initiatives yet exhibited a culture of antiblackness. Consider Caldwell's

good-faith efforts to invest in diversity—hiring a director of equity and
inclusion as opposed to simply tacking on more responsibilities to someone holding an existing position, instituting a Multicultural Engineering
Office (MEO), and funding NSBE activities and subsidizing travel to conferences. Their diversity work is noteworthy. Yet, working with diversity
in mind does not always mean working with Black students in mind.
The extremely limited numbers of Black students stood in stark contrast
to Caldwell's diversity efforts. Black students' unique needs were diluted
under the guise of diversity.

Gloria Ladson-Billings and William Tate IV, in their foundational
"Toward a Critical Race Theory of Education," make clear that they are
not saying that "class and gender are insignificant, but rather, as West
suggests, that 'race matters,' and, as Smith insists, 'blackness matters in
more detailed ways'" (1995, 52). Similarly, in the case of engineers at WSU,
Blackness mattered in a more detailed way. Recall how the MEO served a
wide variety of stakeholders, including women of all races, Asian students,
Latinx students, LGBTQ students, and Black students. The accounts of
interactions between Black and nonblack engineers are useful here. The
shared status of being a "person of color" was not a cause for unification
or studying together. Their shared classification or membership in the
MEO did not result in shared experiences of oppression. Rather, nonblack
students of color were often the perpetrators of antiblack racism, themselves. Black students were rendered a problem or, "the least assimilable
to this multicultural imagination" (Dumas and ross 2016, 430). My point
here is not to vilify a particular group of students. Rather, my point is
to question the assumed community or sameness within the "people of
color" construct and to show how antiblack sentiments exist even within
other minoritized racial groups.

Antiblack racism and microaggressions toward Black people, as students explained, came from a diverse group of nonblack students, from
Latinx, to Asian American, to White. The changing racial demographics
of America calls for fresh lenses to understand cross-racial transactions.
CRT in education, as Michael Dumas and kihana ross (2016) articulated
in their theorization of BlackCrit in Education, is not equipped with the
tools to analyze the specificity of antiblackness. As such, I drew upon
BlackCrit and Afropessimist concepts throughout this text such as Black
suffering (2014), antiblack racism (Dumas and ross 2016), and people of
color blindness (Sexton 2010) to better understand the unique oppressions Black students faced. BlackCrit, lesser-used concepts in CRT such

as racial realism, or even Bourdieu coupled with other theories, might provide generative directions to further understand and complicate how scholars study race and higher education.

The three interrelated concepts I highlighted here—linked fate, labor, and antiblackness—undergird the boundaries and tensions I highlighted in each chapter. From examining Black engineers' lives as they were, this study shed light on student engagement and Black student life at an HWI. In the remainder of the text, I offer findings especially pertinent to Black students in engineering and a brief reflection concerning how scholars study race relations on campus.

Black Engineering Students and Engineering Career Capital

The *engineering career field* spans multiple communities and social worlds. Certain social worlds facilitate more engineering *career capital* than others. Engineering-related internships, research, high grades, the creation of mobile apps or websites, and a portfolio of engineering projects are examples of *career capital*. Engineering majors implicitly vie for distinction in the engineering career field for greater chances of engineering employment.

Different social worlds provide different supports. Participation in the mainstream WSU community did not facilitate engineering capital. Students spent less time at WSU community events in order to acquire more career capital. Students often skipped campus-wide events for the sake of studying for engineering classes. For many engineers, engagement with the mainstream campus seemed less important than engagement with their engineering courses.

BLACK SOCIAL WORLDS AND ACHIEVEMENT

But what of the Black WSU community? Foundational work on Black people in STEM suggests a tension between Black peer group involvement and Black people's achievement in STEM (Seymour and Hewitt 1997). Indeed, some Black WSU engineering students sometimes face an implicit dilemma in regard to their level of engagement with the Black community. As the Black Student Union (BSU) president and Black Cultural Center (BCC) leaders admitted, involvement in the Black community requires an element of time that is sometimes too much for Black engineers and other students with more stringent course requirements. Because the BSU and Black community social world had little alignment with engineering in particular, NSBE was a more logical use of time.

Involvement in the Black community, however, does not lessen a student's likelihood of success as an engineer. Limited involvement in the Black community demonstrated by Black Caldwell students was not a byproduct of exclusion or avoidance, but a result of limited free time outside of their studies. This point is contrary to Seymour and Hewitt's (1997) work on why Black engineers leave engineering majors, who argued,

> The culture of Black peer groups offers no affective support for members who are doing well. Black students either isolate or mock those of their group who are earning good grades. The group offers commiseration in adversity, but invokes negative sanctions against celebrating individual (rather than group) success. (351)

In both the Black and NSBE communities, however, the idea of achievement "for the culture" was touted and appreciated. BSU and BCC representatives articulated why Black engineers could not be very present in the community without malice. Further, Black engineers did not express a culture of anti-intellectualism in the Black community either. My findings, therefore, directly contradict Seymour and Hewitt's (1997) arguments concerning the "dysfunctionality of Black peer groups" (354).

NSBE, a Black social world, played a formative role in socializing Black engineers, providing them with career capital. Students go through a process of "becoming" engineers and adopt engineering identities through their studies (Carlone and Johnson 2007; Perna et al. 2008; Stevens et al. 2008). NSBE, in particular, helps Black students "become" engineers and grow in their engineering identities.

Consider, however, the tension in the NSBE social world between a family focus and an engineering focus. As a group, forming a community with a family-like atmosphere was integral to their functioning. I mention this neither to suggest that NSBE should focus more on technical engineering skills nor to imply that NSBE sacrifices an engineering focus for a family focus. Rather, I want to highlight the fact that people, and Black engineers in this case, are not cold, automatons working with the express goal of gaining career capital. For many Black engineers, NSBE provided a family and space of belonging. A family, rather than a few extra hours of studying or fine-tuning their craft, for many of these participants, was invaluable. Thus, given the goals and purpose of NSBE, the amount of engineering capital NSBE can provide is limited.

Friend groups, potential study partners, and support networks take the form of social capital in NSBE. One's social capital can be understood as the amount and quality of resources within the network as well as the size and maintenance of the network (Portes 1998). Students heard of research opportunities and received referrals for jobs from other Black engineers in NSBE. Nina's fervent request for more Black student representation in the Student Ambassador program in front of two "industry reps" at a NSBE meeting intending to promote a scholarship for Black engineering students is exemplary. NSBE provided a venue for Nina to both recommend and implore NSBE students to participate in a selective Caldwell organization and also a place for Black engineering professionals to advertise an opportunity. The WSU NSBE chapter served as a hub of social capital—a place of connections between students, staff, and industry professionals alike.

THE PROBLEM OF STUDENT COLLABORATION

Engineering career capital gained from participation in the Caldwell community takes the form of social capital, capital found in groups or engineering fraternities, and technical skills from engineering societies. In groups, students often worked more efficiently and were able to finish homework in faster times. Study groups also aided in exam preparation and furnished a consistent team for group projects. A close cohort in classes, beyond collaboration, also provided unorthodox academic supports. For a lack of better words, study groups could facilitate cheating. In the form of someone to sit next to during exams and discreetly share answers or with whom to gather old exams, some students had unfair advantages for accessing higher "achievement" and success. Black students, however, often did not have access to groups or the more unorthodox academic supports. While some majors within Caldwell were exceptions, many participants worked by themselves. Their solitude, however, often came as a result of being ostracized or being made to feel unwelcome by nonblack students.

This finding in particular provides greater nuance to the research showing that Black students study by themselves (Seymour and Hewitt 1997; Treisman 1992). While Seymour and Hewitt (1997) suggested that "students of color who experienced academic difficulty often did not ask questions or seek help" (361), my work shows a more complex picture. Relationship building in college is not a one-way process (Emirbayer 1997; McCabe 2016). Rather, some groups form organically with students of the same race and some nonblack students alienate Black students, making study group membership difficult for Black engineers. In conflict with Treisman's findings on Black students in a college calculus class (1992), I found that Black engineers sought help and wanted to work with groups, yet they were often made to feel unwelcome.

Recall that Ayana said students, during exams, sat with their respective races to better work off of each other's papers. For Black students who were typically the only ones of their race in the class, this was an impossibility. Think back to the ways in which Grace and Chantelle characterized the unorthodox if not unethical collaboration of some Asian students in their classes. Students of other races or students with tight study groups might have an unfair advantage in classes by way of illicit methods. Capital acquisition, in this way, was exclusive, alienating Black students and leaving nonblack students with that unfair advantage.

A Note on Studying Race on Campus

Students move between worlds and sometimes are in the different social spheres at the same time. Recall the unique interplay of the Black Community's social world and the mainstream WSU social world during the Midnight Dinner. This event was simultaneously a Black place and a mainstream space. While technically an event for all students, Black students created a celebratory, validating event for themselves, within and because of the larger dinner. Such complexities in campus life and race relations are often taken for granted.

A relational understanding of the campus racial climate accounts for the complexity of identity and the situated nature of practice and behavior (Emirbayer 1997). Through a relational perspective a climate is not a substance or something that exists outside of students. Rather, a climate is dynamic; a process and product of various relationships between stakeholders on campus, policies, the unique moment, and dependent upon a student's background (Tichavakunda 2020). A relational approach to studying campus climate also engages with the social positioning of people within groups, attuned to the processes that make the climate positive for some and negative for others. Recall that Martin, for example, easily adjusted to WSU and joined a fraternity on Frat Row, an area the majority of Black undergraduates avoided. Further, think back to his leadership in an engineering society and his passive, albeit appreciative role in NSBE. Without understanding his background, Martin's experience deviates from what many might expect from a Black engineer at an elite, historically White institution. What do we make of Martin and other Black engineers who buck the trends? His elite prep school pedigree shaped his habitus to align with that of WSU. The relationships he made in his historically White fraternity and general interactions with nonblack students are likewise familiar to his experiences prior to higher education.

On a survey, Black engineers reporting a positive campus climate might seem similar. Yet consider how students such as Dajuan—who spend the bulk of their social lives in the Black social worlds—and students like Martin or Kareem—who spend the bulk of their social lives in the Caldwell and mainstream WSU worlds—might report positive interpretations of the campus climate. A relational understanding of campus racial climates helps us analyze why their positive experiences are different dependent on their social locations and backgrounds.

Frazier (1968) argued that "studies of race relations have often been based upon individual reactions, without reference to the behavior of men as members of a social group" (44). My work, using a Bourdieusian analysis and engaging with the various social worlds students traverse, does just that. My findings also reiterate and provide nuance to the importance of studying friend groups (e.g., antonio 2001; McCabe 2016) and ethnic student organizations (e.g., Harper and Quaye 2007; Museus 2008; Park 2014) to better understand campus racial climates in higher education. Certainly, I could conduct a full study of just the Black community in relation to the NSBE community. In this work, however, I provide a more expansive portrait. Such communities or enclaves should be objects of sociological analysis, not simply referential groups. NSBE, as a social world, has its own processes of engagement and tensions. Consider the NSBE party, Brown Sugar, which occurred around the same time as the Caldwell Engineering Ball. Black engineers were not necessarily excluded from the Engineering Ball. Rather, they created their own party, with their own music, in their own space. Scholars miss events such as this when they view Black students as, "merely atomized individuals who have been excluded from full participation in the life of the White society" (Frazier 1957, 291). Sociologically, Black enclaves or social worlds are useful sites of study to better understand campus racial climates. More work, I believe, should be dedicated to exploring how such communities are *made*. *Black Campus Life* is only scratching the surface of a sociological analysis of Black social worlds on campus. I briefly mentioned that one student suggested that the Black community comes in "waves." The liveliness of Black campus communities is not a given. Deeper exploration is needed to better understand how institutions can better support and facilitate the creation of Black campus communities.

Implications for Practice

Given the permanence of antiblackness, how can we support Black students' current practices? I highlight four practical implications for faculty, student affairs staff, and administrators in higher education: (1) rethink group work; (2) adopt multipronged support systems; (3) avoid diversity dilution; and (4) invest in Black students.

Group work is part of higher education and the campus experience (see Boud et al. 2014). Faculty seemed to take for granted the obstacles students face in forming and joining groups. While important for engineers and other working professionals, group work does not always meet its goal. In the process of teaching students how to work together, Black students might be ostracized and disrespected. Faculty might consider how they can format group work so that students are doing work in a collegial manner without alienating students of different races. Faculty might take a more active role in the formation of study groups, mandating that students "check in" with other students in faculty-created groups. For example, an obligatory "buddy system" coupled with a class session on working in a collegial manner and with students of different races might be a worthy initiative. Race matters in the classroom, shaping how students interact with each other. Because of the assumed race-neutral nature of the engineering discipline, administrators and faculty might consider that engineering students, in particular, need guidance in working across difference with civility and respect.

My work also suggests a need for a multipronged system of supporting Black students, or engineers in this case, at an HWI. One cannot assume that Black students, by virtue of their race, will associate with the Black Student Union or that a Black engineer might associate with NSBE. In other words, institutional support for one Black organization does not necessitate that all Black students are members of this organization and will benefit. While student affairs representatives might suggest that students learn about these groups, staff must also understand that students foster a sense of engagement through different social worlds and communities. Student affairs practitioners, administrators, and other stakeholders might examine the unique context of their institutions—Black Student Union meetings might be the hub of Black social life at one university and a Black Cultural Center might be the hub at another. Campus spaces, organizations, and relationships that facilitate or inhibit student engagement are contextually bound. As such, institutions might map sites of support and engagement for specific populations, conducting context-specific student engagement assessments. From such assessments, institutions will be more knowledgeable about how to pragmatically support students.

Lastly, higher education staff working on diversity efforts might endeavor to avoid diversity dilution. Well-intentioned programs do not always meet the needs of Black students or other specific racial groups. While umbrella terms such as *underrepresented minority* or *person of color* are useful in some ways, they are confusing in others. Aware of the limitations of such terms, faculty and staff might better serve specific racial populations to meet their unique needs. A simple step in avoiding diversity dilution is disaggregating data—even if the data are not ideal. For example, school brochures and websites might tout a "student population of 65 percent women and students of color." As we have learned throughout this text, however, such statistics are deceiving. Institutions will have to be honest about demographics rather than hiding areas of growth under the overarching terms of "diversity" or "students of color."

The last, overarching, recommendation is to invest in Black students. I mean this in three main ways. (1) Recruit and enroll Black students; regardless of programs or initiatives geared toward Black students, a school with less than a 2 percent Black population cannot be understood as investing in Black students. (2) Provide scholarships specifically for Black students. Black students engage in equity labor every day through activism, through turning interactions with nonblack peers into teaching moments after racist interactions, through dealing with the humiliation of being picked last for group work, and through exercising restraint in the face of peers who are being outwardly antiblack. Compensating Black students is a small step schools can take to acknowledge Black collegians' equity labor. (3) Invest in Black student organizations. Students and administrators know the integral role of such organizations. Recall how some participants pointed to NSBE as their reason for persisting in engineering.

Diversity and equity officers can and do play an important role in Black student life, but student organizations, often carry the uncompensated burden of building and maintaining campus Black communities. Paying Black student leaders and ensuring that Black student organizations have ample operating funds is one way to compensate them for labor creating a welcoming campus community that all students benefit from.

Conclusion

I sought to learn how Black engineers themselves understood their experiences. Understanding how Black students experience and respond to racism is important work, but it is not the only work. To say that Johnson, while Milly Rocking during the Midnight Brunch, or Jasmine, while studying for an electrical engineering exam, or Martin, while delegating tasks during an Engineers Without Borders meeting, were each engaging in various forms of resistance is limiting, if not false. To be clear, I am not arguing that racism is overstated in research concerning Black students at historically White institutions of higher education. Racism has played and will continue to play a formative and influential role in society and higher education for the foreseeable future. My point, however, is that by studying more than how students experience or understand racism in college, we can learn about the various processes and mechanisms by which Black students foster a sense of engagement.

Centering the clashes between races and responses to racism are logical epistemological impulses in campus climate research. Yet, such an approach leaves much of the multifarious Black student experience untold and unexamined by the sociological eye. Thus, the inner workings of NSBE meetings, politics of Black Student Unions, and creative, agentic processes Black students engage in, because or in spite of institutional structures, are rendered less important. In this work, I did something different; studying Black engineers as they were, learning about how they traverse different social worlds, and appreciating the complexities of their identities.

The four students that I highlighted in detail gave me feedback on their chapters. Johnson was the only student to read his section in front of me. Through laughs, sighs, questions, and corrections, we got through it. Yet, one exchange in particular encapsulates the complexity of Black student engagement, campus life, identity, and campus racial climate at a historically White university.

◆◆◆

Johnson looks up from the computer screen. With a hint of aggravation, he frowns at me saying that his group does not simply "throw parties." "We plan events," he says with certitude. I push back, asking what types of events they hold outside of parties. I also let him know that I said "parties" so readers could get a better idea of their work. He does not budge. "Nah," he says, "Party planner makes me sound like I'm some type of slacker. You know? I do more than that. I'm making the events." Expressing frustration, not necessarily with me, he goes on to explain that he curates events for the Black community. He makes his point clear saying, "What do you think Black WSU would do on weekends without our events? We're enhancing the Black student experience."

◆◆◆

Johnson is far from a slacker. He is a critical thinker, creative, charismatic, and intelligent. Johnson shapes the culture of Black student organizations at WSU and even helped create two organizations. Johnson co-creates social worlds for other Black students at WSU. In many regards, he does it for the culture. Yet, how does his investment in the Black community relate to his potential to accrue engineering career capital? A Bourdieusian analysis might suggest that competing interests in different social worlds results in a distraction from the acquisition of career capital. A Critical Race analysis might point to the vast underrepresentation of Black students at WSU, arguing that Johnson overexerts himself to make up for what the school neglected to provide in a critical mass of Black students. Both analyses, to an extent, might have a degree of truth. Neither analysis, however, captures Johnson's resolve and joy in building and creating events for other Black students at WSU. For those invested in Black student life, endeavoring to understand the textured, dynamic campus lives of Black students is critical.

As Johnson showed, college life is a balancing act rife with tensions. For Black students at HWIs, and Black engineering majors especially, navigating tensions and boundaries within social worlds can have serious implications on educational outcomes and experiences. By better understanding the tensions and complexities of negotiating identities within and across social worlds, scholars and student affairs professionals might learn how to better support and invest in Black student life.

At a base level, however, we also stand to learn about life from Black students. Black students at HWIs, such as the participants in this study, are remarkable. Their capacity to navigate inequitable campus social worlds structured against them, achieve academically, and not be completely demoralized is nothing short of incredible. As I showed throughout this book, Black students contort their circumstances to better meet their needs, yet, in the process they must also contort themselves—doing group work by themselves, working to set nonblack peers at ease around them, and even growing numb to racism. This is inequity. HWIs such as WSU can be understood as sites of Black suffering—a result of constant microaggressions, outright racist verbal assaults, and institutional neglect. In the face of antiblack racism, however, students did not fall into the clutches of despair (West 2018). Rather, students resisted and even stared down racism. This is the blues of campus life—wrestling with the fact of oppression and the despair it brings without allowing hopelessness and pessimism to determine one's life. And the blues is not about being a passive agent to racism. Beyond facing reality, the blues is about creatively improvising a life within, against, or outside of structures with the possibility of changing the structures, themselves in the process. The blues of campus life reminds us that while racism's hold on campuses remains, Black student life persists.

Appendix

Notes on Theory and Methods

For the sake of narrative voice, I reserved more in-depth discussion concerning methods and theory for this section. Here I tie up loose ends, addressing questions that might arise concerning my theoretical and methodological approach.

WHY SOCIAL WORLDS?

Scholars study campus life in different ways with different frameworks under different names, but often to the same end of studying student cultures. Some might call the social worlds in this book "sub communities" (e.g., Foster 2003), "subcultures" (e.g., Kuh 1995a), or simply "peer cultures" (e.g., Renn and Arnold 2003). Informed by such concepts, I use the term *social worlds* for three main reasons.

1. *Social worlds* acknowledges the dynamic, lively nature of campus communities. Each world I highlight could be the topic of an in-depth project of its own.

2. *Social worlds* serve as a reframing. I did not want to understand certain communities or cultures as "sub" or "counter," potentially positioning these communities through a lens of mainstream/dominant communities or groups (see Kuh 1995a, 570).

3. *Social worlds* acknowledges the roles of staff, faculty, and other stakeholders or forces that shape campus life for students.

WHY CRT AND BOURDIEU?

I take theoretical cues from Ralph Ellison, specifically his critique of Richard Wright's *Native Son* (see Ellison 1964). Richard Wright's *Native Son*, Ellison argued, was an achievement, yet Ellison did not recognize the humanity in the novel's protagonist, Bigger Thomas. Ellison continues, arguing that Black people are not simply products of their sociopolitical context; rather, a Black person is "a product of the interaction between his racial predicament, his individual will, and the broader American cultural freedom in which he finds his ambiguous existence. Thus, he, too, in a limited way, is his own creation" (1964, 112). *Black Campus Life* examines the interaction between Black students' racial predicament and individual will. In order to examine this interplay of agency, or will, and structure, I use Bourdieu's Theory of Practice, as informed by Critical Race Theory (CRT).

All theories have limitations and strengths—the same is true for CRT and Bourdieu. I tried to use the theories in a mutually informing manner, playing to their strengths to engage with the other's limitations. CRT, for example, while instrumental in a number of ways, especially in naming race and racism, is not enough to articulate the scope of Black students' unique experiences. How, for example, might CRT account for the life students make in spite of, or perhaps because of, the racial climate?

And what of Bourdieu? While created with enough malleability to be used in different contexts, Bourdieu theorized cultural reproduction in the French context in particular with a focus on class and did not engage with race (Lofton and Davis 2015; Musoba and Baez 2009). While a number of identities shape inequality in the United States, race, in the American context, plays an integral role in domination, which forces scholars to reconfigure their model of the dominant class's attributes. Further, Bourdieu, in an effort to avoid overintellectualizing the behaviors of people, devalued the voices and reflexive capabilities of the common person. Bourdieu has thus been critiqued for underestimating the ability of the average person to understand their social situations (Winant 2012).

Given the limitations of both frameworks, I employed CRT and Bourdieu in tandem. I used Bourdieu to understand students' networks, cultures, and the relationship between students' agency and structures. CRT—especially racial realism—played an informative role in understanding the racial context of society and taking seriously Black students' voices.[1]

ARE SOCIAL WORLDS FIELDS?

I began this work likening the four social worlds to four *fields*. The initial construction of social worlds as fields was useful. Understanding these student communities as overlapping, dynamic, temporal worlds with their own unique traditions and practices, I believe, helped me loosen student communities from static, a priori constructions. As such, I highlighted tensions within each community to better demonstrate how these communities were in flux. Further, taking cues from the relational nature of fields, I sought to interview more than just the Black engineers themselves. For the Black community's social world, for example, I also interviewed Black Student Union leaders and Black Cultural Center administrators.

Campus social worlds display *illusio*—a key characteristic of Bourdieu's *field*—which is characterized by the investment in traditions, symbols, and practices unique to a specific field. As Bernard Lahire (2015) argues, however, investment in the illusio of a social world does not necessarily mean that a social world should be understood as a field. The NSBE social world, for example, displays illusio—members recognize the e-board as its governing body, meet at similar times, stand to recite the NSBE mission at the end of meetings, and wear apparel with the NSBE insignia. The NSBE world, and other worlds I analyzed, however, are not fields.

From a Bourdieusian sense, actors compete over capital, or distinction, within a given field (Bourdieu and Passeron 1990). The NSBE community, for example, did not have a distinct form of capital or a struggle for status within the community. Similarly, I found that an argument resting on the idea that students in the Black community were competing for Black capital for greater status cumbersome if not incorrect. Findings demonstrated that students sought participation or membership in such social worlds—not necessarily status.

Data Collection Methods

Research is far from glamorous. Research entails waiting more than half an hour for interviews in empty front offices while being told the administrator will be with you in a moment. Research with college students involves flexibility; expecting texts asking to reschedule or students forgetting about interviews. Research also involves unanswered texts, e-mails, and uninterested students. Ethnographic research is awkward. I confused students, forgot names, and apologized often. Research is running from building to building on campus to squeeze in observations at different events, factoring in the eleven minute walk from the student union to the engineering school, nine minutes if I hustled.

My challenge was being as systematic as possible within the inherent messiness of ethnography. Between Spring 2017 to the end of the Fall 2017 semester, I collected data. Much of the raw data for this project came from field notes as well as interview transcripts of participants. I conducted formal interviews with all participants as well as informal interviews while observing.

ACCESS

The National Society of Black Engineers (NSBE) was the entry point to Black engineering culture. After speaking with an executive board member, I pitched my research idea to the rest of the members. With their approval, I presented my research idea to the entire organization. None of the students objected to my studying them, but I made sure to provide them with informed consent sheets. I attended weekly NSBE executive board meetings and general body meetings. I also familiarized myself with Black culture at the school by attending BSU meetings weekly. Through my attendance and participation, I became a familiar face. I also volunteered to help with NSBE events. During Caldwell's STEM week, I signed up to work events with other NSBE members. As a result of my presence at nearly every NSBE event and meeting and BSU meetings, I was able to establish and maintain rapport with students.

PARTICIPANT SELECTION

I included all of the NSBE members who attended meetings in my study. With the exception of first-years who started during Fall 2017, the latter half of data collection, I did not restrict my interviews to certain classes. I also included Black graduate students in the school of engineering as some attended NSBE meetings and acted as mentors to undergraduates. Further, from student interviews I learned of faculty and staff prevalent in their lives, and tried to interview these parties as well. Using snowball sampling, I also received contact information of Black engineers who did not attend NSBE meetings.

INTERVIEWS AND OBSERVATION

I interviewed and audio-recorded participants with a semi-structured protocol. Later, I either transcribed the interviews verbatim or sent recordings
to a third-party transcription service. Interviews varied in length. Faculty
interviews were between twenty and thirty minutes in length. Staff and
administrator interviews ranged between thirty and fifty minutes. Student
interviews were the longest, between thirty and seventy minutes, with an
average interview time of forty-three minutes.

I also interviewed ten Black engineering students, five times each,
during the summer. All but one of the students was involved in a summer
internship related to their field. I chose five men and five women and
ensured they were returning to campus in the Fall. While I had interviewed
more than thirty Black undergraduates already, some were more likely than
others to chat with me. The ten students I interviewed were also chosen
because they were generally responsive to my texts and emails. Summer
interviews with the students did not last longer than twenty minutes.
With the students' permission, I recorded our phone calls and, similarly,
I transcribed each interview transcript verbatim. I gave each student a
$45 Amazon gift card as an incentive to participate.

Observation occurred through shadowing and attending weekly
BSU meetings, NSBE general body meetings, NSBE e-board meetings,
and NSBE study nights. I also spent time (ten hours during one month)
studying in the MEO to observe how students made use of that space. As
The Fall semester came to a close, I began to exit the field, and stopped
attending NSBE e-board meetings and study nights.

Given that much of the "hanging out" with students coincided with
studying, I was able to record many quotes verbatim by typing them on
my laptop. Other quotes, outside of those in formal interviews, I wrote
down in my mobile phone or asked students during conversation if I could
record them.

Table A.1. Interview Sample

Interviewee Description	# of Participants
Black Undergraduate Engineering Students	45
Black Engineering Graduate Students	9
Black Undergraduates in Different Majors	3
Engineering Faculty	5
Engineering Administrators and Staff	11
WSU Black Student Support Staff	2

I also drew data from artifacts. I sifted through the WSU archives and went through more than fifty years of quarterly magazines to learn about the history of Caldwell in relation to Black students. Digital artifacts also proved useful. From texts, tweets, to GroupMe messages, I learned more about Black undergraduates' lives.

Given my time in the field, I was able to triangulate data across a year-long span and used different sources of data collection such as interviews and observations. I also sent each of the four students I highlighted a draft of their section for feedback and advice about getting their story "right." Further, I presented my findings to Black engineers present at a NSBE general body meeting for verification.

My Identity and Positionality

I am a cisgender Black man. While some participants affectionately called me "NSBE dad" or, in an attempt to crack a joke, "NSBE granddad," I was close to them in age. We were familiar with similar celebrity gossip, listened to similar music, and often used the same slang. From using profanity around me, inviting me to parties, calling me an honorary NSBE member, cracking jokes on each other, and sharing gossip with me, beyond developing rapport with students—we became friends. Some students at WSU even thought I was a Caldwell undergraduate myself. Yet, I was, and the participants, too, were always aware of our differences. In order to provide a glimpse of the nature and tensions of my role as a participant observer and ethnographer, I offer brief insight into my relationship with Bianca, a sophomore engineering student.

◆ ◆ ◆

Bianca has a dry sense of humor and speaks in a frank manner. She says things that leave me laughing, but wondering how much was a joke and how much was her truth. Our first meeting is tense. I volunteered to help out with a fundraiser for NSBE, selling churros outside of a campus library. Running ten minutes late to help out with the fundraiser, I see that Bianca has mentioned me in the WSU NSBE chapter GroupMe messaging application, "yo @Antar, wya [where ya at]? these churros are calling your name." Less than three weeks into fieldwork, I am still getting to know many of the engineers and I have not yet spoken with

Bianca. When I get to the library, Bianca says with a smile, "Took you long enough. I've been here for an hour already." I chuckle, make small talk, asking about her luck selling churros and her plans for the day. She asks, "What are you majoring in by the way?" At that moment I realize Bianca was not present the day I introduced myself and my project to the NSBE chapter. I explain to her my project and that I want to hang out with Black engineers at WSU to better understand their lives. "So you're not actually in NSBE? Hm. I probably shouldn't have yelled at you," she says in a matter of fact way. I laugh, "Low key . . . But no sweat though." She shrugs, "Well, you still should have been on time."

Two months later, after interviewing Bianca and more than twenty other Black engineers, consistent participation in the NSBE chapter, and forging closer bonds with participants, Bianca again brings attention to my researcher role. I have volunteered to drive some of the engineers to laser tag during the second half of the NSBE executive board retreat. On the walk to my car, Allen thanks me for helping. Before I can respond, Bianca says, "Antar doesn't really care about us. He wouldn't be here if he didn't have to. This is just his job." The four engineers laugh, Bianca included. I chuckle, "I mean, this is work, and y'all know I'm writing about y'all. But y'all are my friends first." On our walk I ask Bianca if she is still okay with me hanging out with her for research or if she would rather me not include her stories or information about her. She stops me, "Antar. You know I'm just giving you a hard time."

◆ ◆ ◆

These two interactions with Bianca demonstrate some of the complexities of my identity and ethnographic research—the ongoing process of maintaining rapport, being mistaken as an engineer, negotiating the role of researcher and friend, and reminding participants that I would write about our daily interactions. Such potential encumbrances are unique to the immersive practice of ethnography. The challenges or tensions in fieldwork, however, were a result of access—a deep level of access I likely would not have been given were it not for my identity.

My personal background informed my experience in the field. I attended an HWI myself and was heavily involved in the Black campus community, joining a Black Greek Letter Organization, and leading Black student organizations. While my experience and viewpoint aided me in some ways, I remained vigilant about not simply telling a version of my own story. What I had thought I was going to find based on my own experiences was not what I found. In cases where I might have understood a situation as racist, some participants did not. In cases where I might have been offended, some were not. I had to avidly overcome biases that I held and trust the accounts of students. The differences between my alma mater and WSU, however, were many and I was a foreigner to the engineering field. Such differences, centering voices of participants, careful observation, and guidance from my theoretical frameworks, I believe, kept my data collection process honest.

Data Representation

To increase the trustworthiness of this project, I worked to make clear distinctions between direct observations and secondhand accounts from participants or other sources. Without disrupting the narrative, I make an effort to show where I make assumptions as the researcher with words such as *perhaps* or *maybe*. I also make clear throughout my writing the source of my data, so as not to confuse the reader.

I represented the participants, to the best of my ability, with their quirks, hopes, regrets, joys and other characteristics in an effort to portray their humanity. I also took steps to protect their identities, providing pseudonyms of students and altering other identifying information. At base, I think most people are well-intentioned, doing the best that they can in their fields; myself as a researcher, students as engineers, faculty as professors, administrators as leaders, and so on. There are no "bad guys" in this study. I do, however, highlight the forces and antiblack structures that might result in social reproduction and negatively influence Black engineers' student engagement, perception of the campus climate, and academic success.

I also represented myself in the first person. While the participants and their experiences are the focus, I included my voice to help provide context. I was there, attending meetings, going to events, asking questions, fundraising, or even participating in an NSBE-sponsored Black History Month debate. In the writing, I try to represent myself as a bystander whenever possible, but I do not shrink away from my involvement.

I attended the same amount of meetings, if not more, as NSBE executive board members, helped fundraise, and even was asked to be a tie-breaking vote on where the executive board would go for their retreat. I shared inside jokes with students, studied with them, ate with them, and became friends with many of them. Whether in the capacity of "NSBE dad," essay editor, friendly face in meetings, or researcher, my presence was felt and, in some capacity, I influenced the spaces I entered. As such, I do not attempt to minimize my involvement in the field.

QUOTATIONS

Any quotations included are verbatim. I collected quotes either from transcribed interviews, field notes that I typed during meetings, or informal conversations that I recorded with students (with their permission). I recorded a good number of quotations verbatim during observations because much of my time with students was spent in meetings or studying. I could therefore type on my laptop in an unobtrusive manner. In other cases of observation, I wrote notes on my cell phone. During a party, for example, I used my phone to type snippets of conversation as well as details of the event.

TALKING ABOUT RACISM

Microaggressions and other perceived racialized aggressions are important to understand in an effort to learn more about campus racial climate. Yet, a challenge in studying racial slights is the subjective nature of the offense. While one student might find nothing wrong with being mislabeled as a student athlete another might find the assumption racist and a microaggression. I made an effort, in representing the data, to represent students' voices and sentiments themselves and try not to insert myself. By that I mean I took seriously the Critical Race Theory tenets of valuing students experiential knowledge (Solórzano et al. 2000) as well as racial realism (Bell 1992). At times, adhering to both tenets posed a tension. What did I do if a student found another student's action neutral, but I viewed the same action as racist? While racism is permanent in society, the interpretation of racial slights is often subjective—I try to make clear the participants' understandings of such incidents.

Limitations

This book, while entitled *Black Campus Life*, should not be read or understood as a definitive work on Black students' experiences at HWIs. For example, while I do attempt to engage with participants' intersecting identities, I prioritize race. In prioritizing race, however, I missed opportunities to deeply explore how other important aspects of identity, such as religion, sexuality, class, gender, and ethnicity shape students' experiences. Further, as I have made clear throughout the text, this work draws from and is inspired by much prior research on Black students' experiences at HWIs.

Engineers' lack of leisure time, in some ways, proved a challenge in data collection. Shadowing students meant sitting in silent libraries with them. Other students studied at their apartments or residence halls, so I opted not to join. Recall Dr. Pittman's question of where the Black engineers were. More often than not, they were studying by themselves. Laurie once asked me about my data collection process. I confided in her, telling my difficulties of trying to have conversations with introverted engineers. She laughed saying, "Yeah there are definitely some people I just say 'Hi' to because if I try anything else it's not going to happen." I followed up, saying, "You know, I never really see y'all hanging out." She nodded, saying, "Yeah, like it's only if we're at a [NSBE] meeting. [Or] If I like linger after to talk with people, but that's it."

The data collection process was also limited by sampling as well as my identity. I only interviewed five engineering faculty—two of whom worked with diversity at the school of engineering. While I sent out a general e-mail to faculty in various engineering programs, only three took the time to meet with me. Further, in terms of sampling and observing, some students were easier to shadow than others. Aware of my status as a heterosexual cisgender Black man, close in age to students, I took steps to build and maintain rapport with students in a professional yet friendly manner. I found it easiest, however, to foster relationships with men.

While my identity and unique positionality was a strength in data collection, I also had to fight the belief or reflex that I "would understand" my participants when they explained their experiences to me. During some observations, I am sure, I would have asked different questions had I not shared the same race as my participants. Other things I took for granted because they were familiar. The tendency to jokingly insult someone— playing the dozens—I did not question. The unspoken "nod" Black people sometimes give other Black folk in spaces where they are the minority, I did not question either. While I view my identity as more of a strength than a limitation in this study, I do admit an encumbrance of perhaps accepting some practices as given. I took steps, however, through reflective writing in memos, to keep my assumptions to a minimum. Despite my access in racial identity, my ethnographic analysis was limited because of my lack of an engineering identity. As my participants reminded me on occasion, "You're not even an engineer, Antar." While I could study with them on occasion or shadow them to class, I neither have nor sought to build the engineering discipline they developed over time.

How might the data have been different had I been a White man or an engineer myself? I might have had less inclination to take observations in Black spaces for granted or perhaps as an engineer I would have had a better idea of what mattered in engineering courses and success. Yet I do not think I would have obtained such rich descriptions. Take into account the 113 interviews and 180 hours of observation I conducted, in addition to the fact that I interviewed nearly 80 percent of the entire Black undergraduate engineering population. In ethnography, the researcher is the primary research instrument. While I constantly grappled with reflexivity, the benefits of my positionality and resultant access, I argue, served as a net positive for this research.

Notes

Chapter 1

1. Predominantly White Institutions of higher education report at least a 50 percent White student population. Historically White Institutions of higher education might report less than a 50 percent White student population yet also have a history of excluding/limiting the numbers of Black students. Historically White Institutions' traditions, practices, and symbols were largely designed for and by Whites (see Allen, Epps, and Haniff 1991). In this text, I use historically White institution expansively to include PWIs as well.

2. The name of the school and participants are all pseudonyms.

3. I asked the NSBE president at the time why none of the members attended the BSU election. She was not aware of the election and asked members at the next meeting if anyone knew about election; no one in attendance knew about the meeting either.

4. Ajay Sharma (2016) has provided evidence indicating that the espoused need for STEM workers is likely exaggerated. Others question the goal of increasing the number of STEM graduates, arguing that the STEM emphasis is more about global dominance, bolstering the American military, and lowering the salaries of STEM workers than about equity or knowledge production (e.g., Sengupta-Irving and Vossoughi 2019; Tarnoff 2017).

5. United States Census Bureau (2008) projections, for example, show that racial minorities will comprise the majority of the nation by 2042.

6. Students had varying experiences based on their intersecting identities. However, in order to give race analytic primacy, I could not fully address all such identities in this work. For example, this text would be very different had I employed a Black feminist analytic lens. As such, my work is necessarily limited and only tells part of the story of campus racial life in giving race analytic primacy.

7. Consider two popular ethnographies of campus culture, Rebekah Nathan's *My Freshman Year* (2005) and Michael Moffatt's *Coming of Age in New Jersey* (1989). Moffatt admittedly had difficulty interviewing Black students and mentioned feeling intimidated by some Black male students. Nathan likewise struggled with access to Black campus communities. In both pieces, Black students' lives are rendered a mystery.

8. A dance where one quickly dips their head into the crook of their bent elbow.

Chapter 2

1. America can refer to countries in North, South, or Central America. For the purposes of narrative voice, I use America and the United States of America interchangeably in this text.

2. Data in this section concerning the history of the Caldwell school of engineering came from the West Side University Archives, Special Collections. The campus library provided hard copies of *The West Side* magazine for me to examine in their Special Collections room. I was granted permission to take pictures of relevant material on my mobile phone and take notes. I do not include any other information concerning the data source, to protect the school.

3. Student organizations are led by executive boards, or e-boards. Students on the e-board adopt leadership roles such as president, vice president, and communications chair.

Chapter 3

1. I tried to make it clear to the participants that if they ever needed someone to edit a paper or needed help brainstorming for a writing assignment that I would help.

Chapter 4

1. Johnson's GPA has since risen almost a full point to 2.7.

2. Engineering career capital includes different types of capitals, in a Bourdieusian sense. For example, the resources found in networks is often understood as social capital. For the purposes of this analysis, I included social capital that might facilitate internship placement simply as a form of career capital.

3. Approached by cops.

Chapter 5

1. Racial essentialism arose as a theme in the non-engineering-related WSU Black community as well. However, given my extended time with NSBE and following Black engineers, I had more data to provide examples of racial essentialism within the Black engineering social world.

2. While students of all races are welcome to join SWE, only White women were present for this event.

3. Technical interviews are skills-based. Computer science/programming jobs, for example, may require interviewees to answer computer science–related questions.

Chapter 6

1. While "woke" is defined in different ways, "woke" in this context might be considered a form of critical race consciousness toward various social issues.

Chapter 7

1. Shropshire (2004) coined the term *diversity dilution dilemma* to address how professional sports organizations engage with the broadening understanding of what diversity entails. I use the term differently, specifically highlighting how in an effort to meet the needs of all groups under the umbrella of "diverse," the unique needs of specific groups are not met.

2. Staff in MEO directed me to the American Society for Engineering Education website where I found data concerning student representation.

Chapter 8

1. "Becky" is a stock name sometimes used for White women.

2. "Taking an L" is short for "taking a loss," and is akin to admitting defeat.

3. Dumbledore is the school headmaster in the Harry Potter series and is especially known for his wisdom.

4. Derrick Bell makes use of the same exchange from Toni Morrison's *Beloved* to articulate a racial realist philosophy (see Bell 1992, 29).

Chapter 11

1. "Getting lit" in this context can mean going to parties or drinking alcohol or a combination of the two.

Appendix

1. I say more about the theoretical compatibility between Critical Race Theory and Bourdieu's thinking in a journal article entitled "An Overdue Theoretical Discourse: Pierre Bourdieu's Theory of Practice and Critical Race Theory in Education" (see Tichavakunda 2019).

References

Abrica, E. J., C. García-Louis, and C. D. J. Gallaway. 2020. "Antiblackness in the Hispanic-Serving Community College (HSCC) Context: Black Male Collegiate Experiences through the Lens of Settler Colonial Logics." *Race Ethnicity and Education* 23, no. 1: 55–73.

Agyepong, M. 2017. "The Struggles of Invisibility: Perception and Treatment of African Students in the United States." In *Erasing Invisibility, Inequity and Social Injustice of Africans in the Diaspora and the Continent*, edited by O. N. Ukpokodu and P. O. Ojiambo, 56–75. Newcastle-upon-Tyne: Cambridge Scholars.

Ahmed, S., and E. Swan. 2006. "Introduction: Doing diversity." *Policy Futures in Education* 4, no. 2: 96–100.

Allen, Q. 2018. "(In)visible Men on Campus: Campus Racial Climate and Subversive Black Masculinities at a Predominantly White Liberal Arts University. *Gender and Education*: 1–19.

Allen, W. R. 1992. "The Color of Success: African-American College Students Outcomes at Predominantly White and Historically Black Public Colleges and Universities." *Harvard Educational Review* 62; 26–44.

———, E. G. Epps, and N. Z. Haniff, eds. 1991. *College in Black and White: African American Students in Predominantly White and in Historically Black Public Universities.* Albany: State University of New York Press.

Anderson, E. 2000. *Code of the Street: Decency, Violence, and the Moral Life of the Inner City.* W. W. Norton.

———. 2015. "The White Space." *Sociology of Race and Ethnicity* 1, no. 1: 10–21.

Anderson, M. L., and P. H. Collins. 2004. *Race, Class, and Gender: An Anthology.* 5th ed. Belmont, CA: Wadsworth/Thompson.

antonio, a. l. 2001. "Diversity and the Influence of Friendship Groups in College." *The Review of Higher Education* 25, no. 1: 63–89.

Armstrong, E. A., and L. T. Hamilton. 2013. *Paying for the Party.* Cambridge: Harvard University Press.

Astin, A. W. 1984. "Student Involvement: A Developmental Theory for Higher Education." *Journal of College Student Development* 25: 297–308.

Austin, R. 1991. "The Black Community, Its Lawbreakers, and a Politics of Identification." *Southern California Law Review* 65: 1769–1817.

Bailey, M., and Trudy. 2018. "On Misogynoir: Citation, Erasure, and Plagiarism." *Feminist Media Studies* 18, no. 4: 762–68.

Baldridge, B. J. 2019. *Reclaiming Community: Race and the Uncertain Future of Youth Work*. Stanford: Stanford University Press.

Bell, D. A. 1992. *Faces at the Bottom of the Well: The Permanence of Racism*. New York: Basic Books.

———. 1992. "Racial Realism." *Connecticut Law Review* 24, no. 2: 363–79.

Beddoes, K. 2017. "Institutional Influences that Promote Studying Down in Engineering Diversity Research." *Frontiers: A Journal of Women Studies* 38, no. 1: 88–99.

Biondi, M. 2012. *The Black Revolution on Campus*. Berkeley: University of California Press.

Bix, A. S. 2004. "From 'Engineeresses' to 'Girl Engineers' to 'Good Engineers': A History of Women's US Engineering Education." *NWSA journal*: 27–49.

Bonilla-Silva, E. 2019. "Feeling Race: Theorizing the Racial Economy of Emotions." *American Sociological Review* 84, no. 1: 1–25.

Boud, D., R. Cohen, and J. Sampson, eds. 2014. *Peer Learning in Higher Education: Learning from and with Each Other*. Sterling, VA: Stylus.

Bourdieu, P. 1984. *Distinction: A Social Critique of the Judgement of Taste*. Cambridge: Harvard University Press.

———, & Passeron, J. C. 1990. *Reproduction in Education, Society, and Culture*. 4th ed.). Thousand Oaks, CA: Sage.

Bowman, N. A., and J. J. Park. 2015. "Not All Diversity Interactions are Created Equal: Cross-Racial Interaction, Close Interracial Friendship, and College Student Outcomes. *Research in Higher Education* 56, no. 6: 601–21.

Boyer, E. 1987. *College: The Undergraduate Experience in America*. New York: Harper and Row.

Brasher, J. P., D. H. Alderman, and J. F. Inwood. 2017. "Applying Critical Race and Memory Studies to University Place Naming Controversies: Toward a Responsible Landscape Policy. *Papers in Applied Geography* 3, no. 3–4: 292–307.

Brooms, D. R. 2015. " 'We didn't let the neighborhood win': Black Male Students' Experiences in Negotiating and Navigating an Urban Neighborhood." *The Journal of Negro Education* 84, no. 3: 269–81.

———. 2017. *Being Black, Being Male on Campus: Understanding and Confronting Black Male Collegiate Experiences*. Albany: State University of New York Press.

————. 2018a. " 'Building Us Up': Supporting Black Male College Students in a Black Male Initiative Program." *Critical Sociology* 44, no. 1: 141–55.

————. 2018b. "Exploring Black Male Initiative Programs: Potential and Possibilities for Supporting Black Male Success in College." *The Journal of Negro Education* 87, no. 1: 59–72.

Brooms, D. R., and A. R. Davis. 2017. "Staying Focused on the Goal: Peer Bonding and Faculty Mentors Supporting Black Males' Persistence in College." *Journal of Black Studies* 48, no. 3: 305–26.

Brooms, D. R., and A. R. Perry. 2016. " 'It's Simply Because We're Black Men' Black Men's Experiences and Responses to the Killing of Black Men." *The Journal of Men's Studies* 24, no. 2: 166–84.

Bullock, E. C. 2017. "Only STEM Can Save Us? Examining Race, Place, and STEM Education as Property." *Educational Studies* 53, no. 6: 1–14.

Burt, B. A., K. L. Williams, and W. A. Smith. 2018. "Into the Storm: Ecological and Sociological Impediments to Black Males' Persistence in Engineering Graduate Programs." *American Educational Research Journal* 55, no. 5: 965–1006.

Cabrera, N. L. 2018. "Where Is the Racial Theory in Critical Race Theory?: A Constructive Criticism of the Crits." *The Review of Higher Education* 42, no. 1: 209–33.

————, J. S. Watson, and J. D. Franklin. 2016. "Racial Arrested Development: A Critical Whiteness Analysis of the Campus Ecology. *Journal of College Student Development* 57, no. 2: 119–34.

Carlone, H. B., and A. Johnson. 2007. "Understanding the Science Experience of Successful Women of Color: Science Identity as an Analytic Lens. *Journal of Research in Science Teaching* 44, no. 8: 1187–218.

Carter Andrews, D. J. 2008. "Achievement as Resistance: The Development of a Critical Race Achievement Ideology among Black Achievers." *Harvard Educational Review* 78, no. 3: 466–97.

————. 2012. "Black Achievers' Experiences with Racial Spotlighting and Ignoring in a Predominantly White High School. *Teachers College Record* 114, no. 10: 1–46.

Carter, P. L. 2006. "Straddling Boundaries: Identity, Culture, and School." *Sociology of education* 79, no. 4: 304–28.

Chadderton, C. 2013. "Towards a Research Framework for Race in Education: Critical Race Theory and Judith Butler." *International Journal of Qualitative Studies in Education* 26, no. 1: 39–55.

Chambers, C. R., ed. 2011. *Diversity in Higher Education: Vol. 8. Support Systems and Services for Diverse Populations: Considering the Intersections of Race, Gender, and the Diverse Needs of Black Female Undergraduates.* New York: Emerald Group.

————, and M. C. Poock. 2011. "Does Engagement = Positive Outcomes for African American Women College Students? A Cursory Analysis of NSSE 2009–2010 Data." In *Support Systems and Services for Diverse Populations*, edited by C. R. Chambers, 1–20. New York: Emerald Group.

Chambliss, D. F., and C. G. Takacs. 2014. *How College Works*. Cambridge: Harvard University Press.

Chan, H. Y., H. Choi, M. F. Hailu, M. Whitford, and S. Duplechain DeRouen. 2020. "Participation in Structured STEM-Focused Out-of-School Time Programs in Secondary School: Linkage to Postsecondary STEM Aspiration and Major." *Journal of Research in Science Teaching*.

Chang, M. J. 1999. "Does Racial Diversity Matter? The Educational Impact of a Racially Diverse Undergraduate Population." *Journal of College Student Development* 40, no. 4: 377–95.

————, J. Sharkness, S. Hurtado, and C. B. Newman. 2014. "What Matters in College for Retaining Aspiring Scientists and Engineers from Underrepresented Racial Groups." *Journal of Research in Science Teaching* 51, no. 5: 555–80.

Chao, M. M., Y. Y. Hong, and C. Y. Chiu. 2013. "Essentializing Race: Its Implications on Racial Categorization. *Journal of Personality and Social Psychology* 104, 4: 619.

Charles, C. Z., M. J. Fischer, M. A. Mooney, and D. S. Massey. 2009. *Taming the River: Negotiating the Academic, Financial, and Social Currents in Selective Colleges and Universities*. Princeton: Princeton University Press.

Charleston, L. J., P. L. George, J. F. Jackson, J. Berhanu, and M. H. Amechi. 2014. "Navigating Underrepresented STEM Spaces: Experiences of Black women in US Computing Science Higher Education Programs Who Actualize Success." *Journal of Diversity in Higher Education* 7, no. 3: 166–76.

Cohen, C. J. 1999. *The Boundaries of Blackness: AIDS and the Breakdown of Black Politics*. Chicago: University of Chicago Press.

Cohen, J. J. 1998. "Time to Shatter the Glass Ceiling for Minority Faculty." *Journal of the American Medical Association* 280, no. 9: 821–22.

Cole, D. 2007. "Do Interracial Interactions Matter? An Examination of Student-Faculty Contact and Intellectual Self-Concept." *The Journal of Higher Education* 78, no. 3: 249–81.

Collins, P. H. 2000. *Black Feminist Thought: Knowledge, Consciousness, and the Politics of Empowerment*. New York: Routledge.

Cox, A. M. 2015. *Shapeshifters: Black Girls and the Choreography of Citizenship*. Durham: Duke University Press.

Crenshaw, K. W. 1989. "Demarginalizing the Intersection of Race and Sex: A Black Feminist Critique of Antidiscrimination Doctrine, Feminist Theory, and Antiracist Politics." *University of Chicago Legal Forum* 139: 139–67.

Crenshaw, K. 1991. "Mapping the Margins: Intersectionality, Identity Politics, and Violence against Women of Color." *Stanford Law Review* 43: 1241–99.

————, N. Gotanda, G. Peller, and K. Thomas, eds. 1995. *Critical Race Theory: The Key Writings that Formed the Movement*. New York: NYU Press.

Dache, A., and J. A. White. 2016. "College Students or Criminals? A Postcolonial Geographic Analysis of the Social Field of Whiteness at an Urban Community College Branch Campus and Suburban Main Campus." *Community college review* 44, no. 1: 49–69.

Dache, A., S. J. Quaye, C. Linder, and K. McGuire, eds. 2019. *Rise Up!: Activism as Education*. East Lansing: Michigan State University Press.

Dancy, T. E., K. T. Edwards, and J. Earl Davis. 2018. "Historically White Universities and Plantation Politics: Antiblackness and Higher Education in the Black Lives Matter Era." *Urban Education* 53, no. 2: 176–95.

Davis, J. E. 1994. "College in Black and White: Campus Environment and Academic Achievement of African American Males." *The Journal of Negro Education* 63, no. 4: 620–33.

Dawson, M. C. 1994. *Behind the Mule: Race and Class in African American Politics*. Princeton: Princeton University Press.

De Fina, A. 2007. "Code-Switching and the Construction of Ethnic Identity in a Community of Practice." *Language in Society* 36, no. 3: 371–92.

Delgado, R., and J. Stefancic. 2012. *Critical Race Theory: An Introduction*. New York: New York University Press.

Desmond, M. 2016. *Evicted: Poverty and Profit in the American City*. New York: Broadway Books.

Donovan, R. A., and L. M. West. 2015. "Stress and Mental Health: Moderating Role of the Strong Black Woman Stereotype." *Journal of Black Psychology* 41, no. 4: 384–96.

Douglass, P., B. Hesse, T. K. Nopper, G. Thomas, and C. Wun. 2016. *Conceptual Aphasia in Black: Displacing Racial Formation*. Lanham, MD: Lexington Books.

Du Bois, W. E. B. 2008. *The Souls of Black Folk*. Oxford: The Independent (Original work published in 1903.)

————. 2013. "A Negro Student at Harvard at the End of the 19th Century." *The Massachusetts Review* 54, no. 3: 364–80. (Original work published in 1960.)

Dumas, M. J. 2014. " 'Losing an Arm': Schooling as a Site of Black Suffering." *Race Ethnicity and Education* 17, no. 1: 1–29.

————, and k. m. ross. 2016. " 'Be Real Black for Me': Imagining BlackCrit in Education." *Urban Education* 51, no. 4: 415–42.

Edgerton, J. D., and L. W. Roberts. 2014. "Cultural Capital or Habitus? Bourdieu and Beyond in the Explanation of Enduring Educational Inequality." *Theory and Research in Education* 12, no. 2: 193–220.

Ellison, R. 1945. "Richard Wright's Blues." *The Antioch Review* 5, no. 2: 198–211.

Emirbayer, M. 1997. "Manifesto for a Relational Sociology." *American Journal of Sociology* 103, no. 2: 281–317.

Espinosa, L. 2011. "Pipelines and Pathways: Women of Color in Undergraduate STEM Majors and the College Experiences that Contribute to Persistence." *Harvard Educational Review* 81, no. 2: 209–41.

Essed, P. 1991. *Understanding Everyday Racism: An Interdisciplinary Approach.* Newbury Park, CA: Sage.

Esters, L. L., and I. A. Toldson. 2013. "Supporting Minority Male Education in Science, Technology, Engineering, and Mathematics (STEM) Disciplines." *Texas Education Review* 1: 209–19.

Evans, L., and W. L. Moore. 2015. "Impossible Burdens: White Institutions, Emotional Labor, and Micro-Resistance." *Social Problems* 62, no. 3: 439–54.

Fanon, F. 2003. "The Fact of Blackness." In *Identities: Race, Class, Gender, and Nationality*, edited by L. M. Alcoff and E. Mendieta, 62–74. Oxford: Blackwell.

Feagin, J., and M. Sikes. 1994. *Living with Racism: The Black Middle Class Experience.* Boston: Beacon Press.

Feagin, J. R., H. Vera, and N. Imani. 1996. *The Agony of Education: Black Students at White Colleges and Universities.* New York: Routledge.

Feinberg, A., R. Branton, and V. Martinez-Ebers. 2019, March 22. Counties that Hosted a 2016 Trump Rally Saw a 226 Percent Increase in Hate Crimes. *The Washington Post.* https://www.washingtonpost.com/politics/2019/03/22/trumps-rhetoric-does-inspire-more-hate-crimes/?noredirect=on&utm_term=.0a0031b215f9#click=https://t.co/bYXsN60xzH.

Ferguson, A. A. 2010. *Bad Boys: Public Schools in the Making of Black Masculinity.* Ann Arbor: University of Michigan Press.

Fleming, J. 1984. *Blacks in College: A Comparative Study of Student Success in Black and White Institutions.* San Francisco: Jossey-Bass.

Fordham, S. 1996. *Blacked Out: Dilemmas of Race, Identity, and Success at Capital High.* Chicago: University of Chicago Press.

Foster, K. M. 2003. "The Contours of Community: The Formation and Maintenance of a Black Student Community on a Predominantly White Campus." *Race, Ethnicity and Education* 6, no. 3: 265–81.

Frazier, E. F. 1957. "The Negro Middle Class and Desegregation." *Social Problems* 4, no. 4: 291–301.

———. 1968. *E. Franklin Frazier on Race Relations.* Edited by G. Edwards. Chicago, IL: University of Chicago Press.

Fries-Britt, S., C. A. George Mwangi, and A. M. Peralta. 2014. "Learning Race in a US Context: An Emergent Framework on the Perceptions of Race among Foreign-Born students of Color." *Journal of Diversity in Higher Education* 7, no. 1: 1–13.

Garcia, G. A., M. P. Johnston, J. C. Garibay, F. A. Herrera, and L. G. Giraldo. 2011. "When Parties Become Racialized: Deconstructing Racially Themed Parties." *Journal of Student Affairs Research and Practice* 48, 1: 5–21.

Gasiewski, J. A., M. K. Eagan, G. A. Garcia, S. Hurtado, and M. J. Chang. 2012. "From Gatekeeping to Engagement: A Multicontextual, Mixed Method

Study of Student Academic Engagement in Introductory STEM Courses." *Research in higher education* 53, no. 2: 229–61.

Gaston Gayles, J., and K. N. Smith. 2018. "Advancing Theoretical Frameworks for Intersectional Research on Women in STEM." *New Directions for Institutional Research* 2018, no. 179: 27–43.

Gieryn, T. F. 2000. "A Space for Place in Sociology." *Annual review of sociology* 26, no. 1: 463–96.

Gilkes Borr, T. 2018. "The Strategic Pursuit of Black Homophily on a Predominantly White Campus." *The Journal of Higher Education* 90, no. 2: 1–25.

Golash-Boza, T. 2016. "A Critical and Comprehensive Sociological Theory of Race and Racism." *Sociology of Race and Ethnicity* 2, no. 2: 129–41.

Gonzales, L. D. 2014. "Framing Faculty Agency inside Striving Universities: An Application of Bourdieu's Theory of Practice." *The Journal of Higher Education* 85, no. 2: 193–218.

Grier-Reed, T., and R. J. Wilson. 2016. "The African American Student Network: An Exploration of Black Students' Ego networks at a Predominantly White Institution." *Journal of Black Psychology* 42: 374–86.

Griffin, K. A., E. L. Cunningham, G. Mwangi, and A. Chrystal. 2016. "Defining Diversity: Ethnic Differences in Black Students' Perceptions of Racial Climate." *Journal of Diversity in Higher Education* 9, no. 1: 34.

Griffith, A. N., N. M. Hurd, and S. B. Hussain. 2019. " 'I Didn't Come to School for This': A Qualitative Examination of Experiences with Race-Related Stressors and Coping Responses among Black Students Attending a Predominantly White Institution." *Journal of adolescent research* 34, no. 2: 115–39.

Guiffrida, D. A. 2003. "African American Student Organizations as Agents of Social Integration." *Journal of College Student Development* 44, no. 3: 304–19.

Gurin, P., E. Dey, S. Hurtado, and G. Gurin. 2002. "Diversity and Higher Education: Theory and Impact on Educational Outcomes." *Harvard Educational Review* 72, no. 3: 330–67.

Gusa, D. L. 2010. "White Institutional Presence: The Impact of Whiteness on Campus Climate." *Harvard Educational Review* 80: 464–90.

Hailu, M. F., and M. Sarubbi. 2019. "Student Resistance Movements in Higher Education: An Analysis of the Depiction of Black Lives Matter Student Protests in News Media." *International Journal of Qualitative Studies in Education* 32, no. 9: 1108–24.

Harper, S. R. 2004. "The Measure of a Man: Conceptualizations of Masculinity among High-Achieving African American Male College Students." *Berkeley Journal of Sociology* 48: 89–107.

———. 2010. "An Anti-Deficit Achievement Framework for Research on Students of Color in STEM." *New Directions for Institutional Research* 148: 63–74.

———. 2012. "Race without Racism: How Higher Education Researchers Minimize rRacist Institutional Norms." *Review of Higher Education* 36, no. 1: 9–29.

————. 2013. "Am I My Brother's Teacher? Black Undergraduates, Racial Socialization, and Peer Pedagogies in Predominantly White Postsecondary Contexts."
Review of Research in Education 37, no. 1: 183–211.

————. 2014. "(Re)setting the Agenda for College Men of Color: Lessons Learned
from a 15-Year Movement to Improve Black Male Student Success." In *Men
of Color in Higher Education: New Foundations for Developing Models for
Success*, edited by R. A. Williams, 116–43. Washington, DC: Stylus.

————, and S. Hurtado. 2007. "Nine Themes in Campus Racial Climates and
Implications for Institutional Transformation." *New Directions for Student
Services* 120: 7–24.

Harper, S. R., L. D. Patton, and O. S. Wooden. 2009. "Access and Equity for African
American Students in Higher Education: A Critical Race Historical Analysis of Policy Efforts." *The Journal of Higher Education* 80, no. 4: 389–414.

Harper, S. R., and S. J. Quaye. 2007. "Student Organizations as Venues for Black
Identity Expression and Development among African American Male Student Leaders." *Journal of College Student Development* 48, no. 2: 127–44.

Harris, A. P. 1990. "Race and Essentialism in Feminist Legal Theory." *Stanford
Law Review* 42, no. 3: 581–616.

Harris III, F., R. T. Palmer, and L. E. Struve. 2011. "'Cool Posing' on Campus:
A Qualitative Study of Masculinities and Gender Expression among Black
Men at a Private Research Institution." *The Journal of Negro Education* 80,
no. 1: 47–62.

Harris, J. C., and L. D. Patton. 2017. "The Challenges and Triumphs in Addressing Students' Intersectional Identities for Black Culture Centers." *Journal of
Diversity in Higher Education* 10, no. 4: 334.

Harris-Perry, M. V. 2011. *Sister Citizen: Shame, Stereotypes, and Black Women in
America*. New Haven: Yale University Press.

hooks, b. 1981. *Ain't I a Woman: Black Women and Feminism*. Boston: South
End Press.

Horowitz, H. L. 1987. *Campus Life: Undergraduate Cultures from the End of the
Eighteenth Century to the Present*. Chicago: University of Chicago Press.

Hotchkins, B. K., and T. Dancy. 2017. "A House Is not a Home: Black Students'
Responses to Racism in University Residential Halls." *Journal of College &
University Student Housing* 43. No. 3: 42–52.

Hull, G. T., P. B. Scott, and B. Smith, eds. 1982. *All the Women Are White, All the
Blacks Are Men, but Some of Us are Brave*. Old Westbury, NY: Feminist Press.

Hunter, M. A., M. Pattillo, Z. F. Robinson, and K. Y. Taylor. 2016. "Black Placemaking: Celebration, Play, and Poetry." *Theory, Culture & Society* 33, no.
7–8:. 31–56.

Hunter, M. A., and Z. Robinson. 2018. *Chocolate Cities: The Black Map of American
Life*. Berkeley: University of California Press.

Hurtado, S. 1992. "The Campus Racial Climate: Contexts of Conflict." *The Journal
of Higher Education* 63, no. 5: 539–69.

Hurtado, S., C. L. Alvarez, C. Guillermo-Wann, M. Cuellar, and L. Arellano. 2012. "A Model for Diverse Learning Environments." In *Higher Education: Handbook of Theory and Research*, edited by J. C. Smart and M. B. Paulsen, 41–122. Dordrecht: Springer.

Hurtado, S., N. L. Cabrera, M. H. Lin, L. Arellano, and L. L. Espinosa. 2009. "Diversifying Science: Underrepresented Student Experiences in Structured Research Programs." *Research in Higher Education* 50, no. 2: 189–214.

Hurtado, S., K. A. Griffin, L. Arellano, and M. Cuellar. 2008. "Assessing the Value of Climate Assessments: Progress and Future Directions." *Journal of Diversity in Higher Education* 1, no. 4: 204–21.

Hurtado, S., C. B. Newman, M. C. Tran, and M. J. Chang. 2010. "Improving the Rate of Success for Underrepresented Racial Minorities in STEM Fields: Insights from a National Project." *New Directions for Institutional Research* 148: 5–15.

Hypolite, L. I. 2020. "People, Place, and Connections: Black Cultural Center Staff as Facilitators of Social Capital." *Journal of Black Studies* 51, no. 1: 37–59.

Ignatiev, N. 2012. *How the Irish Became White*. New York: Routledge.

Inwood, J. F., and D. G. Martin. 2008. "Whitewash: White Privilege and Racialized Landscapes at the University of Georgia." *Social & Cultural Geography* 9, no. 4: 373–95.

Ireland, D. T., K. E. Freeman, C. E. Winston-Proctor, K. D. DeLaine, S. McDonald Lowe, and K. M. Woodson. 2018. "(Un) Hidden Figures: A Synthesis of Research Examining the Intersectional Experiences of Black Women and Girls in STEM Education." *Review of Research in Education* 42, no. 1: 226–54.

Jack, A. A. 2014. "Culture Shock Revisited: The Social and Cultural Contingencies to Class Marginality." *Sociological Forum* 29, 2: 453–75.

Jackson, J. L. 2001. *Harlemworld: Doing Race and Class in Contemporary Black America*. Chicago: University of Chicago Press.

James, S. A. 1994. "John Henryism and the Health of African-Americans." *Culture, medicine and psychiatry* 18, no. 2: 163–82.

Jenkins, D. A., A. A. Tichavakunda, and J. A. Coles. 2020. "The Second ID: Critical Race Counterstories of Campus Police Interactions with Black Men at Historically White Institutions." *Race Ethnicity and Education* 24, no. 2: 149–66.

Jourian, T., and L. McCloud. 2020. "'I Don't Know Where I Stand': Black Trans Masculine Students' Re/De/Constructions of Black Masculinity." *Journal of College Student Development* 61, no. 6: 733–49.

Keels, M. 2020. *Campus Counterspaces: Black and Latinx Students' Search for Community at Historically White Universities*. Ithaca: Cornell University Press.

Kuh, G. D. 1995a. "Cultivating 'High-Stakes' Student Culture Research." *Research in higher education* 36, no. 5: 563–76.

———. 1995b. "The Other Curriculum: Out-of-Class Experiences Associated with Student Learning and Personal Development." *The Journal of Higher Education* 66, no. 2: 123–55.

Ladson-Billings, G. J., and W. F. Tate IV. 1995. "Toward a Critical Race Theory of Education." *Teachers College Record* 97, 1: 47–68.

Lahire, B. 2015. "The Limits of the Field: Elements for a Theory of the Social Differentiation of Activities." In *Bourdieu's Theory of Social Fields: Concepts and Applications*, edited by M. Hilgers and E. Mangez, 62–101. New York: Routledge.

Leath, S., and T. Chavous, T. 2018. "Black Women's Experiences of Campus Racial Climate and Stigma at Predominantly White Institutions: Insights from a Comparative and Within-Group Approach for STEM and Non-STEM Majors." *The Journal of Negro Education* 87, no. 2: 125–39.

Leonardo, Z. 2013. *Race Frameworks: A Multidimensional Theory of Racism and Education*. New York: Teachers College Press.

Lewis, J. A., R. Mendenhall, S. A. Harwood, and M. B. Huntt. 2013. "Coping with Gendered Racial Microaggressions among Black Women College Students." *Journal of African American Studies* 17, no. 1: 51–73.

Lerma, V., L. T. Hamilton, and K. Nielsen. 2020. "Racialized Equity Labor, University Appropriation, and Student Resistance." *Social Problems* 67, no. 2: 286–303.

Linder, C., S. J. Quaye, A. C. Lange, M. E. Evans, and T. J. Stewart. 2019. *Identity-based Student Activism: Power and Oppression on College Campuses*. New York: Routledge.

Linder, C., S. J. Quaye, A. C. Lange, R. E. Roberts, M. C. Lacy, and W. K. Okello. 2019. " 'A Student Should Have the Privilege of Just Being a Student': Student Activism as Labor." *The Review of Higher Education* 42, no. 5: 37–62.

Lofton, R., and J. E. Davis. 2015. "Toward a Black Habitus: African Americans Navigating Systemic Inequalities within Home, School, and Community." *The Journal of Negro Education* 84, no. 3: 214–30.

Love, B. L. 2016. "Antiblack State Violence, Classroom Edition: The Spirit Murdering of Black Children. *Journal of Curriculum and Pedagogy* 13, no. 1: 22–25.

Margolis, J., and A. Fisher. 2002. *Unlocking the Clubhouse: Women in Computing*. Cambridge: MIT Press.

Marra, R. M., L. Steege, C. L. Tsai, and N. E. Tang. 2016. "Beyond 'Group Work': An Integrated Approach to Support Collaboration in Engineering Education. *International Journal of STEM Education* 3, no. 1: 17.

McCabe, J. M. 2016. *Connecting in College: How Friendship Networks Matter for Academic and Social Success*. Chicago: University of Chicago Press.

McGee, E. O., and L. Bentley. 2017. "The Troubled Success of Black Women in STEM." *Cognition and Instruction* 35, no. 4: 265–89.

McGee, E. O., and D. B. Martin. 2011. " 'You Would not Believe What I Have to Go Through to Prove My Intellectual Value!' Stereotype Management among Academically Successful Black Mathematics and Engineering Students." *American Educational Research Journal* 48, no. 6: 1347–89.

Mirza, H. S. 2014. "Decolonizing Higher Education: Black Feminism and the Intersectionality of Race and Gender." *Journal of Feminist Scholarship* 7, no. 7: 1–12.

Moffatt, M. 1989. *Coming of Age in New Jersey: College and American Culture.* New Brunswick: Rutgers University Press.

Morgan, D. L., and C. H. F. Davis III, eds. 2019. *Student Activism, Politics, and Campus Climate in Higher Education.* New York: Routledge.

Morgan, D. L., K. B. Davis, and N. López. 2020. "Engineering Political Fluency: Identifying Tensions in the Political Identity Development of Engineering Majors." *Journal of Engineering Education* 109, no. 1: 107–24.

Morrison, T. 1987. *Beloved.* New York: Knopf.

Moses, R., and C. E. Cobb. 2002. *Radical Equations: Civil Rights from Mississippi to the Algebra Project.* Boston: Beacon Press.

Museus, S. D. 2008. "The Role of Ethnic Student Organizations in Fostering African American and Asian American Students' Cultural Adjustment and Membership at Predominantly White Institutions." *Journal of College Student Development* 49, no. 6: 568–86.

Musoba, G., and B. Baez. 2009. "The Cultural Capital of Cultural and Social Capital: An Economy of Translations." In *Higher Education: Handbook of Theory and Research*, edited by J. Smart, Vol. 24, 151–82). Amsterdam: Springer.

Mwangi, C. A. G., and S. Fries-Britt. 2015. "Black within Black: The Perceptions of Black Immigrant Collegians and Their US College Experience." *About Campus* 20, no. 2: 16–23.

Mwangi, C. A. G., N. Daoud, S. English, and K. A. Griffin. 2017. " 'Me and My Family': Ethnic Differences and Familial Influences on Academic Motivations of Black Collegians." *The Journal of Negro Education* 86, no. 4: 479–93.

Nathan, R. 2006. *My Freshman Year: What a Professor Learned by Becoming a Student.* Ithaca: Cornell University Press.

National Academies of Sciences, Engineering, and Medicine. 2020. *Promising Practices for Addressing the Underrepresentation of Women in Science, Engineering, and Medicine: Opening Doors.* National Academies Press: https://doi.org/10.17226/25785.

Newman, C. B. 2015. "Rethinking Race in Student-Faculty Interactions and Mentoring Relationships with Undergraduate African American Engineering and Computer Science Majors. *Journal of Women and Minorities in Science and Engineering* 21, no. 4: 323–46.

———. 2016. "Minority Engineering Programs at a Crossroads." *Journal for Multicultural Education* 10, no. 2: 217–33.

Noble, S. U. 2013. "Google Search: Hyper-visibility as a Means of Rendering Black Women and Girls Invisible." *InVisible Culture* 19. http:// ivc.lib.rochester.

edu/portfolio/google-search-hyper-visibility-as-a-means-of-renderingblack-women-and-girls-invisible/.

Ogunyemi, D., C. Clare, Y. M. Astudillo, M. Marseille, E. Manu, and S. Kim. 2020. "Microaggressions in the Learning Environment: A Systematic Review." *Journal of Diversity in Higher Education* 13, no. 2: 97–119.

Okello, W. K. 2020. "Organized Anxiety: Respectability Politics, John Henryism, and the Paradox of Black Achievement." *Race Ethnicity and Education,* Ahead of Print: 1–19.

Omi, M., and H. Winant. 1986. *Racial Formation in the United States.* New York: Routledge.

O'Neal, J. 2011. "Foreword." In M. Inaba, *Willie Dixon: Preacher of the Blues.* Lanham, MD: Scarecrow Press.

Ong, M., J. M. Smith, and L. T. Ko. 2018. "Counterspaces for Women of Color in STEM Higher Education: Marginal and Central Spaces for Persistence and Success." *Journal of Research in Science Teaching* 55, no. 2: 206–45.

Park, J. J. 2014. "Clubs and the Campus Racial Climate: Student Organizations and Interracial Friendship in College." *Journal of College Student Development* 55, no. 7: 641–60.

———, and Y. K. Kim. 2013. "Interracial Friendship and Structural Diversity: Trends for Greek, Religious, and Ethnic Student Organizations." *The Review of Higher Education* 37, no. 1: 1–24.

Parker, L., and M. Lynn. 2002. "What's Race Got to Do with It? Critical Race Theory's Conflicts with and Connections to Qualitative Research Methodology and Epistemology." *Qualitative inquiry* 8, no. 1: 7–22.

Pascarella, E. T., and P. T. Terenzini. 2005. *How College Affects Students: A Third Decade of Research,* Vol. 2. San Francisco: Jossey-Bass.

Pattillo, M. 2010. *Black on the Block: The Politics of Race and Class in the City.* Chicago: University of Chicago Press.

Patton, L. D. 2006. "The Voice of Reason: A Qualitative Examination of Black Student Perceptions of Black Culture Centers." *Journal of College Student Development* 47, no. 6: 628–46.

———. 2016. "Disrupting Postsecondary Prose: Toward a Critical Race Theory of Higher Education." *Urban Education* 51, no. 3: 315–42.

Perna, L., V. Lundy-Wagner, N. D. Drezner, M. Gasman, S. Yoon,E. Bose, E., and S. Gary. 2009. "The Contribution of HBCUs to the Preparation of African American Women for STEM Careers: A Case Study." *Research in Higher Education* 50, no. 1: 1–23.

Pierce, C. M., J. V. Carew, D. Pierce-Gonzalez, and D. Wills. 1977. "An Experiment in Racism: TV Commercials." *Education and Urban Society* 10, no. 1: 61–87.

Piliawsky, M. 1984. "Racial Equality in the United States: From Institutionalized Racism to 'Respectable' Racism." *Phylon* 45, no. 2: 135–43.

Portes, A. 1998. "Social Capital: Its Origins and Applications in Modern Sociology." *Annual Review of Sociology* 24, no. 1: 1–24.

Posey-Maddox, L. 2017. "Race in Place: Black Parents, Family-School Relations, and Multi-Spatial Microaggressions in a Predominantly White Suburb." *Teachers College Record* 119, no. 11: 1–42.

Quaye, S. J., and S. R. Harper. 2014. *Student Engagement in Higher Education: Theoretical Perspectives and Practical Approaches for Diverse Populations.* New York: Routledge.

Quaye, S. J., S. R. Harper, and S. L. Pendakur, eds. 2019. *Student Engagement in Higher Education: Theoretical Perspectives and Practical Approaches for Diverse Populations.* New York: Routledge.

Quaye, S. J., S. N. Karikari, K. D. Carter, W. K. Okello, and C. Allen. 2020. " 'Why Can't I Just Chill?': The Visceral Nature of Racial Battle Fatigue." *Journal of College Student Development* 61, no. 5; 609–23.

"Racial Tension and Protests on Campuses across the Country." (November 10, 2015). *The New York Times.* https://www.nytimes.com/2015/11/11/us/racial-tension-and-protests-on-campuses-across-the-country.html.

Ray, V. E., A. Randolph, M. Underhill, and D. Luke. 2017. "Critical Race Theory, Afro-Pessimism, and Racial Progress Narratives." *Sociology of Race and Ethnicity* 3, no. 2: 147–58.

Renn, K. A., and K. D. Arnold. 2003. "Reconceptualizing Research on College Student Peer Culture." *The Journal of Higher Education* 74, no. 3: 261–91.

Reyes, D. V. 2018. *Learning to Be Latino: How Colleges Shape Identity Politics.* New Brunswick: Rutgers University Press.

Rincón, B. E., and C. E. George-Jackson. 2016. "Examining Department Climate for Women in Engineering: The Role of STEM Interventions." *Journal of College Student Development* 57, no. 6: 742–47.

Rogers, I. 2012. *The Black Campus Movement: Black Students and the Racial Reconstitution of Higher Education, 1965–1972.* New York: Palgrave MacMillan.

Roulin, N., and A. Bangerter. 2013. "Students' Use of Extra-Curricular Activities for Positional Advantage in Competitive Job Markets." *Journal of Education and Work* 26, 1: 21–47.

Secules, S. 2019. "Making the Familiar Strange: An Ethnographic Scholarship of Integration Contextualizing Engineering Educational Culture as Masculine and Competitive." *Engineering Studies* 11, 3: 196–216.

Sengupta-Irving, T., and S. Vossoughi. 2019. "Not in Their Name: Re-Interpreting Discourses of STEM Learning through the Subjective Experiences of Minoritized Girls." *Race Ethnicity and Education* 22, no. 4: 479–501.

Sexton, J. 2010. "People-of-Color-Blindness Notes on the Afterlife of Slavery." *Social Text* 28, no. 2: 31–56.

Seymour, E., and N. M. Hewitt. 1997. *Talking about Leaving: Why Undergraduates Leave the Sciences.* Boulder: Westview Press.

Sharma, A. 2016. "STEM-ification of Education: The Zombie Reform Strikes Again." *Journal for Activist Science and Technology Education* 7, no. 1: 43–51.

Shropshire, K. L. 2004. "Minority Issues in Contemporary Sports." *Stanford Law & Policy Review* 15, no. 1: 189–215.

Simien, E. M. 2005. "Race, Gender, and Linked Fate." *Journal of Black Studies* 35, no. 5; 529–50.

Slaton, A. E. 2010. *Race, Rigor, and Selectivity in US Engineering: The History of an Occupational Color Line.* Cambridge: Harvard University Press.

Slaughter, J. B., Y. Tao, and W. Pearson. 2015. *Changing the Face of Engineering: The African American Experience.* Baltimore: Johns Hopkins University Press.

Smith, W. A., P. G. Altbach, and K. Lomotey. 2002. *The Racial Crisis in American Higher Education: Continuing Challenges for the Twenty-First Century.* Albany: State University of New York Press.

Smith, W. A., M. Hung, and J. D. Franklin. 2011. "Racial Battle Fatigue and the Miseducation of Black Men: Racial Microaggressions, Societal Problems, and Environmental Stress." *The Journal of Negro Education* 80, no. 1: 63–82.

Smith, W. A., J. B. Mustaffa, C. M. Jones, T. J. Curry, and W. R. Allen. 2016. "'You Make Me Wanna Holler and Throw up Both My Hands!': Campus Culture, Black Misandric Microaggressions, and Racial Battle Fatigue." *International Journal of Qualitative Studies in Education* 29, no. 9: 1189–1209.

Solórzano, D. G., and D. D. Bernal. 2001. "Examining Transformational Resistance through a Critical Race and LatCrit Theory Framework: Chicana and Chicano Students in an Urban Context." *Urban education* 36, no. 3: 308–42.

Solórzano, D. G., M. Ceja, and T. Yosso. 2000. "Critical Race Theory, Racial Microaggressions, and Campus Racial Climate: The Experiences of African American College Students." *The Journal of Negro Education* 69, no. 1: 60–73.

Steele, C. M. 1997. "A Threat in the Air: How Stereotypes Shape the Intellectual Identities and Performance of Women and African-Americans." *American Psychologist* 52: 613–29.

Stevens, M. L., E. A. Armstrong, and R. Arum. 2008. "Sieve, Incubator, Temple, Hub: Empirical and Theoretical Advances in the Sociology of Higher Education." *Annual Review of Sociology* 34: 127–51.

Stevens, R., K. O'Connor, L. Garrison, A. Jocuns, and D. M. Amos. 2008. "Becoming an Engineer: Toward a Three Dimensional View of Engineering Learning." *Journal of Engineering Education* 97, no. 3: 355–68.

Stitt, R. L., and A. Happel-Parkins. 2019. "'Sounds Like Something a White Man Should Be Doing': The Shared Experiences of Black Women Engineering Students." *The Journal of Negro Education* 88, no. 1: 62–74.

Strayhorn, T. L. 2012. "Sense of Belonging and STEM Students of Color." In *College Students' Sense of Belonging*, edited by T. L. Strayhorn, 61–76. New York: Routledge.

Sue, D. W. 2010. *Microaggressions in Everyday Life: Race, Gender, and Sexual Orientation.* Hoboken: John Wiley and Sons.

Tarnoff, B. 2017. "Tech's Push to Teach Coding Isn't about Kids' Success—It's about Cutting Wages." *The Guardian*, September 21. https://www.theguardian.com/technology/2017/sep/21/coding-education-teaching-silicon-valley-wages.

Thelamour, B., C. George Mwangi, and I. Ezeofor. 2019. "'We Need to Stick Together for Survival': Black College Students' Racial Identity, Same-Ethnic Friendships, and Campus Connectedness." *Journal of Diversity in Higher Education* 12, no. 3: 266–79.

Tichavakunda, A. A. 2019. "An Overdue Theoretical Discourse: Pierre Bourdieu's Theory of Practice and Critical Race Theory in Education." *Educational Studies* 55, no. 6: 651–66.

———. 2020. "Relational Sociology and Race Relations: Pushing the Conversation in Higher Education." In *Relational Sociology and Research on Schools, Colleges and Universities*, edited by W. G. Tierney and S. Kolluri, 91–110. Albany: State University of New York Press.

———. 2020. "Studying Black Student Life on Campus: Toward a Theory of Black Placemaking in Higher Education." *Urban Education*, 0042085920971354.

Tierney, W. G. 1999. "Models of Minority College-Going and Retention: Cultural in? tegrity versus Cultural Suicide." *Journal of Negro Education* 68, no. 1: 80–91.

Treisman, U. 1992. "Studying Students Studying Calculus: A Look at the Lives of Minority Mathematics Students in College." *The College Mathematics Journal* 23, no. 5: 362–72.

Turner, C. S. V. 1994. "Guests in Someone Else's House: Students of Color." *The Review of Higher Education* 17, no. 4: 355–70.

Walley-Jean, J. C. 2009. "Debunking the Myth of the 'Angry Black Woman': An Exploration of Anger in Young African American Women." *Black Women, Gender & Families* 3, no. 2: 68–86.

Warikoo, N. K. 2016. *The Diversity Bargain: And Other Dilemmas of Race, Admissions, and Meritocracy at Elite Universities*. Chicago: University of Chicago Press.

West, C. 2018. "Brother Martin Was a Blues Man: A Boston Review Book Talk with Cornel West." *Boston Review*, March 12. http://bostonreview.net/race-podcast/cornel-west-brother-martin-was-blues-man.

West, L. M., R. A. Donovan, and A. R. Daniel. 2016. "The Price of Strength: Black College Women's Perspectives on the Strong Black Woman Stereotype." *Women & Therapy* 39, no. 3–4: 390–412.

Wilder, C. S. 2014. *Ebony and ivy: Race, Slavery, and the Troubled History of America's uUniversities*. New York: Bloomsbury.

Willis, P. E. 1977. *Learning to Labor: How Working Class Kids Get Working Class Jobs*. New York: Columbia University Press.

Winant, H. 2012. "The Dark Matter." *Ethnic and Racial Studies* 35, 4: 600–607.

Winkle-Wagner, R. 2009. *The Unchosen Me: Race, Gender, and Identity among Black Women in College*. Baltimore: Johns Hopkins University Press.

————, and D. L. McCoy. 2018. "Feeling Like an 'Alien' or 'Family'? Comparing Students and Faculty Experiences of Diversity in STEM Disciplines at a PWI and an HBCU." *Race Ethnicity and Education* 21, no. 5: 593–606.

Yosso, T. J. 2005. "Whose Culture Has Capital? A Critical Race Theory Discussion of Community Cultural Wealth." *Race ethnicity and education* 8, no. 1: 69–91.

Zinn, M. B., L. W. Cannon, E. Higginbotham, and B. T. Dill. 1986. "The Costs of Exclusionary Practices in Women's Studies." *Signs: Journal of women in culture and society* 11, no. 2: 290–303.

Index

CPSIA information can be obtained
at www.ICGtesting.com
Printed in the USA
LVHW100334150223
739546LV00001B/4